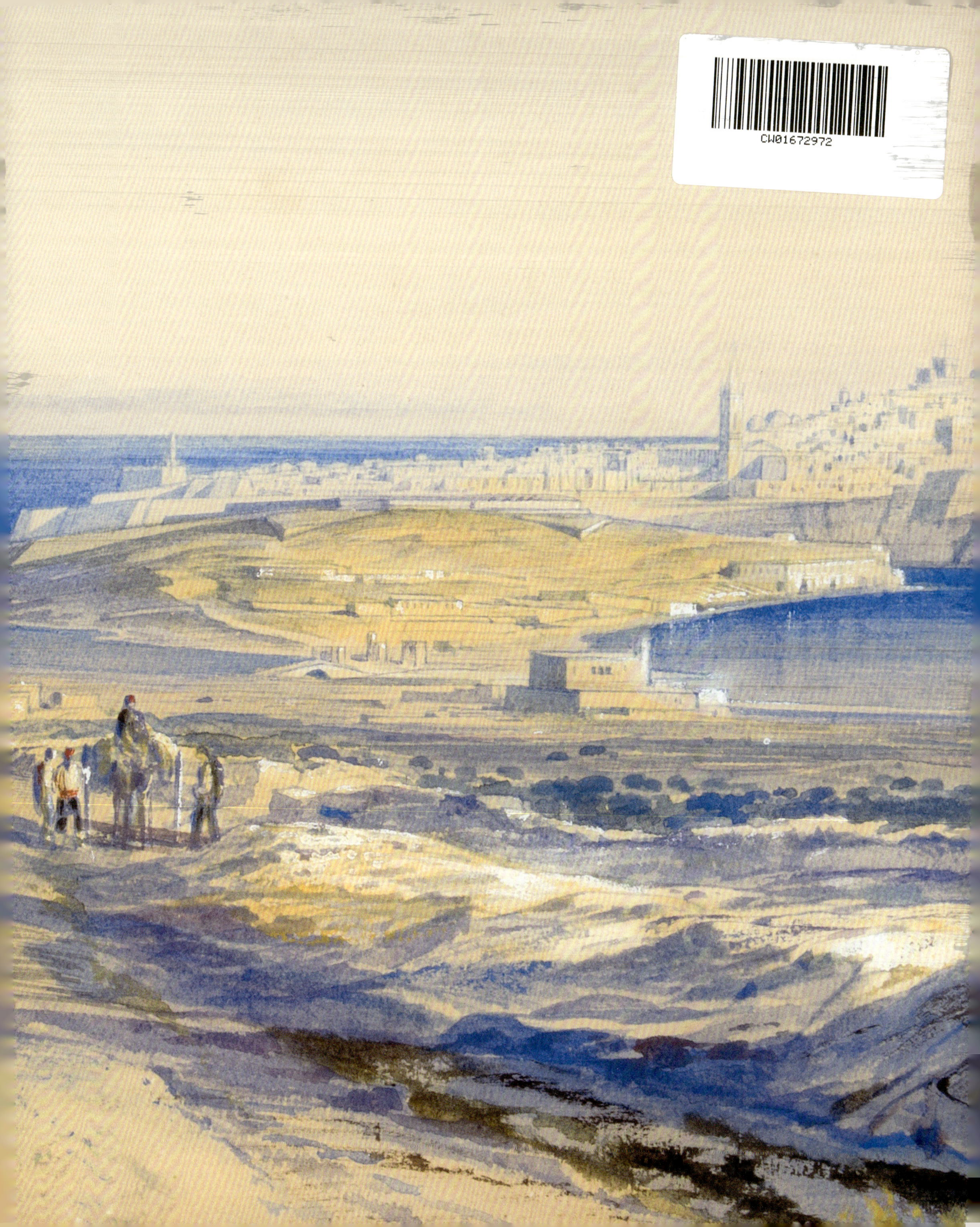

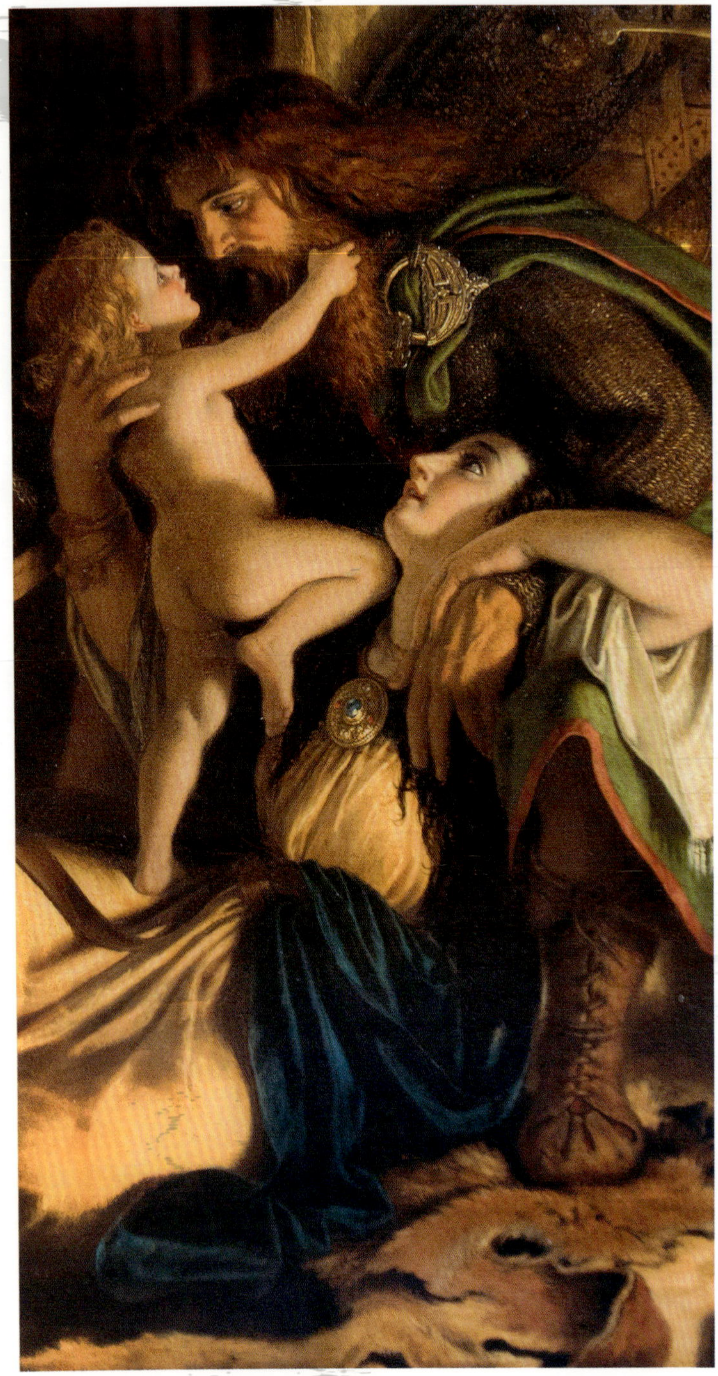

8 & 10 Ryder Street
St James's
London SW1Y 6QB
020 7839 7551
gallery@chrisbeetles.com
www.chrisbeetles.com

ISBN 978-1-905738-96-0

Cataloguing in publication data is available
from the British Library

Researched and written by David Wootton,
with contributions from Alexander Beetles,
and additional research by Fiona Nickerson

Edited by Pascale Oakley and David Wootton

Design by Pascale Oakley

Photography by Julian Huxley-Parlour
Reproduction by www.cast2create.com
Colour separation and printing by Geoff Neal Litho Limited

Front cover:
Albert Chevallier Tayler, *The Dining Room* [**59**]

Front endpaper:
Edward Lear, *Valletta* [**39**]

This page:
Joseph Noel Paton, *The Islesman at Home* [detail of **49**]

Title page:
Robert Walker Macbeth, *The Return of a Whaler*
[detail of **60**]

Pages 106-107:
Herbert Menzies Marshall, *The Embankment with Old Scotland Yard and the Clock Tower of the Palace of Westminster Beyond* [**81**]

Back endpaper:
Robert Thorne Waite, *The Last Load* [**67**]

Back cover:
Alfred Parsons, *A Summer Garden* [**69**]

Chris Beetles
Summer Show
2020

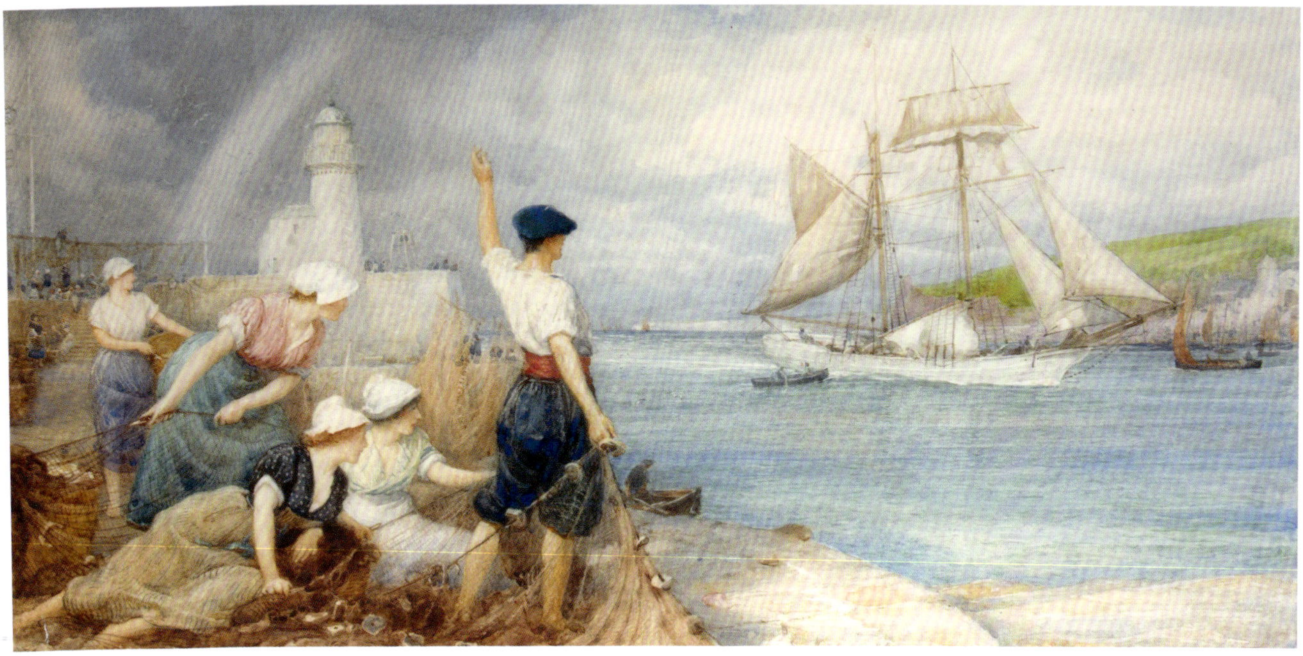

CHRIS BEETLES GALLERY

THOMAS ROWLANDSON

Thomas Rowlandson (1757-1827)

Thomas Rowlandson raised comic art to a new level by representing the panorama of contemporary life with almost unparalleled fluency – adopting lyricism or incisiveness as best fitted the subject. And, in capturing an abundance of picturesque detail, his work provided a parallel to the novels of Henry Fielding or Laurence Sterne.

For a biography of Thomas Rowlandson, please see refer to *Chris Beetles Summer Show*, 2017, page 4.

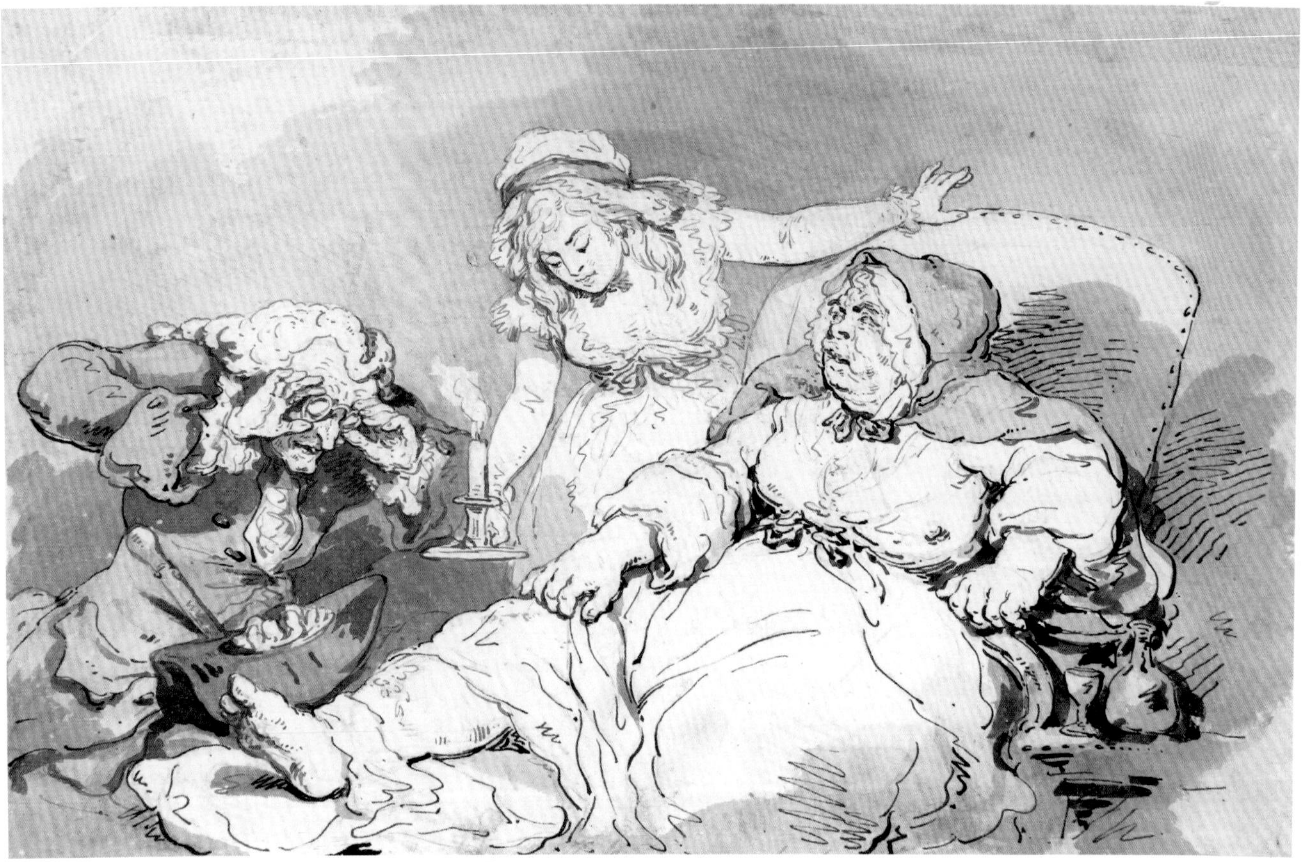

1 A Bawd on Her Last Legs
Pen ink and watercolour on laid paper with the 'Maid of Dort' form of the 'Pro Patria' watermark
9 x 13 inches

Published (in reverse) as an etching and aquatint by S W Fores, No 3 Piccadilly, London, on 1 October 1792

A Bawd on Her Last Legs

The present work by Thomas Rowlandson has been considered to exemplify a vein of eighteenth-century imagery in which a sick prostitute is 'invoked as an object of ridicule, a symbol of vice, a cautionary figure, and much else besides' (Noelle Gallagher, *Itch, Clap and Pox*, New Haven: Yale University Press, 2019, page 62). Having said that, it conveys its message through economy, sensitivity and even beauty, confident draughtsmanship combining with a carefully balanced composition.

An obese brothel keeper reclines in an armchair and reveals a sore leg, indicative of an infected varicose ulcer or, perhaps, a sexually transmitted disease and the lifestyle that has led to it. It is scrutinised through spectacles by a lean and elderly doctor, who sits on a stool at her feet. Between them, a pretty young prostitute leans forward to proffer a candle that is lit but guttering, suggestive of the passing of her own time and the ebbing of her mistress's life.

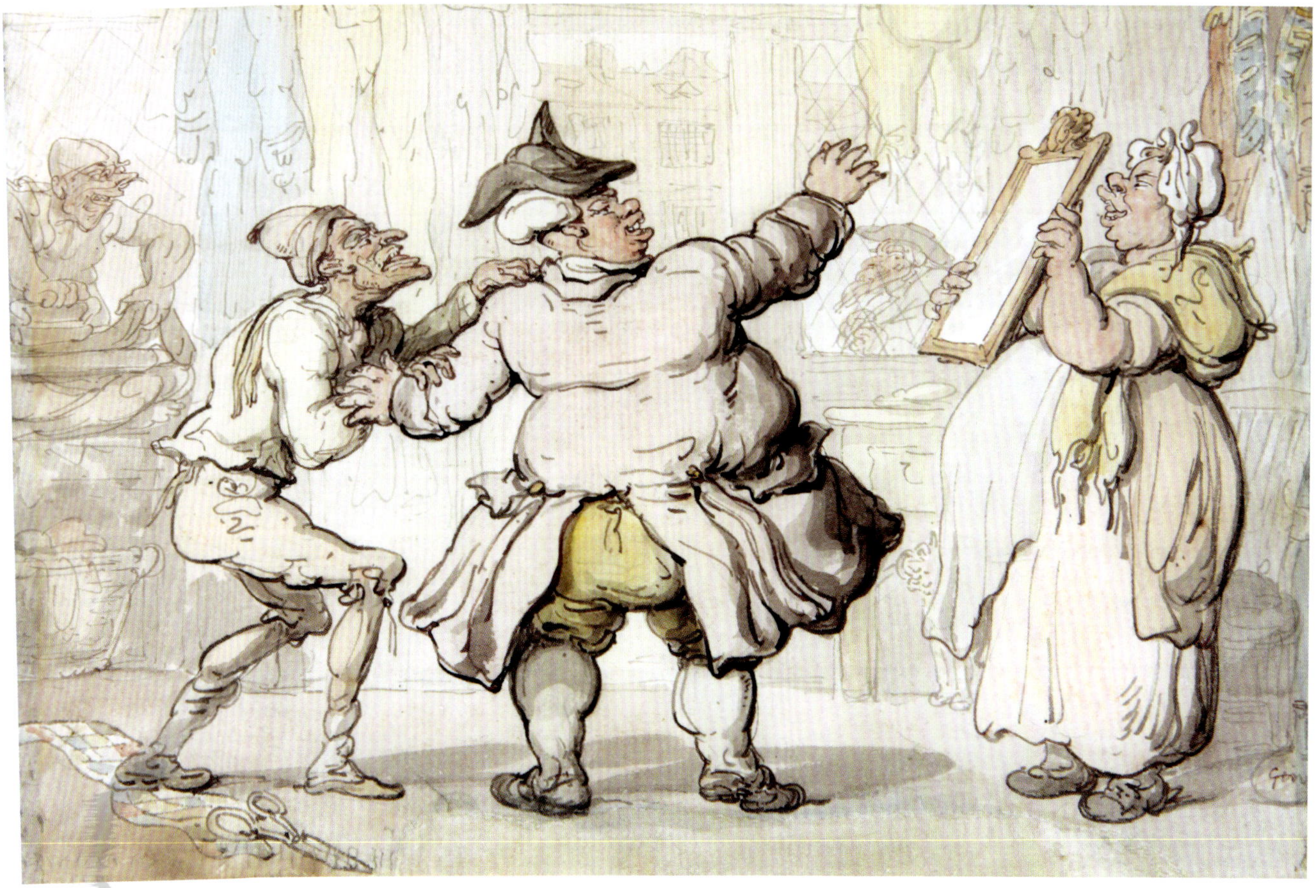

At the Tailor's

By the turn of the eighteenth to the nineteenth century, London had, perhaps unsurprisingly, developed a largescale tailoring industry, catering to many sectors of society. However, alongside it ran a market in second-hand clothing, which was patronised by the mass of the middle and lower classes. There were second-hand shops across London, but some areas were especially known for them, including Houndsditch and Smithfield. That Rowlandson's image depicts such a shop is suggested by a watercolour study for the present work, which is held in the collections of the Fine Art Museums of San Francisco and is entitled *A Tailor's Shop*. Above the door in that study is a sign with the inscription, 'Peter Smith buys & sells old clothes. Gentlemen fitted in the most fashionable taste'. So it seems likely that this gentleman is being fitted into something not originally made for him. It is yet to be ascertained whether or not Peter Smith was a real dealer in second-hand clothing.

2 **At the Tailor's**
Pen ink and watercolour
7 ¼ x 10 ½ inches
Exhibited: 'Bliss was it in that dawn to be alive: British Watercolours & Drawings 1750-1850', Chris Beetles Gallery, October 2008, No 68; 'The Age of Thomas Rowlandson', Chris Beetles Gallery, October-November 2012, No 53

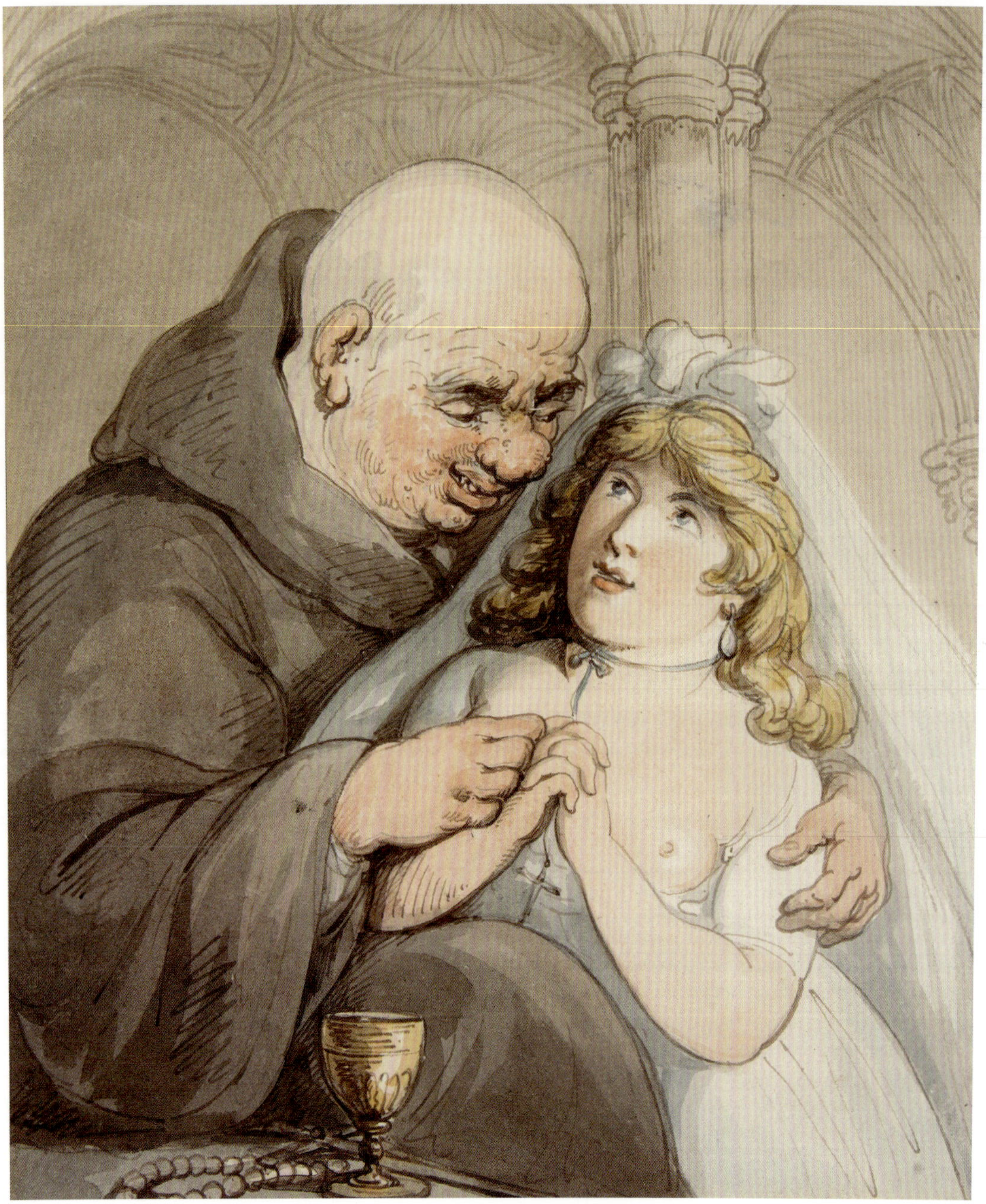

3 Symptoms of Sanctity
Watercolour
9 ¾ x 8 inches
Literature: Joseph Grego, *Rowlandson the Caricaturist*, London: Chatto and Windus, 1880, vol II, page 27

Published as an etching by S W Fores, No 50 Piccadilly, London, on 20 January 1801

Symptoms of Sanctity

This work brings together two of Thomas Rowlandson's favourite themes: the hypocrisy and veniality of the church, and especially, the Roman Catholic church, and a contrast between beautiful youth and ugly age. As a pretty and young communicant kneels at an altar in an attitude of prayer, she receives physical, as well as spiritual, comfort from a monk.

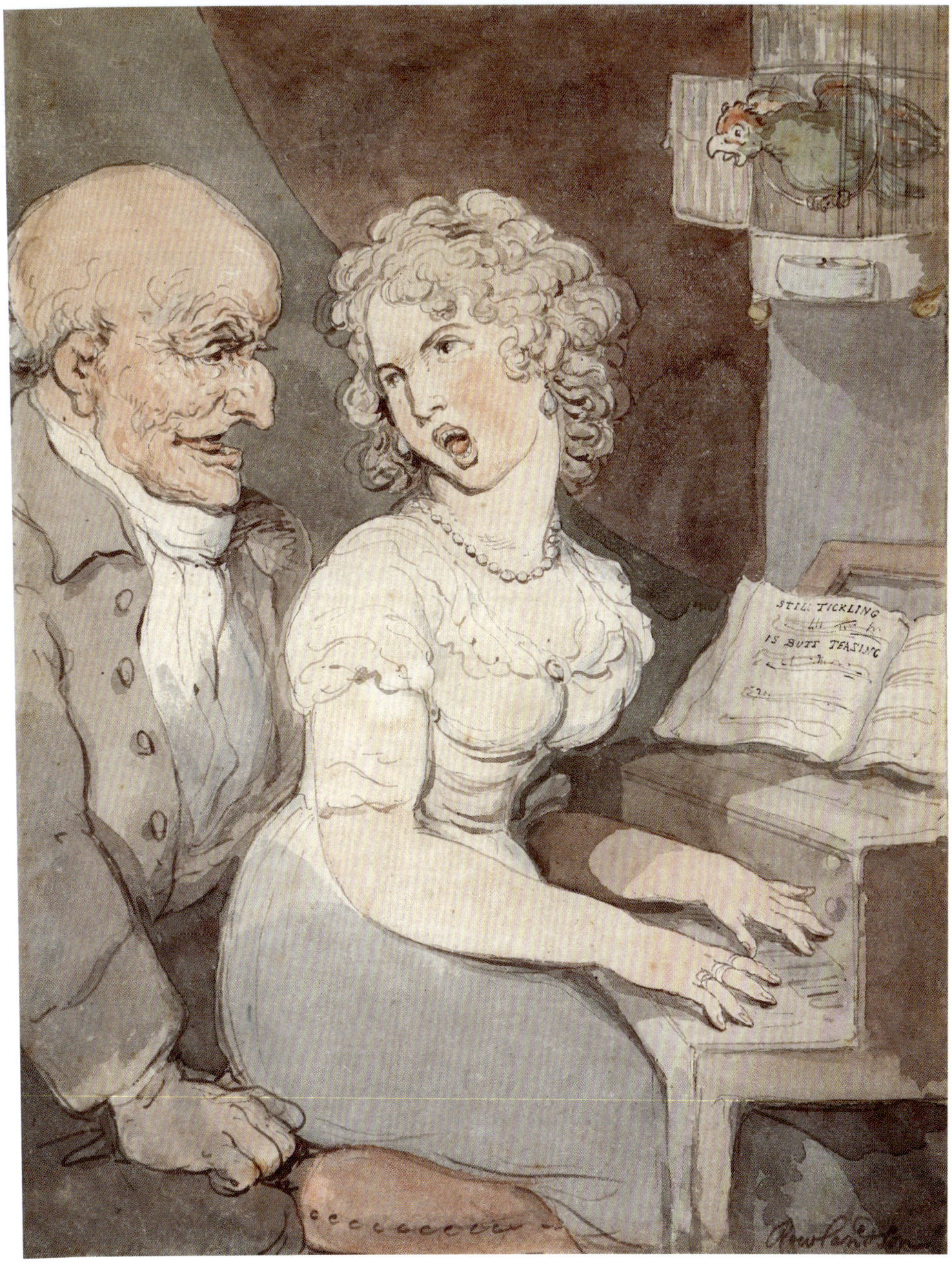

Still Tickling is Butt Teasing
Thomas Rowlandson followed a long cultural tradition in using musical performance as both context and metaphor for desire and seduction. In particular, he explored the visual pun of 'fingering' by depicting pairs or groups of figures around a keyboard, as in the present example in which a young female pianist is surprised by the uncomfortably close proximity of her elderly auditor. The encounter is emphasised by both the title of the piece that she plays and the alarm shown by her pet parrot. The whole provides a contrast to another, much earlier image by Rowlandson – *Music has charms to soothe the savage breast* – in which the man who has been listening to a young female pianist has fallen fast asleep.

4 **Still Tickling is Butt Teasing**
Signed
Watermarked '1825' on wove paper
Pen ink and watercolour
10 ¼ x 7 ½ inches
Provenance: Dr John Birch
Literature: Mike Rendell, *Trailblazing Women of the Georgian Era: The Eighteenth-Century Struggle for Female Success in a Man's World*, Havertown: Pen & Sword Books, 2018 [ebook], page 46
Exhibited: 'The Long Nineteenth Century: Treasures and Pleasures', Chris Beetles Gallery, March-April 2014, No 27

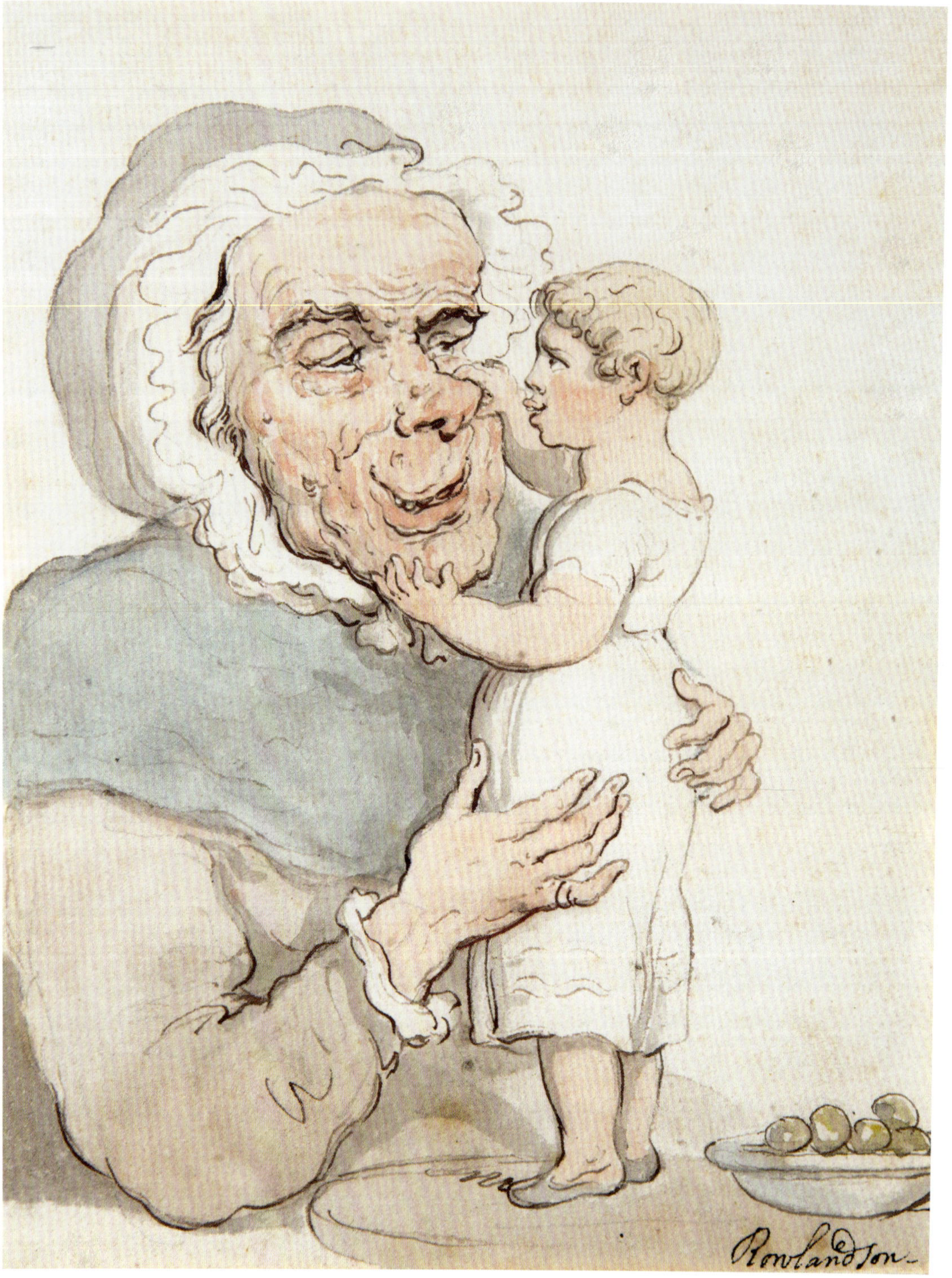

5 **Youth and Age**
Signed
Pen ink and watercolour
6 ½ x 4 ¾ inches
Provenance: Luke Gertler

6 Laughing Grotesques
Pen ink and watercolour
5 x 6 ¾ inches
Exhibited: 'Bliss was it in that dawn to be alive: British Watercolours & Drawings 1750-1850', Chris Beetles Gallery, October 2008, No 75; 'The Age of Thomas Rowlandson', Chris Beetles Gallery, October-November 2012, No 61

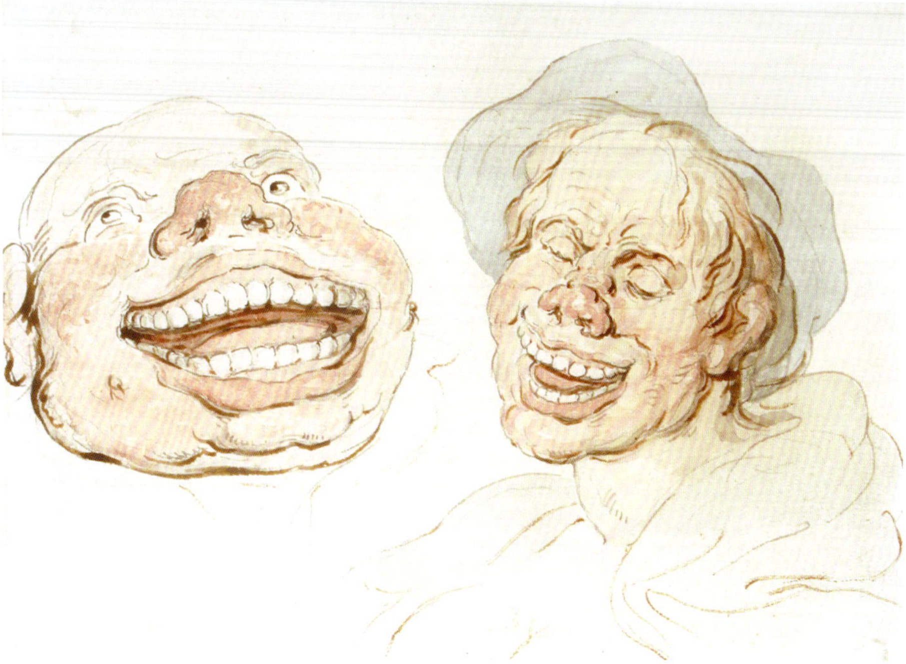

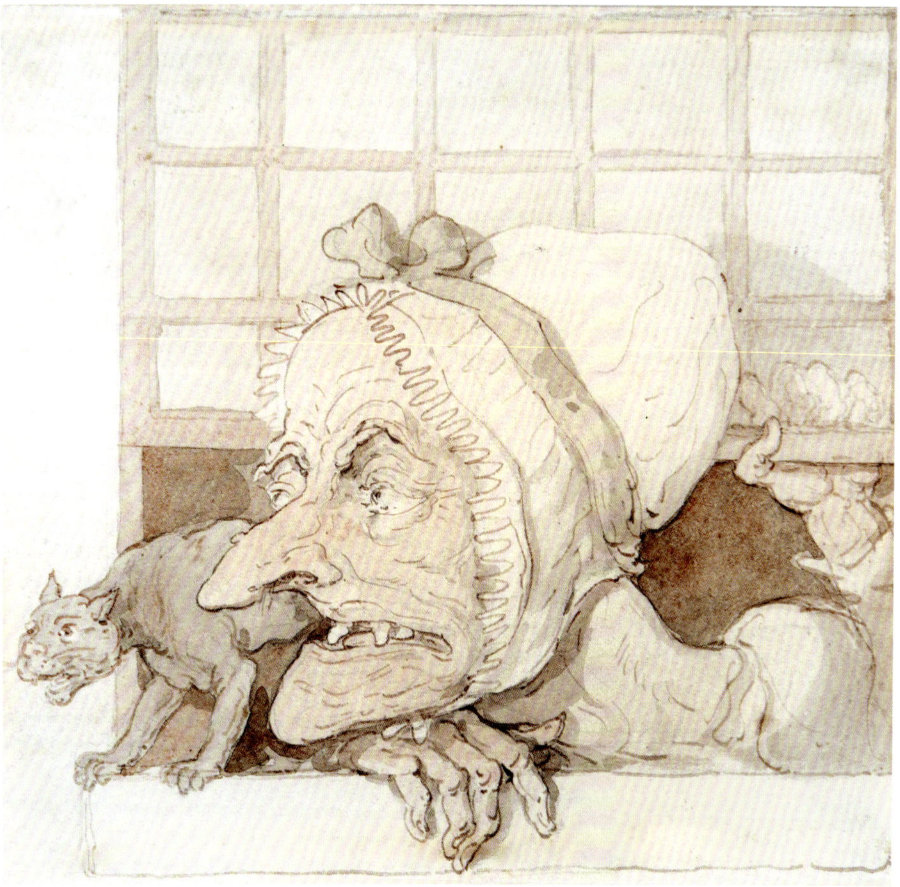

7 The Crone and the Cat
Pen ink and watercolour
6 x 6 inches
Provenance: Luke Gertler

This is possibly the work described as 'An Old Woman and her Cat at a Window', which was formerly in the collection of John Chester Esq of Old Square, Lincoln's Inn. See Joseph Grego, *Rowlandson the Caricaturist*, London: Chatto and Windus, 1880, vol II, page 428.

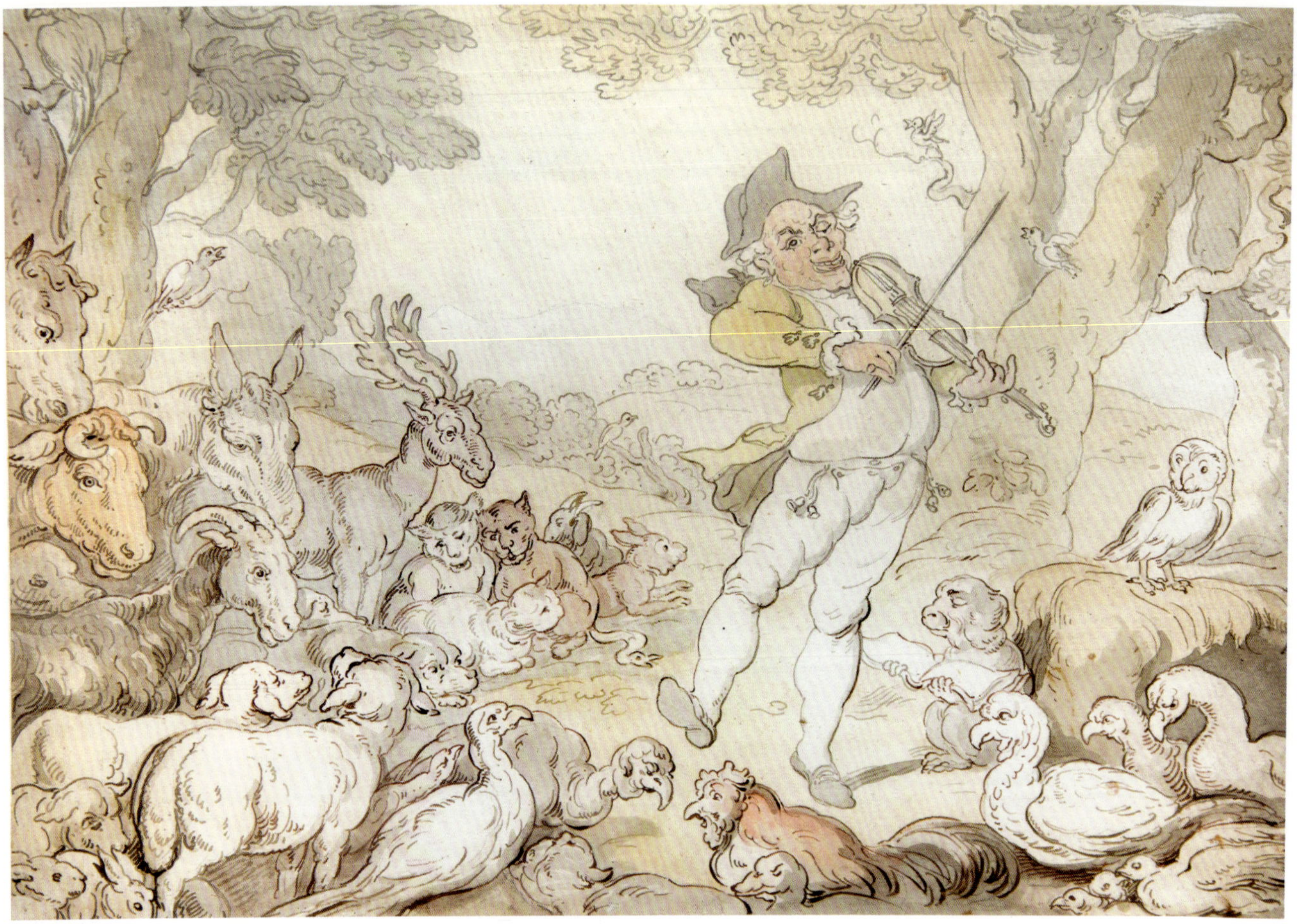

8 An Appreciative Audience
Signed
Watercolour
8 ¾ x 10 ¾ inches

The Inspiration of Classical Mythology: Jupiter & Juno and An Appreciative Audience

As a student of the Royal Academy Schools in the 1770s, Thomas Rowlandson would have been required to emulate classical models by drawing from casts of antique sculpture. At the same time, he would also have absorbed many of the historical and mythological stories that such sculpture represents. He maintained these interests throughout his career, continuing to produce both serious and satirical images based on mythological subjects.

Jupiter & Juno exemplifies Rowlandson's art at its most purely neoclassical, and suggests a response to the outline illustrations by his almost exact contemporary, John Flaxman, to Homer's *The Iliad and The Odyssey*, published in 1793. The king and queen of the Roman gods, Jupiter and Juno (known in Greek as Zeus and Hera) were both siblings and spouses. Rowlandson seems to show them at an early stage in their relationship, before Juno's 'conjugal happiness' became 'frequently disturbed by the numerous amours of her husband' and 'showed herself jealous and inexorable in the highest degree' (as explained by John Lemprière in his highly popular classical dictionary, *Bibliotheca Classica*, first published in 1788).

By contrast, *An Appreciative Audience* shows Rowlandson in a satirical mode, however gentle. Though he is dressed in contemporary clothes, the musician at its centre is based on the mythological figure of Orpheus, 'as his enchanting strain/Soothes beasts, and woods, and all the listening plain' (as expressed by Samuel Croxall in his 1717 translation of Book 11 of Ovid's *Metamorphoses*). As such, it draws on a long history of images of Orpheus charming the animals. It may, of course, caricature a specific musician and, if so, is likely to criticise his talents, implying that his *only* 'appreciative audience' is one that is composed of animals. However, those animals' faces are, at least slightly, anthropomorphic (a result of the artist's interest in 'comparative anatomy'), and some may portray known individuals.

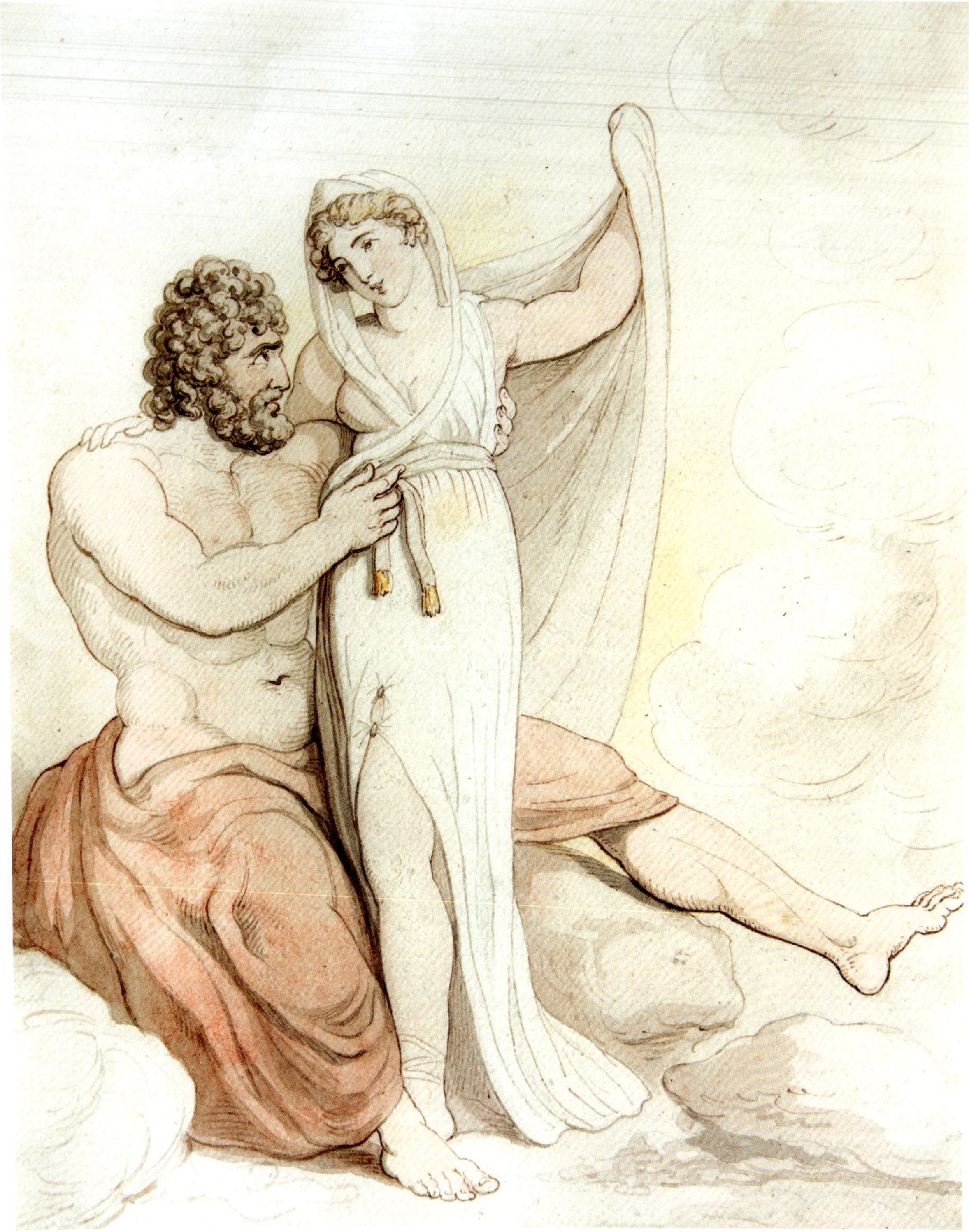

9 Jupiter & Juno
Watercolour
8 x 6 inches

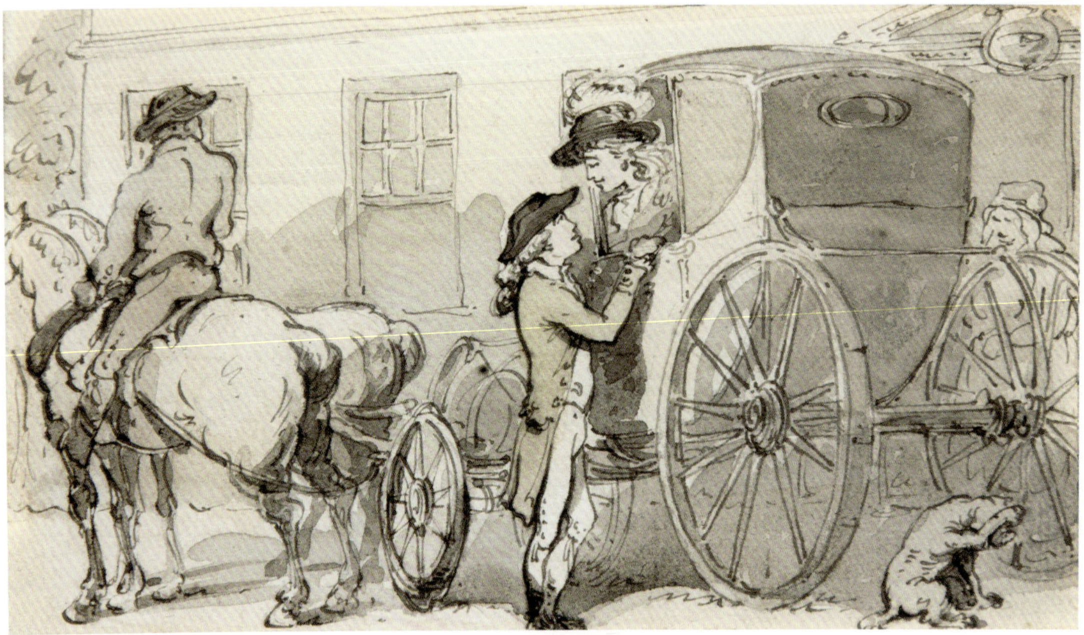

10 Flirting at the Carriage Door
Pen ink and watercolour
3 ½ x 5 ¾ inches

11 Street Scene (below)
Inscribed 'T Rowlandson' in another hand
Pen ink and watercolour
5 ¾ x 9 ¼ inches
Provenance: J Barton Townsend of Philadelphia

Exhibited: 'The Age of Thomas Rowlandson', Chris Beetles Gallery, October-November 2012, No 24

Similar to *Country Town*, exhibited in 'Thomas Rowlandson (1756-1827)', Frank T Sabin, 154 New Bond Street, London, 1933, No 99

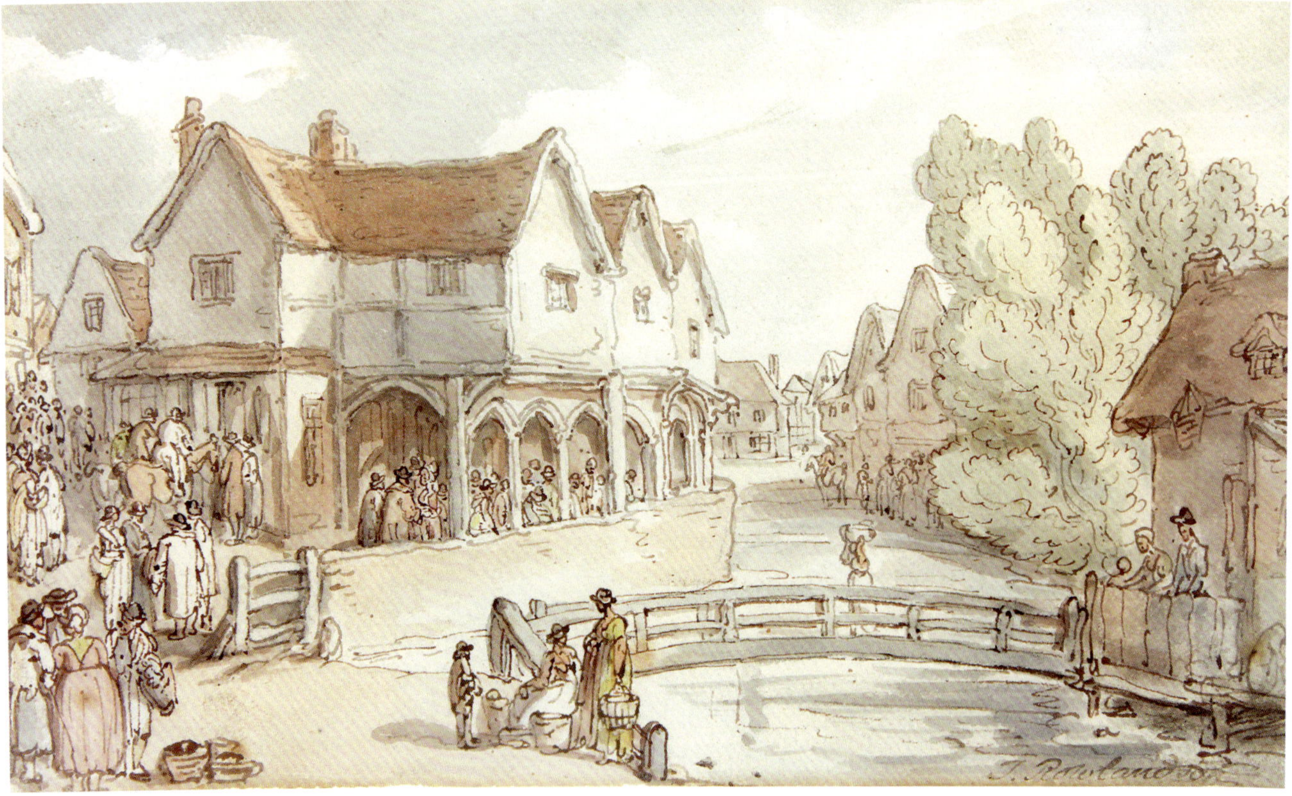

12 Fair Lane
Pen ink and watercolour
4 ¾ x 7 ¼ inches

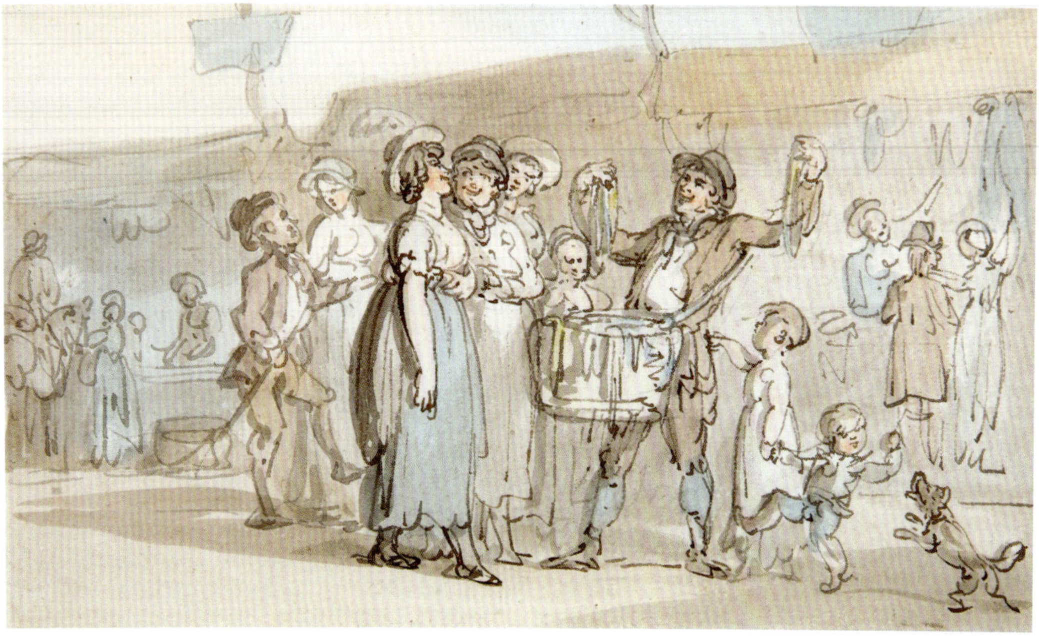

13 Country Fair for Hiring Servants
(below)
Pen ink and watercolour
7 ½ x 10 ¾ inches
Provenance: Louis Delatigny (1854-1936)

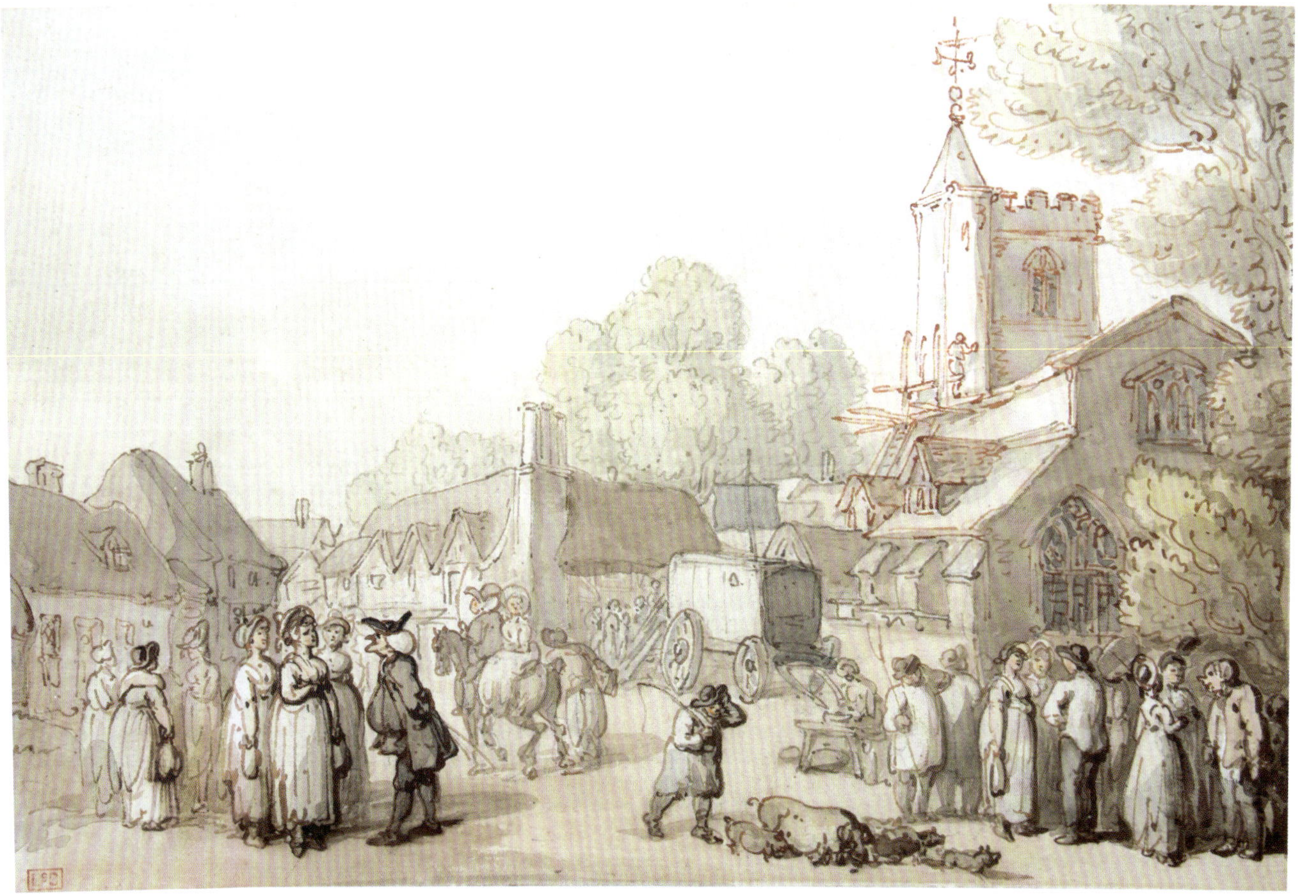

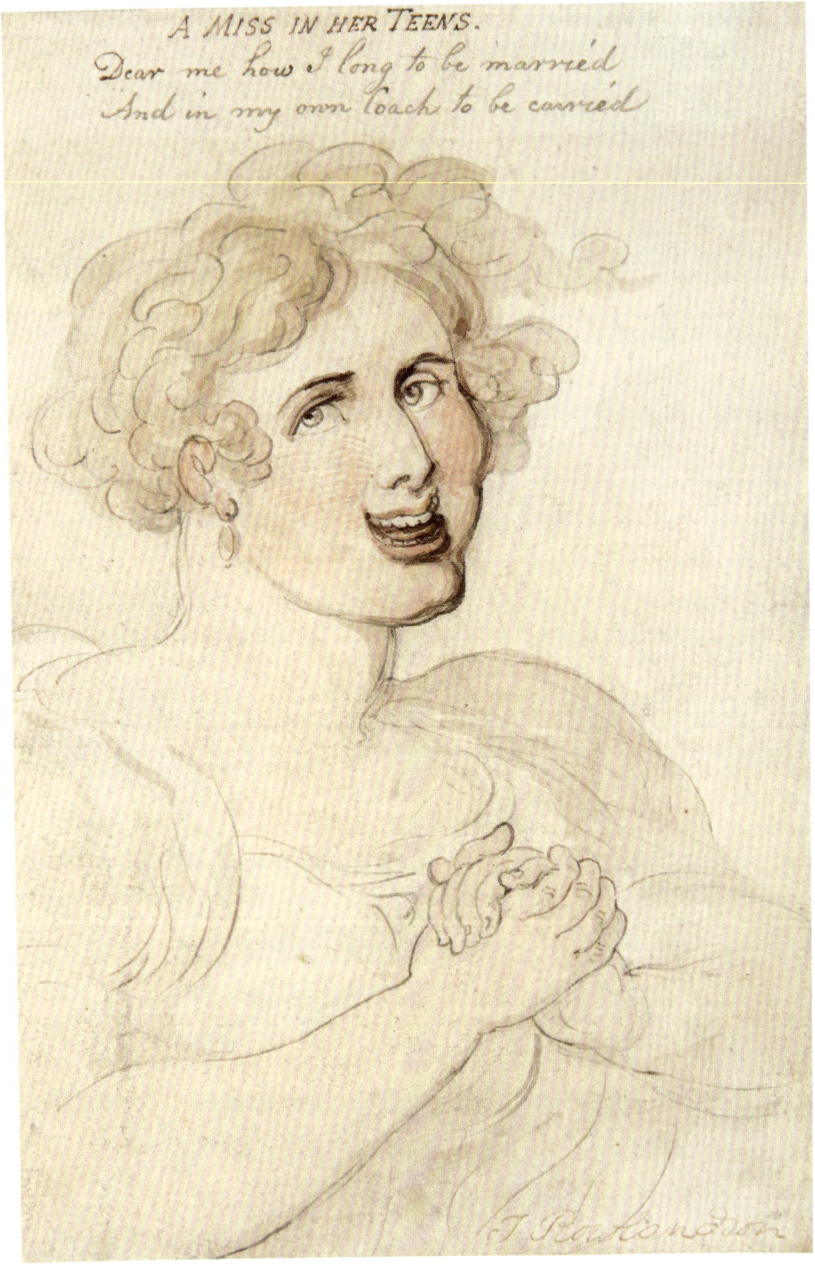

A Miss in her Teens

The title of this work references two popular stage comedies of the eighteenth century. The main title is taken from David Garrick's two act farce, *Miss in Her Teens*, which was adapted from Florent Carton Dancourt's 1691 play, *La Parisienne*. It was first performed at Covent Garden, London, in 1747. However, the couplet that acts as a subtitle is taken from T A Lloyd's *The Romp*, a two-act 'musical entertainment', altered from Isaac Bickerstaff's 1767 ballad opera, *Love in the City*. It was first performed at Covent Garden in 1778.

The two comedies were much revived, and in 1786 both were performed at Covent Garden with Mrs Brown in each leading role: Miss Biddy Bellair in *Miss in her Teens* and Priscilla Tomboy in *The Romp*. It is possible that Thomas Rowlandson saw Mrs Brown perform these roles and then produced the present work as a portrait.

Mrs J Brown was born into the theatrical Mills family and married William Ross, acting under the name of Mrs Ross in Ireland and Norwich. Following the death of her first husband in 1781, she married her fellow actor and singer, J Brown, in the same year. She made her London debut at Covent Garden in January 1786 as Miss Prue in William Congreve's *Love for Love*. Though praised for her performances on the metropolitan stage, she was considered a pale imitation of her more successful younger rival, Dorothea Jordan.

Rowlandson also inscribed the couplet from *The Romp* on a small watercolour entitled *The Wooer Wooed*, which is in the collection of the British Museum.

14 A Miss in her Teens
Dear me how I long to be married
And in my own Coach to be carried
Signed and inscribed with title
Pen and ink with watercolour
7 ¼ x 4 ½ inches

JOHN DOWNMAN

John Downman, ARA (1750-1824)

John Downman was one of the finest and most popular portraitists of the late eighteenth century, who received the patronage of both members of the royal family and icons of fashion. Working mainly in watercolour and pastel, he specialised in small format images that often depicted the half-length of the sitter in profile or semi-profile.

For a biography of John Downman, please refer to page 108.

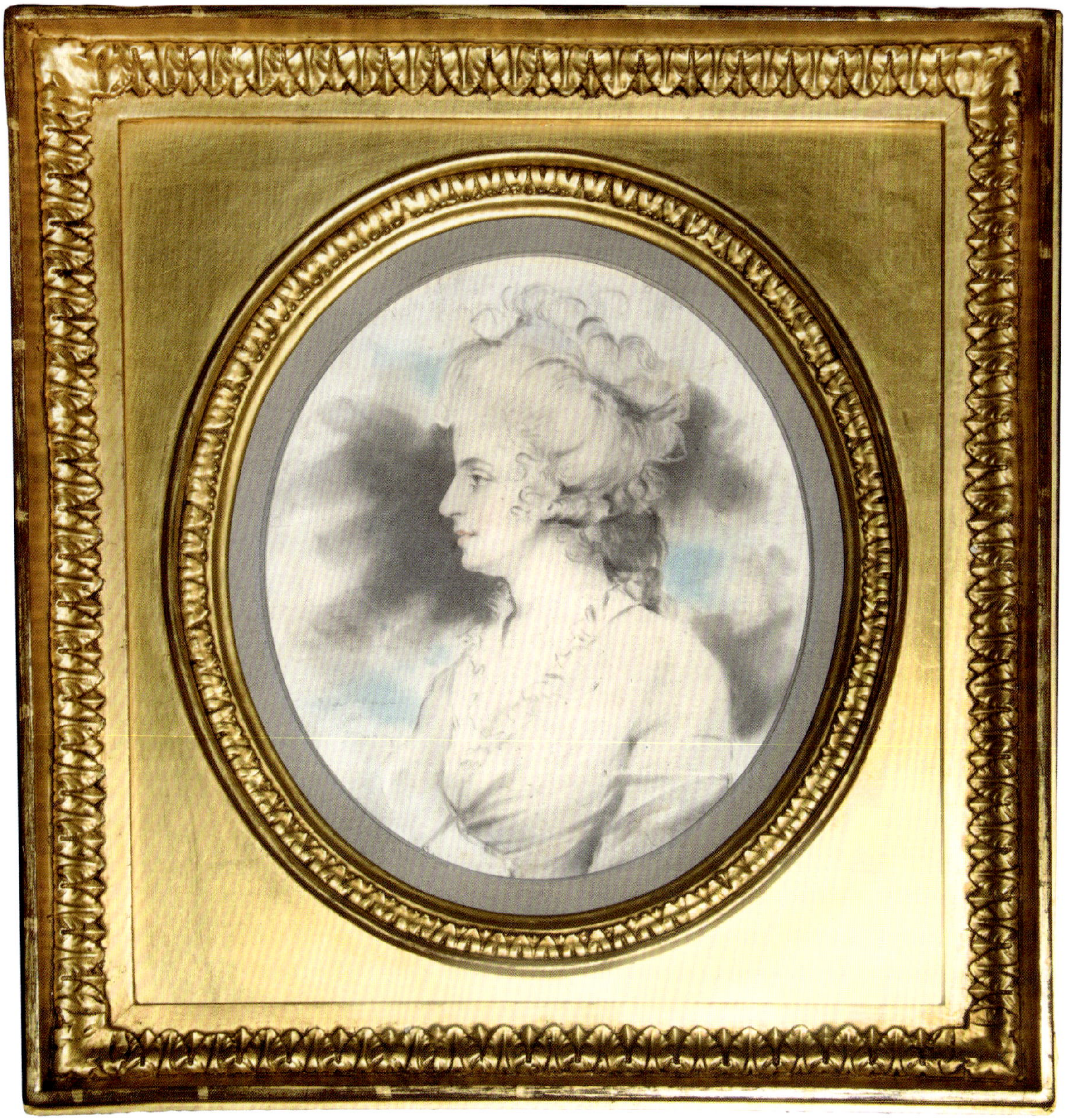

15

15 Portrait of a Lady in Profile
Signed and dated 1793
Watercolour
7 x 6 inches

WILLIAM ALEXANDER

William Alexander (1767-1816)

William Alexander was the only English artist of the late eighteenth century to penetrate the interior of China. As a result, he became well known for his images of the country at a time when Chinoiserie was all the rage. Admired as a technician, he worked as drawing master until 1808, when he accepted a position as one of the first curators at the British Museum.

For a biography of William Alexander, please refer to page 109.

An Inferior Mandarin of Turon Bay

William Alexander acted as junior draughtsman to Lord Macartney's embassy to China during the years 1792-94. For a fortnight of June 1793, the embassy stayed at Turon Bay, and it was during that time that Alexander produced the study on which the present watercolour is based.

Turon is now the city of Dà Nang in Vietnam. In developing trading rights with the country during the seventeenth and eighteenth centuries, the French called the city 'Tourane' as a corruption of the Vietnamese phrase 'Cua Hàn', meaning the mouth of the Han River, on which the city sits. In turn, the name was adapted to 'Turon'. Turon was in Annam, the central one of Vietnam's three provinces, though British visitors often called the region 'Cochin China'. In 1787, just six years before Alexander's visit, the ascendant ruler, Nguyen Ánh, ceded Turon to the French in return for a promise of aid.

On 3 June 1793, Alexander recorded in his journal, 'This morning a Mandarin from court ... came on board to see our ship ... with another of inferior rank who sat a few minutes while I made a slight sketch of him ... I persevered in keeping the sketch so he went out in a huff' (Susan Sloman, *Image of China: William Alexander*, London: Jupiter Books, 1980, page 9). He inscribed the sketch, 'An Inferior Mandarin of Turon Bay'. He also made a sketch of a pipe-bearer, and went on to work up the two drawings into finished watercolours before combining them in a composition. This was then engraved by James Caldwall on 12 April 1796 as *A Mandarine or Magistrate of Tourane Attended by His Pipe-Bearer, and published in Volume 3 of Sir George Staunton's An Authentic Account of An Embassy from the King of Great Britain the Emperor of China*, London: G Nicol, 1797. The original sketches entered the collection of Lord Macartney.

16 An Inferior Mandarin of Turon Bay
Signed with initials
Watercolour with bodycolour
14 ¾ x 9 ½ inches
Exhibited: 'Bliss was it in that dawn to be alive: British Watercolours & Drawings 1750-1850',
Chris Beetles Gallery, October 2008, No 165;
'The Long Nineteenth Century: Treasures and Pleasures', Chris Beetles Gallery, March-April 2014, No 4

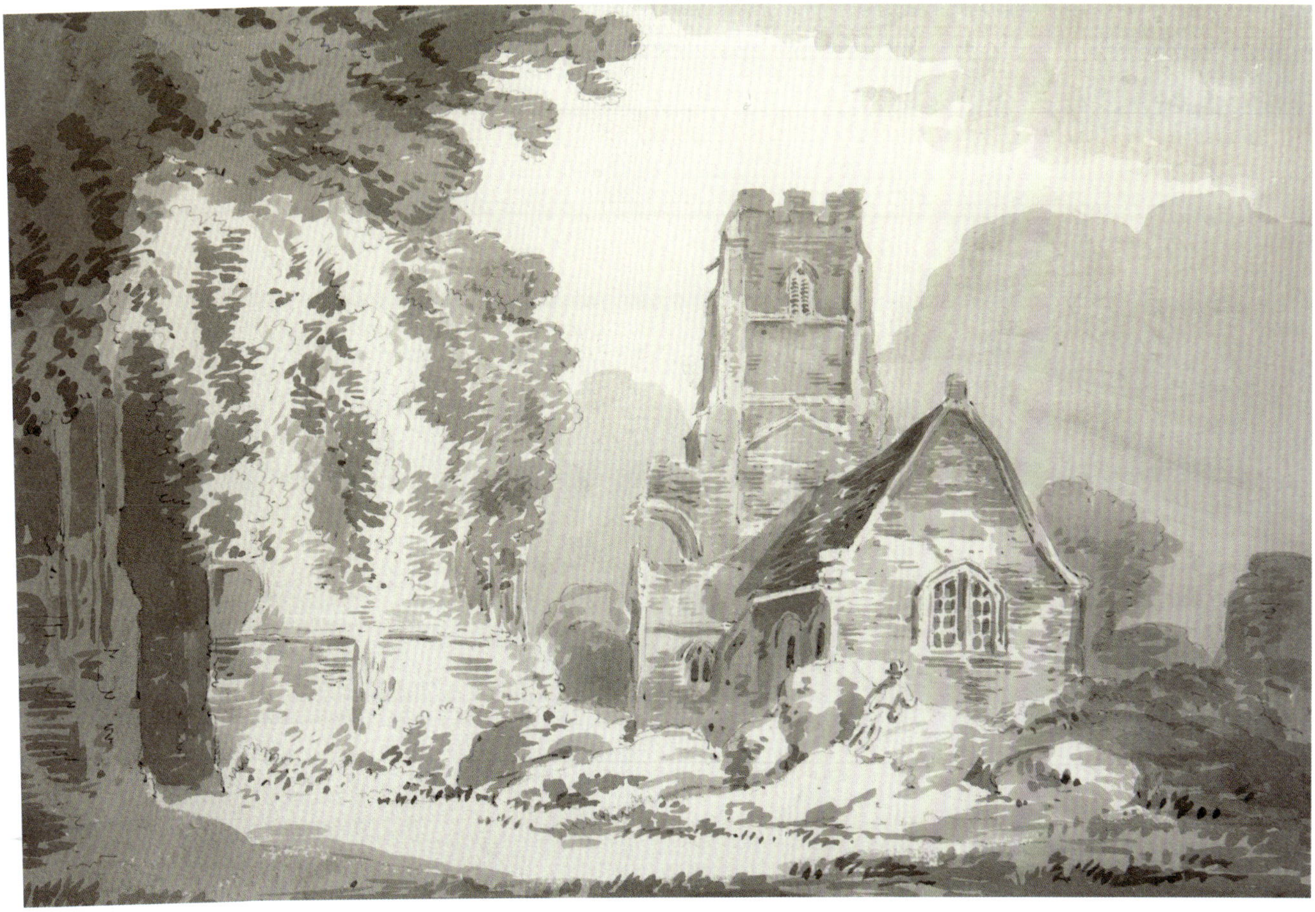

18 **St Andrew's Church, Covehithe, Suffolk**
Watercolour with pencil
6 ¾ x 9 ½ inches

St Andrew's Church, Covehithe, Suffolk
Edward Dayes made a number of drawings of buildings in Suffolk during the late 1780s. The present work almost certainly depicts the highly distinctive church of St Andrew's Covehithe, which stands vulnerably close to the eroding coastline between Southwold and Lowestoft. By the 1670s, the original large fourteenth-century structure was proving too expensive for the few parishioners to maintain; so they successfully sought permission to remove its roof and build a smaller church within it, incorporating its impressive tower in the process. Like Dayes, Cornelius Varley and John Cotman were also drawn to capture its picturesque qualities in watercolour (Norwich Castle Museum, 1781-83, and British Museum, 1804-5, respectively). However, Dayes' image is distinct from theirs in employing a viewpoint from within the ivy-clad ruins and focussing closely on the east end of the rebuilt church. In so doing, it clearly shows a window that would be replaced in the nineteenth century.

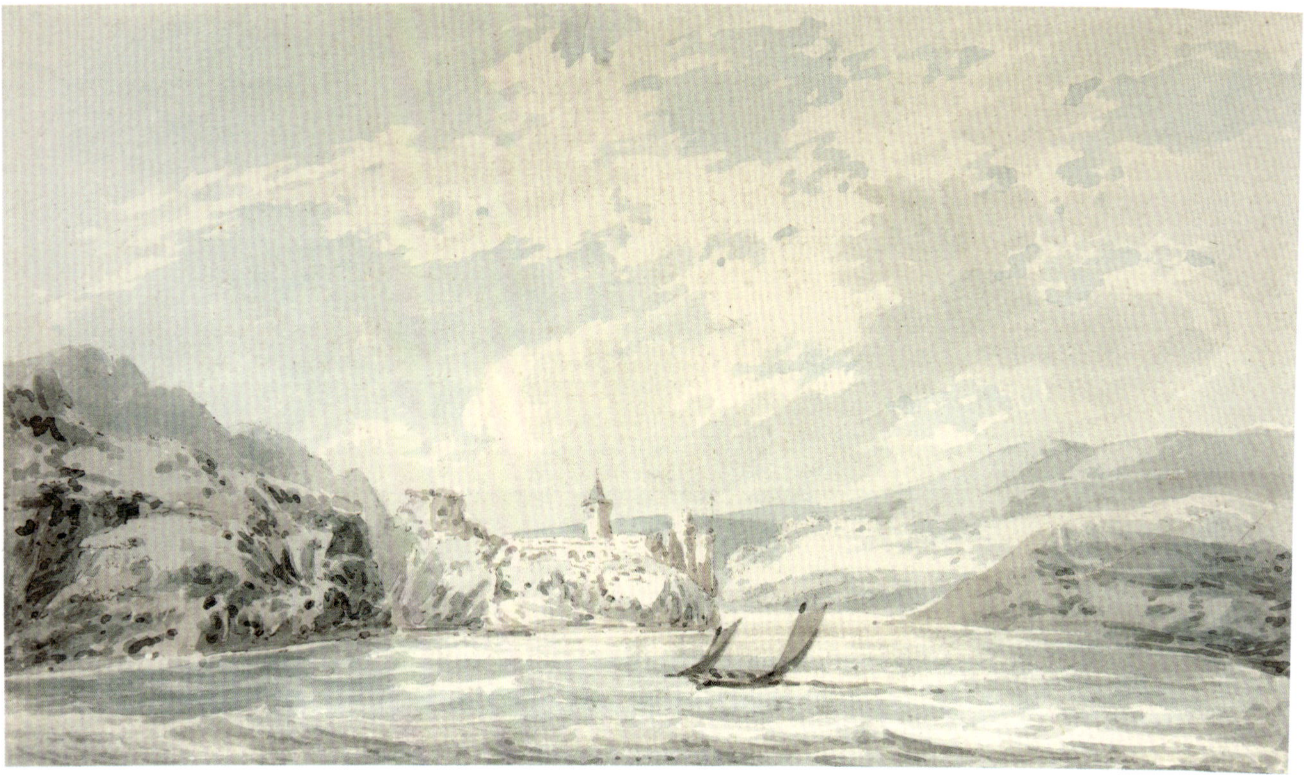

19 Dartmouth Castle
Watercolour
5 ½ x 8 ¼ inches

Dartmouth Castle

Devon proved to be a popular sketching ground for landscape artists during the late eighteenth century, and the picturesque qualities of such castles as that at Dartmouth held a particular appeal. Dartmouth Castle was constructed close to the church of St Petrox from 1388 to guard the estuary of the River Dart, and the towers of the two buildings together comprise a distinctive profile. However, the spire of the church that Edward Dayes included in his watercolour was removed in 1856, following the erection of a lighthouse on the other side of the promontory.

Dayes may have travelled to Devon in or before 1798, as in the August of that year he recorded in his diary that he was painting an oil of Dartmouth Castle. In addition to the present watercolour, there is a least one other by Dayes of the castle; recently in the stock of another London dealer, it presents a view from the other direction, looking out to sea. Dayes' former pupil, Thomas Girtin, also visited Devon in the late 1790s and, among numerous watercolours, produced *Kingswear Seen from Dartmouth*, Devon (Yale Center for British Art).

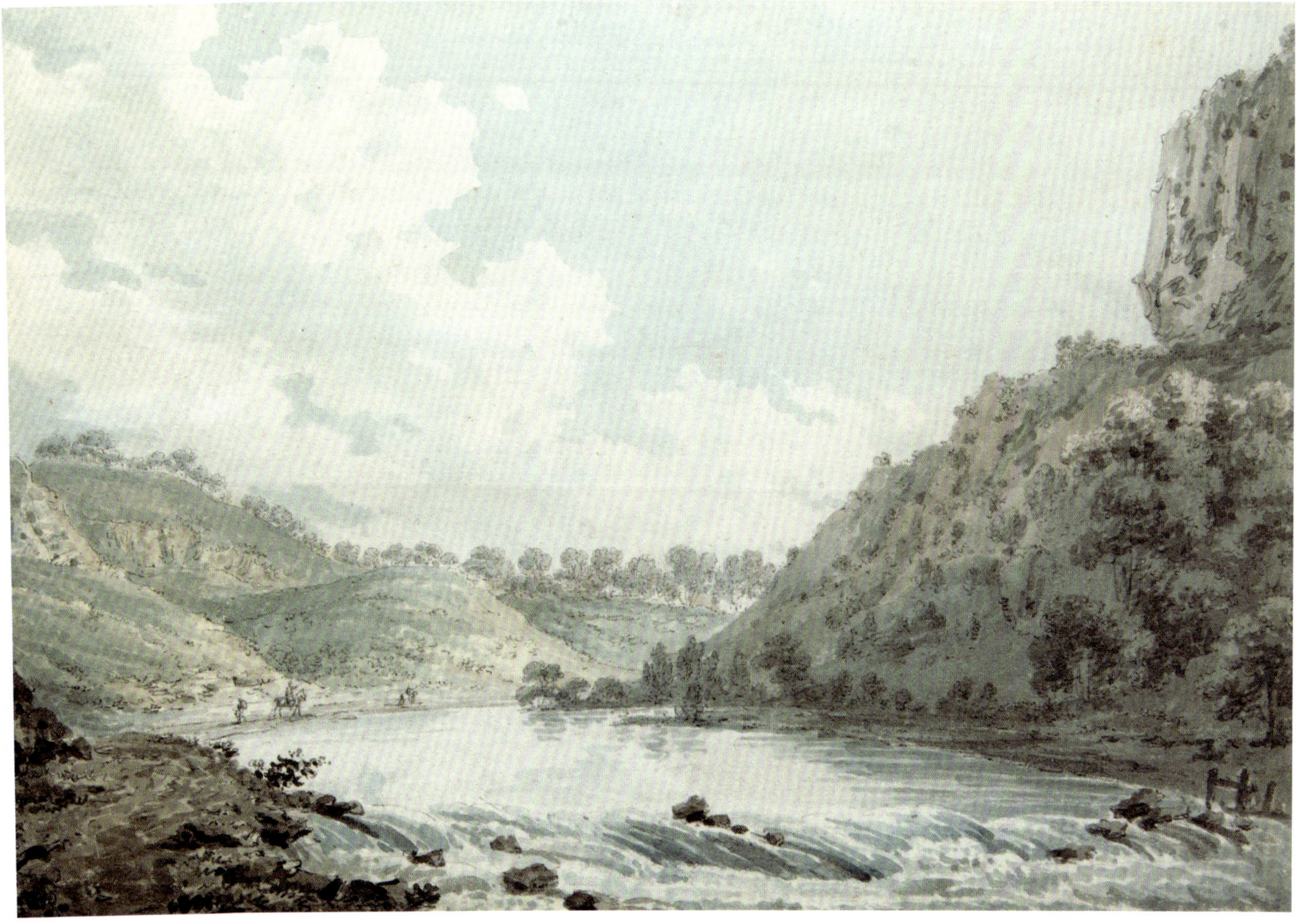

20 High Tor, Matlock
Watercolour
6 ¾ x 9 inches

High Tor, Matlock
The village of Matlock, in Derbyshire's Peak District, developed as a tourist destination through the course of the eighteenth century, as a result of the discovery of warm springs and the establishment of therapeutic baths. Its impressive setting on the steep sided valley of the River Derwent, dominated by the limestone crag of High Tor, made it attractive to artists by the 1770s, including Joseph Wright of Derby and John Warwick Smith.

Edward Dayes made an 'Excursion through Derbyshire and Yorkshire' in 1803, and completed an account of it just before his death in the following year. When it was posthumously published in 1805, its editor, E W Brayley stated that the 'principal object' of the trip was 'to contemplate the romantic Character of Dove-Dale; and to inspect, and to make Drawings of the sublime and picturesque Scenery of the North and West Ridings of Yorkshire'. In a footnote to his account, Dayes wrote of Matlock, that 'between the bath and the village, every twenty yards will afford a new scene, from the sudden turns of the river, and the majestic elevation of Matlock High-tor, which forms a fine abrupt contrast to the opposite and more gentle bank of the Derwent'.

DAVID COX

David Cox, OWS PAA (1783-1859)

The freedom and atmosphere of his mature landscapes of England and Wales made David Cox one of the most influential of Victorian watercolourists.

For a biography of David Cox, please refer to *Chris Beetles Summer Show*, 2017, page 24.

David Cox in North Wales

While living in London in 1805, David Cox made his first sketching tour to North Wales, and there produced his earliest recorded drawings, including *On the Road to Dolgelly* (private collection). He is likely to have been inspired by his mentor, John Varley, who had made his own visits to the region just a few years earlier, as well as by the developing fashion for Picturesque tours around Britain.

North Wales became more accessible to Cox from 1814, following his move to Hereford, where he took up a teaching position at Miss Croucher's School for Young Ladies. In 1818, he returned to Dolgelly (now spelled Dolgellau), and made a number of studies that he probably worked up later, including *Parliament House, Dolgelly* [23] and *Water Mill* [22].

Though Cox went back to London to live in 1827, he remained drawn to North Wales, and made further trips to the region, including a significant one in 1836, during which he prepared the illustrations that he was to contribute to Thomas Roscoe's *Wanderings and Excursions in North Wales*, published in the same year. His drawing of Conway (or Conwy) Castle [21] possibly dates from this period. In 1844, he made the first of annual summer visits to the village of Betws-y-Coed, situated on the confluence of the rivers Conwy, Lledr and Llugwy, and these continued until 1856, just three years before his death.

21 Conway Castle
Pencil
6 ¾ x 10 ½ inches

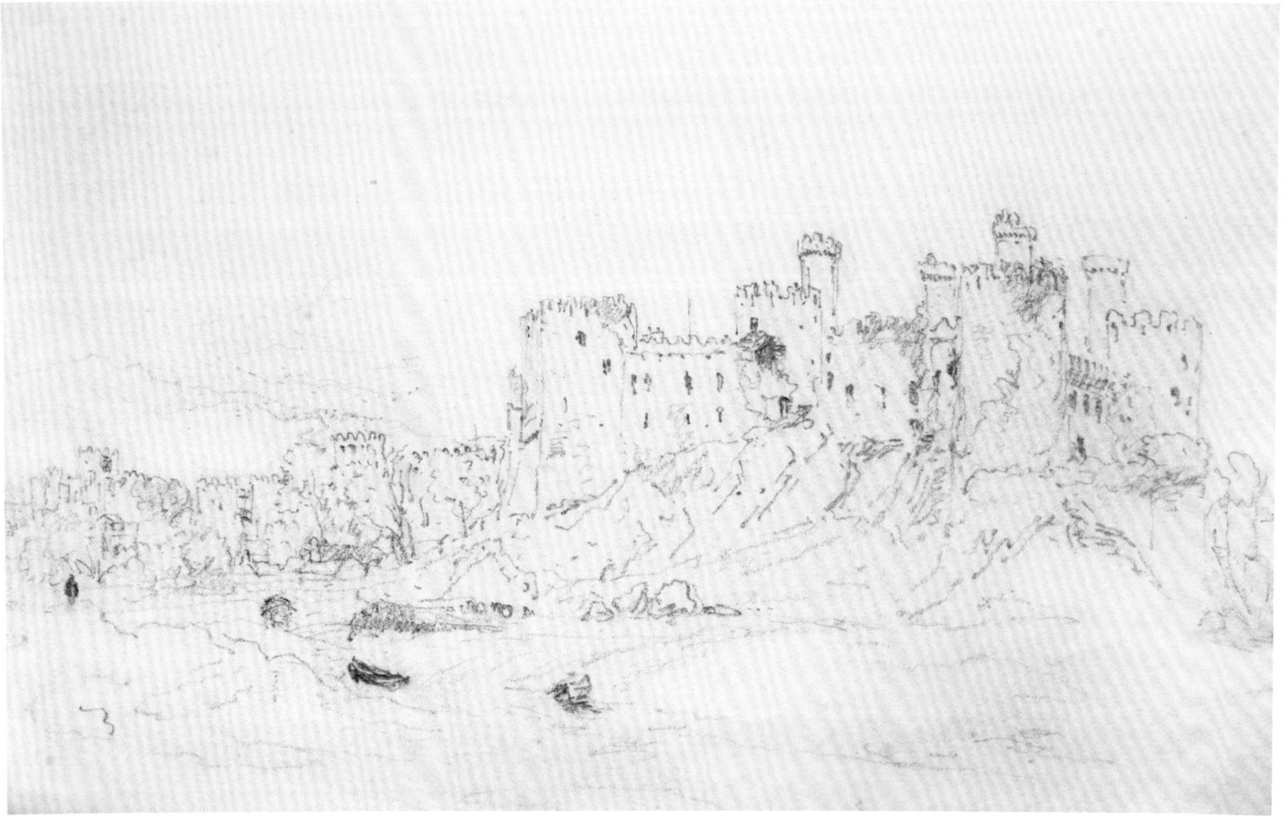

22 Water Mill
Signed on detached slip of paper
Watercolour
4 ¾ x 7 inches

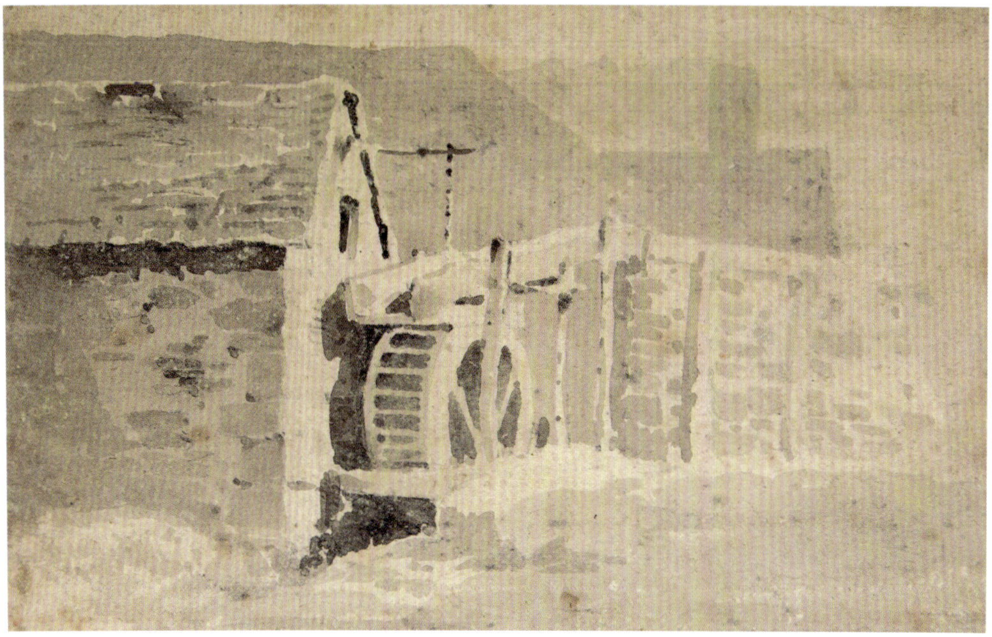

23 Parliament House, Dolgelly
Signed and dated 1819
Inscribed 'In Dolgelly. Owen Glendowr held his meetings' on reverse
Watercolour
4 x 7 ½ inches

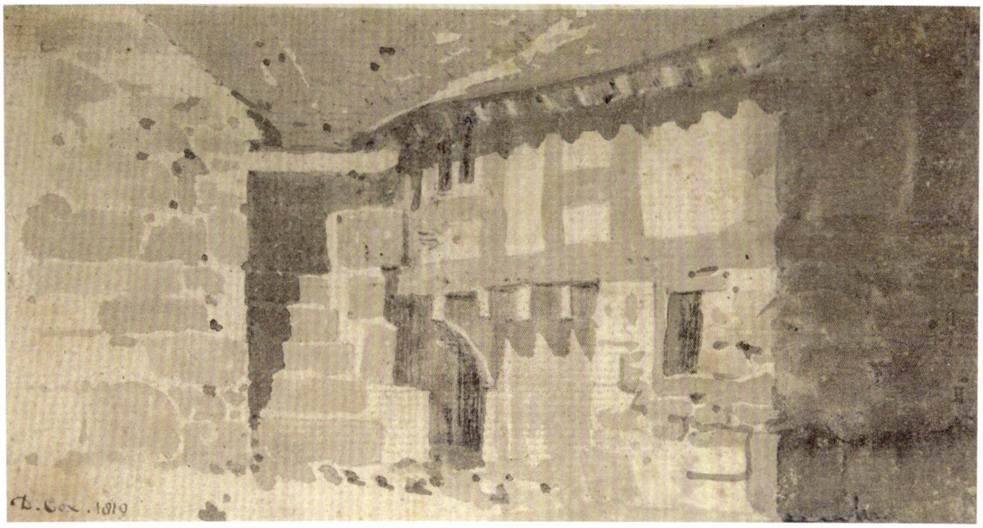

Parliament House, Dolgelly

The present work is of great interest both for its historical association and its relation to drawings of the same subject by John and Cornelius Varley (the one by John being in the British Museum). As noted in the inscription on the reverse of the drawing, the building is believed by some to be that in which 'Owen Glendowr held his meetings'. Owain Glyndŵr (circa 1359-circa 1415) led a long, violent, if ultimately unsuccessful campaign to ensure Wales's independence from England. There is a strong tradition and some evidence that Glyndŵr used the building, also known as Plas Cwrt yn Dre, to assemble his allies. However, others claim that it dates to no earlier than the late fifteenth century.

By the mid eighteenth century, the Old Parliament House was attracting the attention of artists and antiquaries, despite, or perhaps because of, the fact, that it was deteriorating. During the nineteenth century, a campaign was launched to restore the property and convert it into a museum. However, an appeal to raise the funds to purchase it from the then owner was suppressed in favour of another to found a private school for girls. As a result, the timber-framed building was bought in 1886 by the mail order entrepreneur, Pryce Pryce-Jones, who had it dismantled and rebuilt – in an altered form – on his estate at Dolerw Park, Newtown, 30 miles southeast of Dolgellau. Since then, it has been used for a variety of purposes, including, until 2010, as a Quaker meeting house. Though a listed building since 1988, its survival and status continue to be disputed.

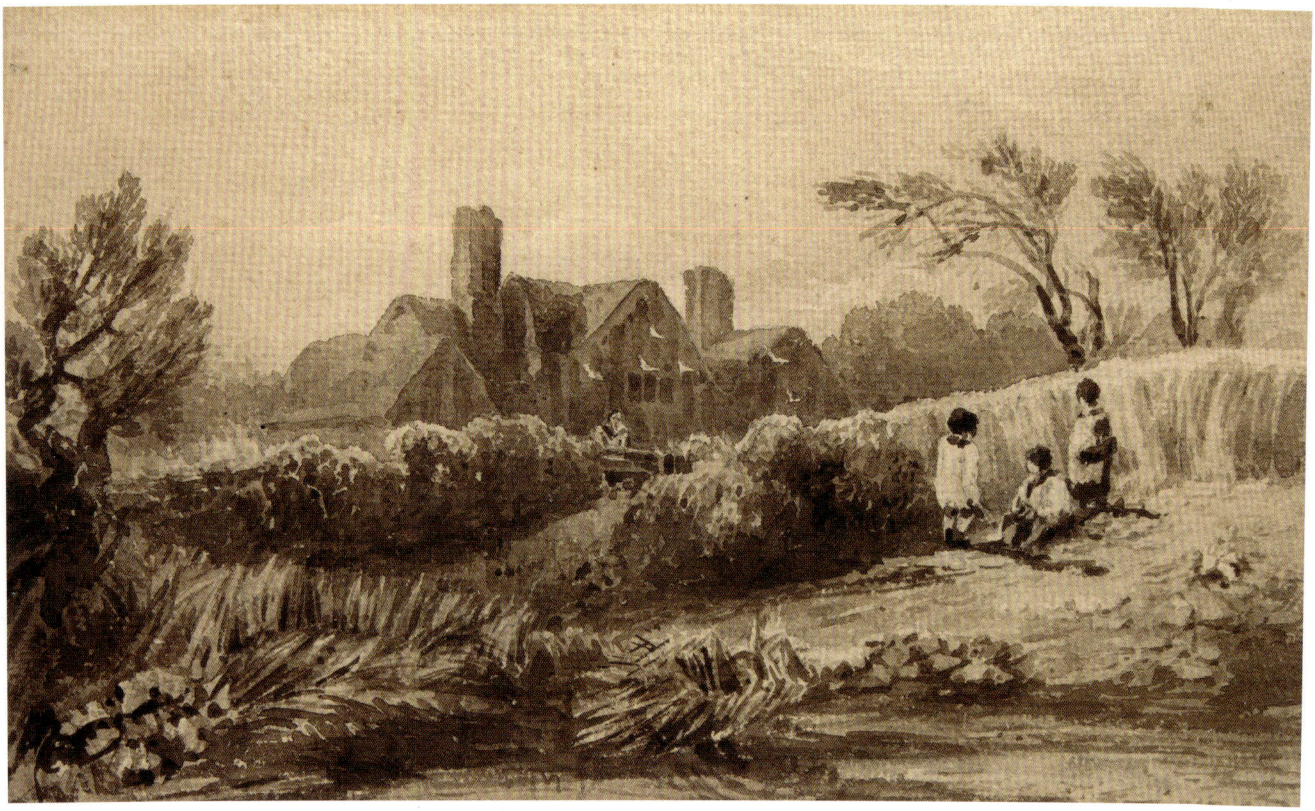

24 Selly Hill Farm
Watercolour
6 ¾ x 10 ¾ inches
Exhibited: 'David Cox, 1873-1859: An Exhibition of His Watercolours', The Wren Gallery, London, March 1973

Selly Hill Farm

While the association between David Cox and Haddon Hall, in Derbyshire, has been explored with some thoroughness, his connection to the humbler dwelling of Selly Hill Farm (now known as Selly Manor) is less well known.

One of Birmingham's oldest buildings, Selly Hill Farm originally stood on a hill in the manor of Selly, to the south of the present city centre. First recorded in the late fifteenth century as a farm known as Smythes tenement, it was leased in 1561 by the landowner, William Gower, to his bailiff, John Setterford, who then made extensive renovations to the house. Following the death of John's widow, Phylis, in 1608, the house went to her grandson, John Pritchett, and the Pritchetts, who were yeomen farmers, continued to own and live in it throughout the remainder of the seventeenth century. During the eighteenth century, the house became more of an investment, and had a number of short-term owners and tenants. By 1775, when it was put up for sale, it had gained the name Selly Hill Farm. Following a further sale, 20 years later, the house lost its status, as the 65 acres on which it had stood were broken in two.

Early in the nineteenth century, the house was divided into two cottages, and fell increasingly into disrepair. To such artists as David Cox, however, this gave it an attractively picturesque quality. He produced the earliest known drawing of the building before 1840, at a time when the two cottages were occupied by the agricultural labourers, Charles Holyoake and Charles Stuckley, and their families. As the Holyoakes were just a couple, while the Stuckleys comprised a household of seven, the three children in the present watercolour may have belonged to the latter.

Around the time of Cox's death in 1859, the building was reapportioned as three cottages and became known as the Rookery, a term suggestive of its increasingly overcrowded and dilapidated state. In 1895, it was bought, along with several other nearby plots of the divided Selly Grove estate, by Edward Oliveri, an Italian-born wine merchant and local councillor. However, it was only after his premature death in 1907 that action was taken to preserve and repair it. It was then bought by George Cadbury, the creator of the famous chocolate company and founder of Bournville, the model village that lies just south of Selly. Under the direction of the architect, William Alexander Harvey, it was removed and rebuilt in Bournville, a painstaking process that took seven years between 1909 and 1916. It then opened as a museum, with the new name of Selly Manor, displaying sixteenth and seventeenth-century furniture and domestic objects that had been collected by George Cadbury's son, Laurence.

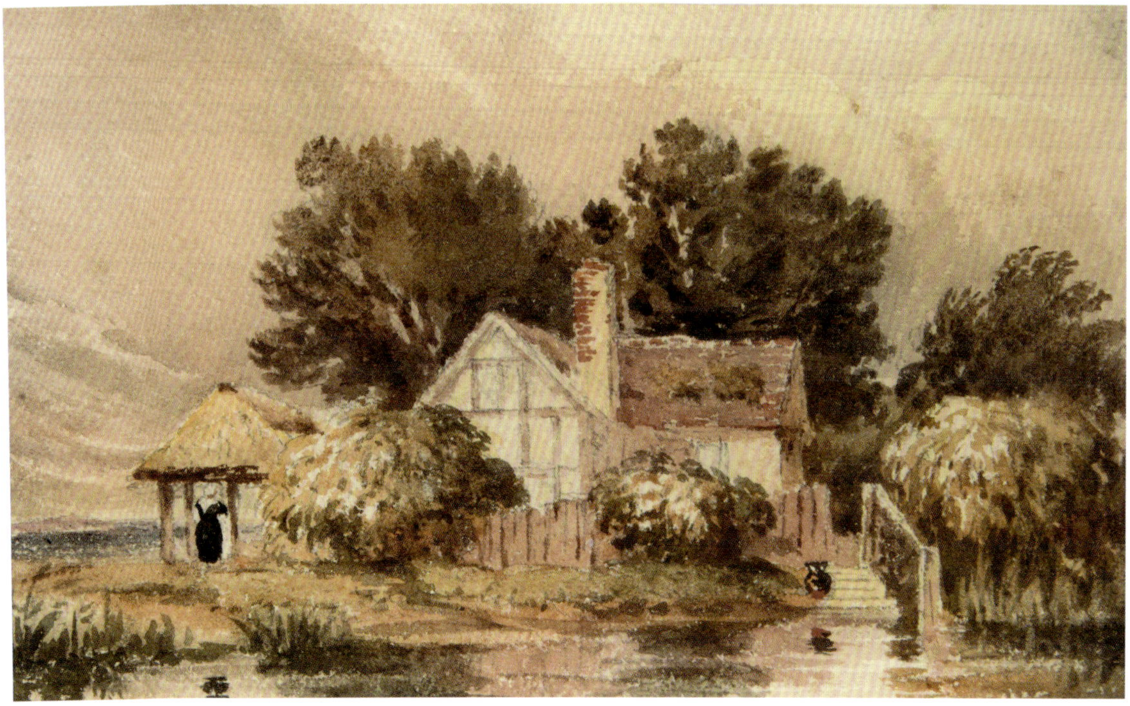

25 **Riverside Cottage** (above)
Pencil and watercolour
5 ½ x 8 ¾ inches

26 **Ruined Cottage** (below)
Pencil
6 ¾ x 8 ¾ inches

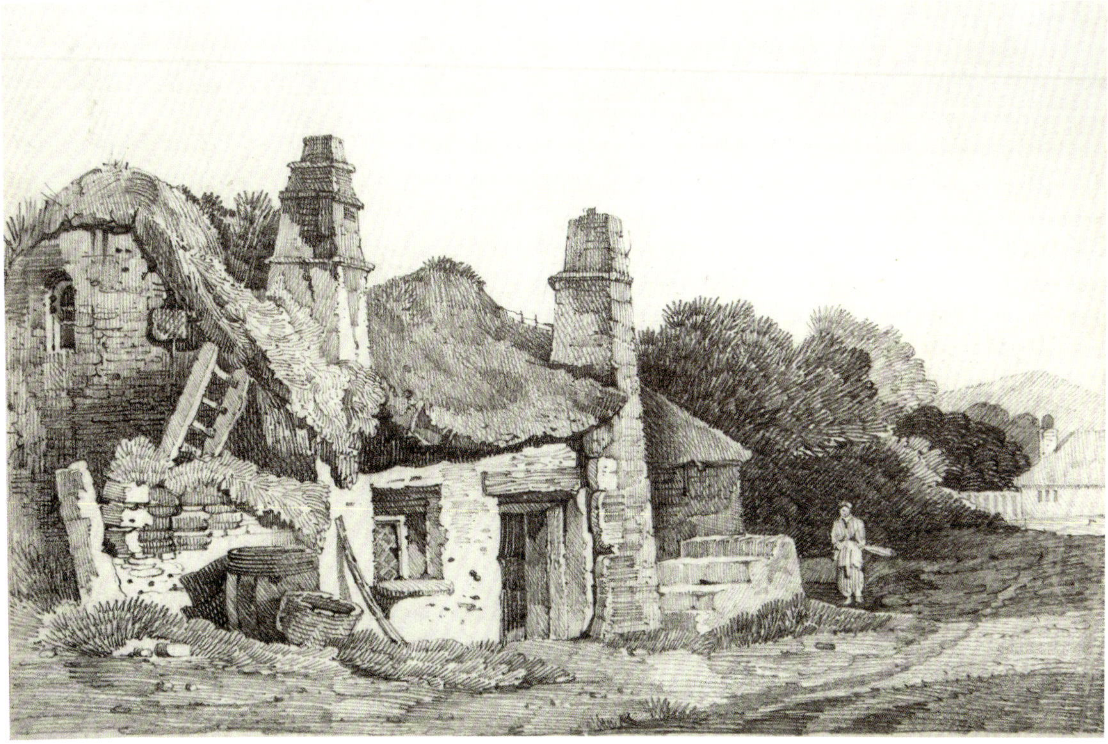

COPLEY FIELDING

Anthony Vandyke Copley Fielding, POWS (1787-1855)

Copley Fielding was one of the most technically impressive watercolourists of his day, both popular as an artist and influential as a teacher.

For a biography of Copley Fielding, please refer to page 111.

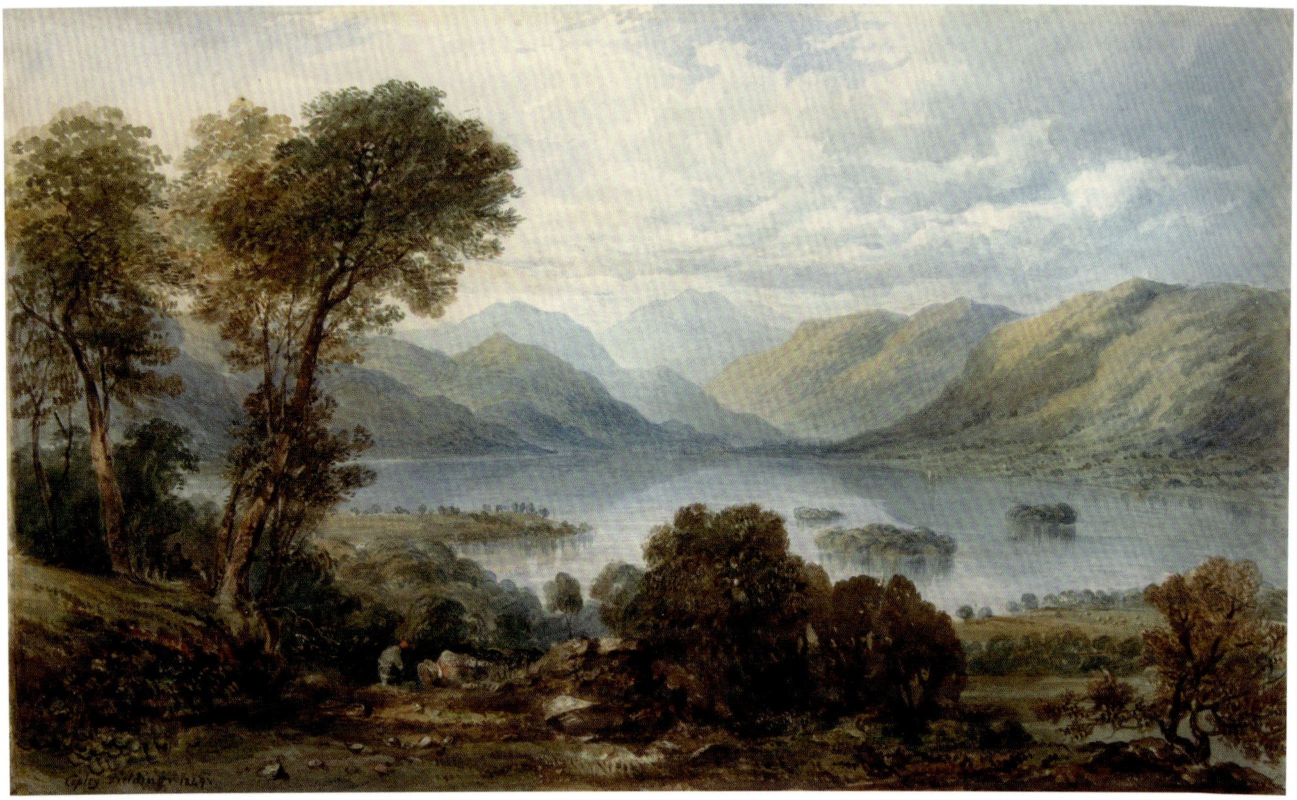

27 **Derwent Water from the Castle Head**
Signed and dated 1849
Watercolour with gum arabic
11 x 17 inches

Derwent Water from the Castle Head
Yorkshire-born Copley Fielding spent his late teenage years, until 1807, with his family in Keswick, on the northern shore of Derwent Water, in Cumberland (now in Cumbria). Though based in Southern England from 1809, he often returned to the Lake District on sketching tours, and exhibited paintings of the area regularly and frequently at the Society of Painters in Water Colours until 1854, the year before his death.

For the present work, Fielding chose a classic viewpoint from which to depict Derwent Water. The low wooded hill of Castlehead, just outside Keswick, allows a panorama looking south that includes Rampsholme Island, Lord's Island and St Herbert's Island in the lake itself and the fell known as Catbells in the background.

Though Fielding would certainly have known the place himself, he seems to have founded his composition on an image by Thomas Allom, which was engraved by Samuel Lacey and published in Thomas Rose's topographical guide of 1832, *Westmoreland, Cumberland, Durham & Northumberland*. In turn, Allom's image must have been based on W F Kangiesser's watercolour of about 20 years earlier (now held in the British Museum), as it is almost identical, even to a similar trio of figures on the left and the same dispersal of boats upon the water.

GEORGE PYNE

George Pyne, AOWS (1800-1884)

Though overshadowed in his early career by the artistic achievements of his father and father-in-law, George Pyne came into his own as a precise, and sometimes intense, architectural draughtsman.

For a biography of George Pyne, please refer to *Chris Beetles Summer Show*, 2017, page 28.

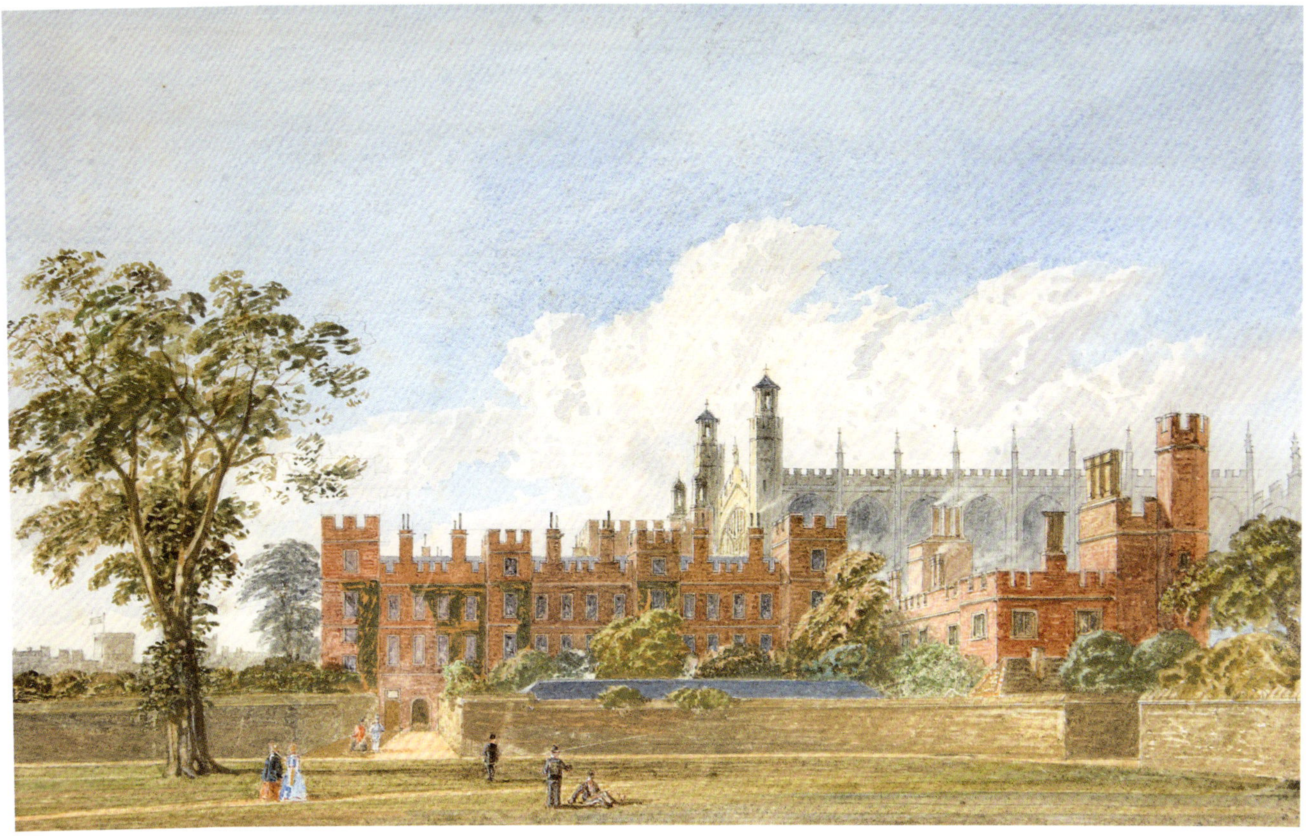

28 **The Provost's House, Eton**
Watercolour with pencil; 8 ¾ x 12 ¾ inches
Provenance: Leger Galleries, London, December 1976;
Peter Lawrence

The Provost's House, Eton

Eton College, Buckinghamshire, was founded by Henry VI in 1440. The institution was originally modelled on Winchester, founded in 1387, as a charity school for 70 less privileged boys. Its red brick buildings include a house for the use of the Provost, the chairman of the college's governing body, which selects a Head Master. It is overshadowed by a fine grey-stone chapel in the Perpendicular style, which was constructed later in the fifteenth century. The upper school was added in 1694, when the college first became fashionable for sons of the nobility. Further expansion occurred as both its fame and its population grew.

During the period of George Pyne's career, Eton had five Provosts, all of whom had been educated at Eton and King's College, Cambridge. These were the long-serving but conservative Joseph Goodall (1809-40); John Lonsdale (1840), who was elected but refused office in favour of Francis Hodgson; Hodgson (1840-53), who proved to be a great reformer; Edward Hawtrey (1853-62), who had served as Head Master under Hodgson; and Charles Goodford (1862-1884), who was Head Master under Hawtrey and was another reformer.

This watercolour was presented to Peter Lawrence in 1977, on his retirement from his position as a house master at Eton. Publishing books and articles on aspects of the history of the college, he founded the Museum of Eton Life in 1985. Until his death in 2005, he was the last surviving master at Eton to have served in the Second World War.

EDWARD LEAR

Edward Lear (1812-1888)

Though now best known for his nonsense poems and drawings for children, Edward Lear made his initial reputation as an ornithological illustrator, and then earned his living as a landscape painter. During extensive travels in Europe, the Middle East and Asia, he made frequent, evocative sketches that acted as the basis for astonishing oils and watercolours.

For a biography of Edward Lear, please refer to *Chris Beetles Summer Show*, 2014, page 5.

29 Collecting Water, Corpo di Cava
Inscribed 'Corpo di Cava' and dated '25 July 1838'
Pencil drawing of mother and child on reverse
Oil on paper
5 ½ x 8 ¾ inches

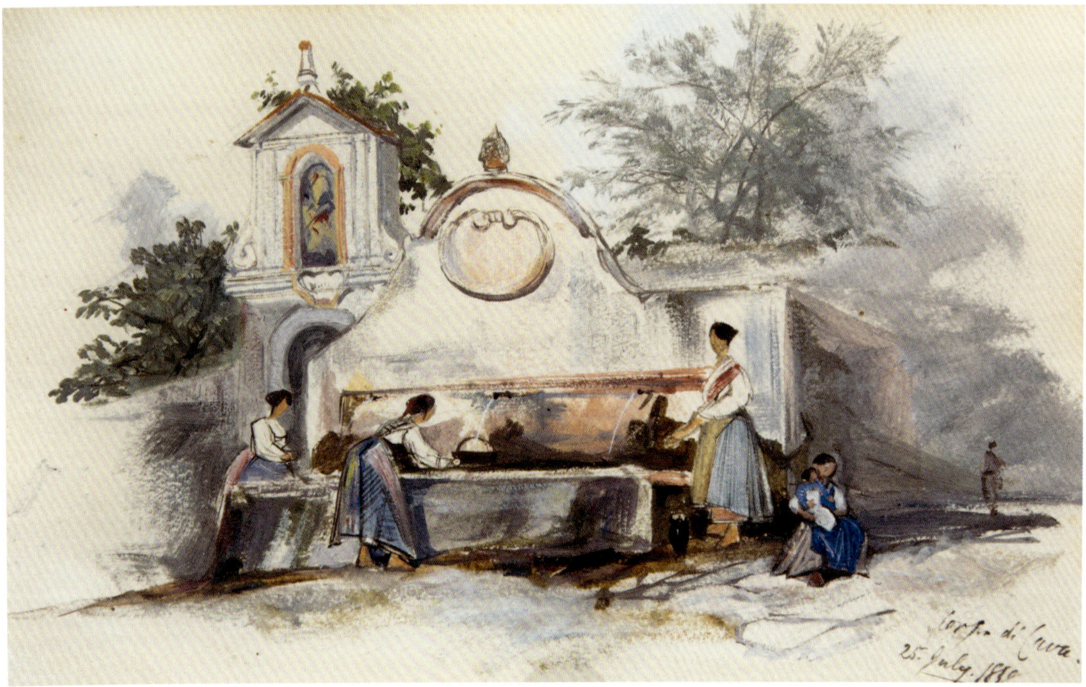

Edward Lear in Italy in 1838

Early in 1837, a group of subscribers, led by the Earl of Derby and his cousin, Robert Hornby, commissioned Edward Lear to go to Rome to produce drawings (and, at the same time, to improve the state of his health). It would be his third trip to the Continent, but his first to Italy. He left England in July that year, and arrived in Rome in the December. Apart from two visits to England in 1841 and 1845-46, he then remained in Italy for a decade.

Each summer of that decade, Lear would travel to a different part of the country. In May 1838, he made a slow journey to Naples in the company of fellow artist, James Uwins. On their arrival, they found that they were staying in the same hotel – the Hotel de La Ville de Rome – as Samuel Palmer and his wife, Hannah, who were in the middle of their Italian honeymoon. However, Lear found Naples 'all noise, horror – dirt, heat – & abomination' (as he expressed in a letter to John Gould in the following year, on 17 October 1839). So, after a few days, he and Uwins moved on.

Travelling in a south-easterly direction, they settled at Corpo di Cava, a village situated at the head of a high wooded valley looking down to the Bay of Salerno. It had been the haunt of artists since the time of Poussin and Rosa, and James Uwins' uncle, Thomas Uwins RA, had painted there 10 years before, which may have prompted his and Lear's visit. There they established a daily pattern of walking and sketching, punctuated by some longer expeditions, including that, in the middle of June, to the classical ruins of Paestum, which dominate the coastline about 30 miles south of Salerno.

Late in June, Lear and Uwins moved from Corpo di Cava to Amalfi, on the coast west of Salerno, and stayed for three weeks at the Albergo Cappucini, until 18 July. The visitors' book reveals that they overlapped with Achille Vianelli and Ercole Gigante, two landscape painters of the School of Posillipo. It was following their return to Corpo di Cava in late July that Lear produced *Collecting Water, Corpo di Cava* [29]. This, and the undated view of Vietri sul Mare, now a suburb of Salerno [31], show Lear experimenting with oil – on paper – for the first time, sometimes purely and sometimes in conjunction with other, water-based media. His decade in Italy is defined in part by his decision to take seriously to oils. He and Uwins finally left Corpo di Cava at the beginning of August, in order to stay in Sorrento, on the southern extreme of the Bay of Naples. At the end of the month, they began their slow return to Rome.

30 On the Road to Vietri sul Mare
Signed, inscribed '[V]ietra' and '13', and dated '[Ju]ly 1838'
Pencil with bodycolour
4 ½ x 6 inches

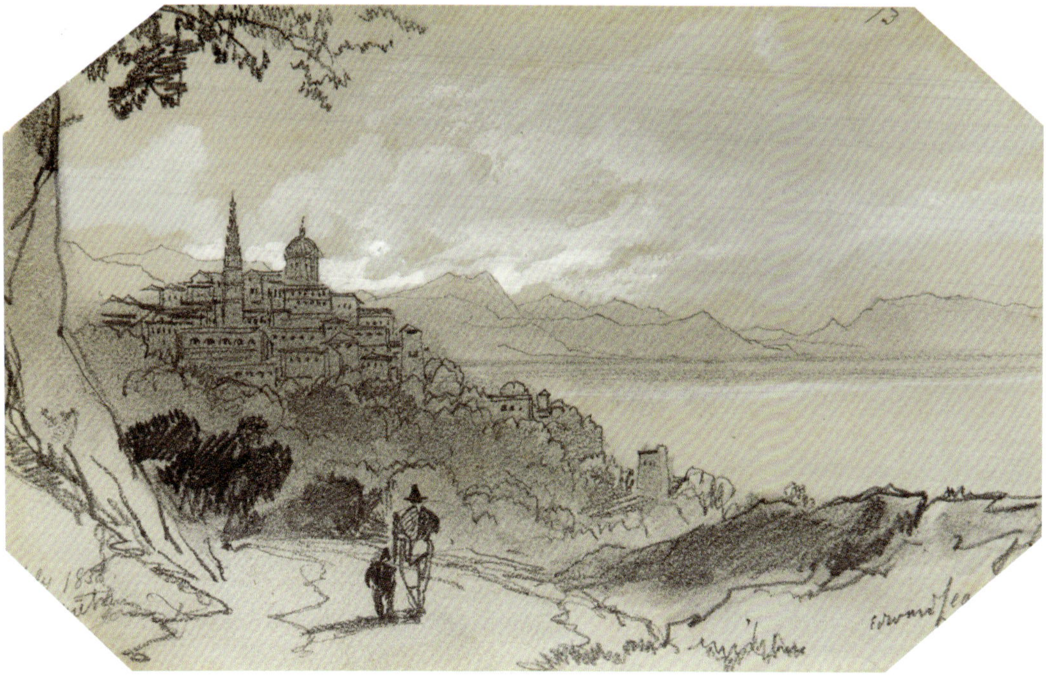

31 Vietri sul Mare
Oil with watercolour and bodycolour
9 ¼ x 13 ½ inches

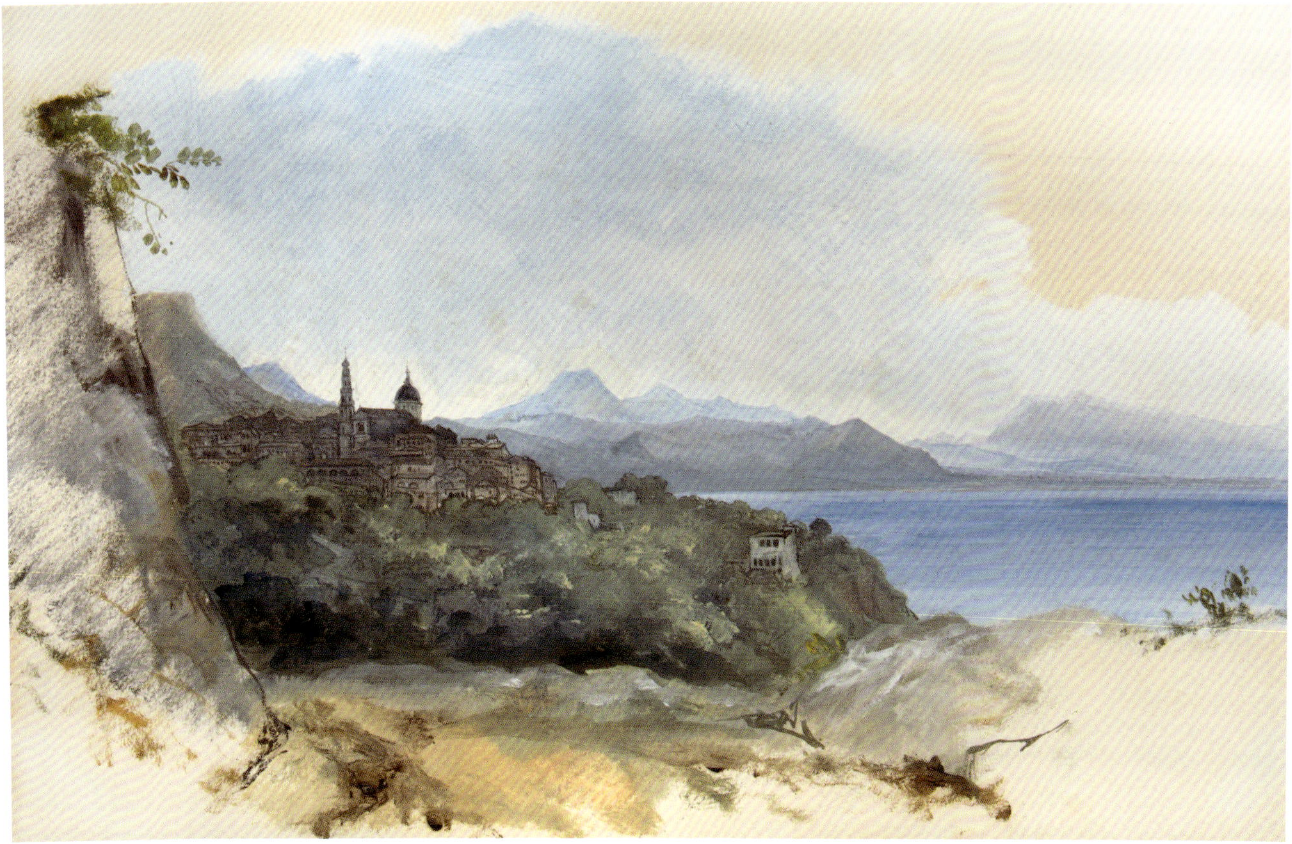

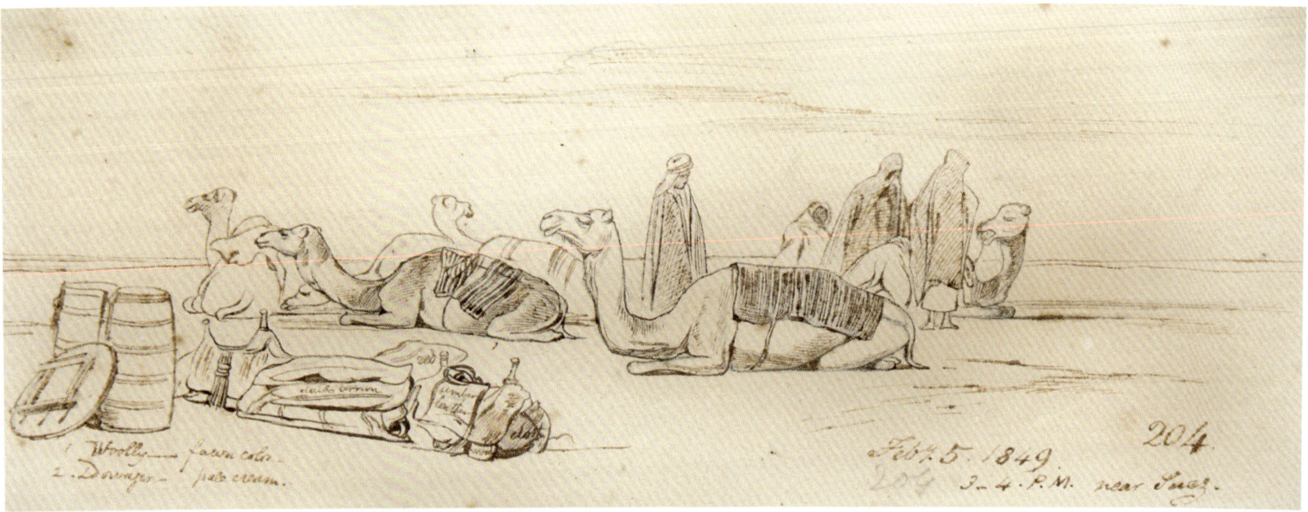

Camels Resting near Suez

Having been thinking about a trip to Egypt from early in 1848, Edward Lear arrived in Cairo in January 1849. There he met his old friend, the Reverend John Cross, who had offered to finance an expedition to Sinai and Palestine. They set out by camel on 13 January, and travelled along a route that can be charted through the many drawings that Lear made on the way, including those around Suez (15-17 January), of the wadis around Abu Zenima (20 January) and of Wadi Ferran (23 January).

Lear and Cross arrived at St Catherine's Monastery, Mount Sinai, on 27 January 1849, and stayed there for three nights. However, during that time, Lear caught a cold, so they decided to turn back to Suez, and on their arrival, Lear was exhibiting signs of fever. They had 'hoped to make Gaza, quarantine, and the Holy Land but, having stayed there for eight days … the weather turned bad and Lear suddenly became miserable and gave up. From Alexandria, he took ship for Malta' (Peter Levi, *Edward Lear: A Life*, London: Tauris Parke paperbacks, 2013 (revised ed), page 121). He would eventually visit Palestine in spring 1858.

The present drawing was made outside Suez on 5 February 1849, near the end of the trip. It is likely to be at least one of five studies of camels produced on that day. Two others are in the collection of the Houghton Library, Harvard University. The first, numbered '200' and drawn at 10 am, focusses on a single camel which has been tethered by its front leg. The second, numbered '201' and drawn at noon, comprises studies of six dead camels in various states of decomposition, one of which is being picked over by vultures. As the present – far more charming – drawing was numbered '204' and drawn between 3 and 4 pm, Lear must have made two further studies in the time in between noon and 3 pm, probably also of camels.

In a letter to his sister, Ann, written between 16 January and 3 February, Lear described his experience of the beasts of burden. He compared the enjoyable sensation of riding one to sitting 'on a rocking chair', but found them to be easily irritated, so that 'If you try to make them go faster – they grown', as he expressed in his punning spelling, and 'if you stop them or try to go slower – they growl also'.

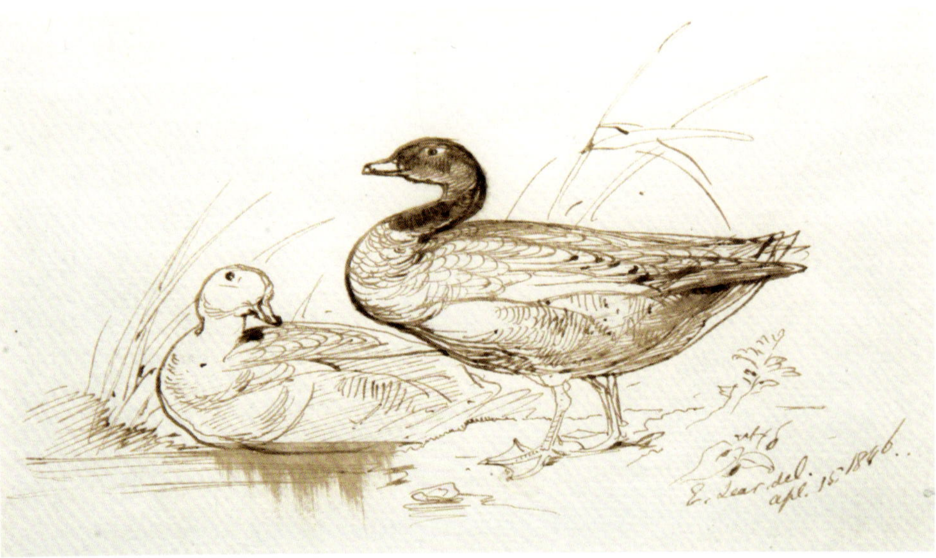

32 Camels Resting near Suez (above)
Inscribed '204', 'near Suez', '1. Woolly – fawn colour' and '2. Dowager – pale cream', and dated 'Feby 5 1849. 3-4 pm'
Pen and ink
4 x 10 inches
Provenance: Andrew McIntosh Patrick; Luke Gertler

33 Two Geese
Signed and dated 'Apl 15. 1846'
Pen and ink
3 ¾ x 5 ¾ inches
Provenance: Fanny and George Coombe of Peppering House, Burpham, Sussex, and by descent; Luke Gertler

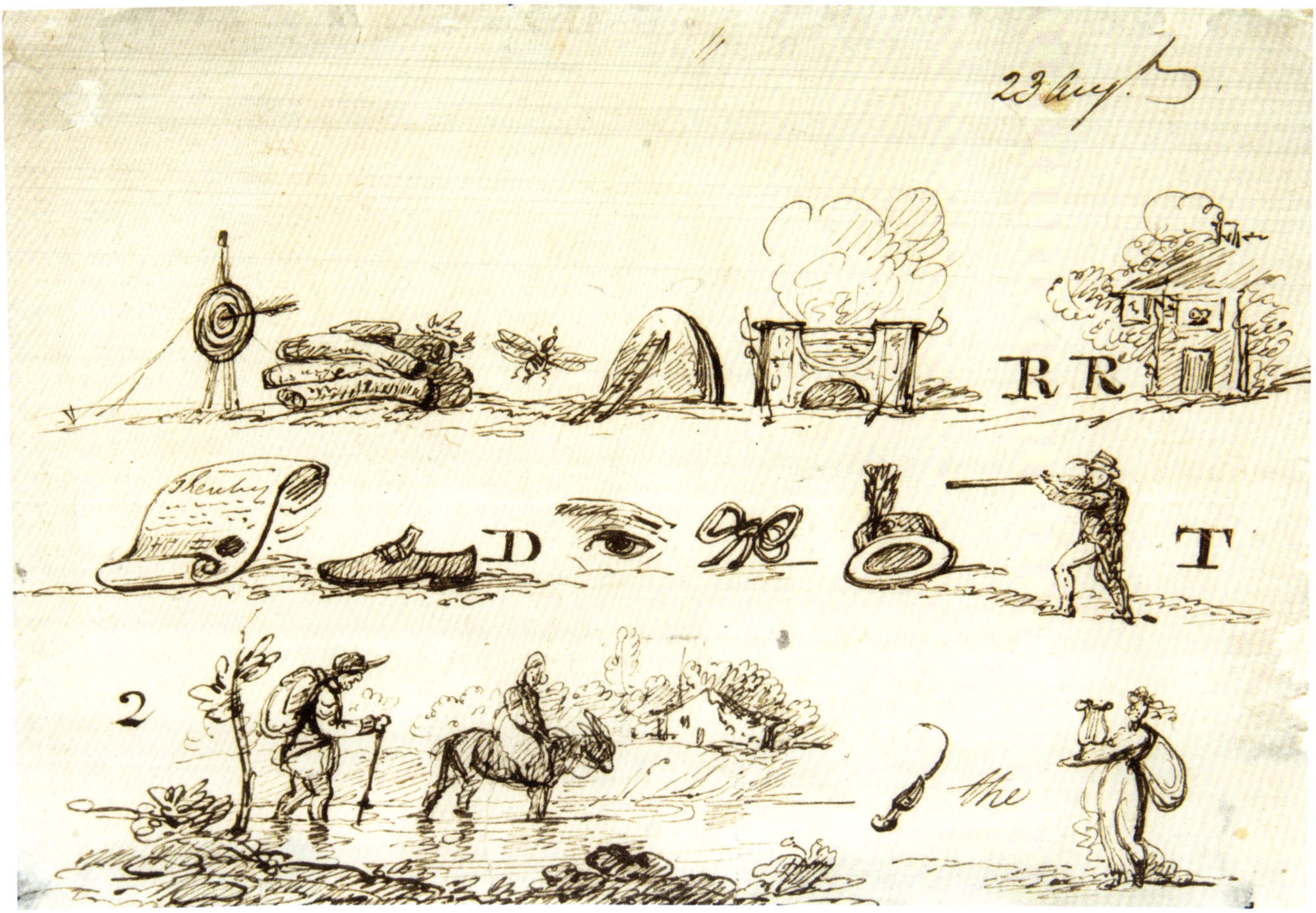

34 The Rebus Letter
Dated '23 August'
Pen and ink
4 ¼ x 5 inches

The Rebus Letter

A rebus is a text that is presented as a combination of images and individual letters. The form may have originated in Egypt as early as 3400 BC, but was certainly popular in England during the eighteenth and nineteenth centuries, both in correspondence and as an entertainment. The present example by Edward Lear may be either the beginning of a letter or an element in a game. It spells out the following message: 'I would be a great arse in/writing should I not attempt/to afford to catch the muse'. The use of the word 'arse' may seem out of character for such a writer as Lear. However, it does appear in his diaries, including the entry for 1 September 1867, when he relays the words of a German tutor spoken during a game of Charades: 'it is Arse: for it says – let it be concealed – certainly I should always conceal my arse: nobody should show his arse'.

Two Geese (opposite)

Edward Lear made the present drawing for the family of his childhood friend, Fanny (née Drewitt), of Peppering House, Burpham, Sussex, and her husband, George Coombe. Dated 'Apl 15 1846', it was probably produced on a rare visit to England, during the years in which Lear was living in Italy. In the same month, the first volume of his *Illustrated Excursions in Italy* – which he dedicated to his patron, the Earl of Derby – was published in London by Thomas M'Lean, and this led to his being appointed drawing master to Queen Victoria. Earlier the same year, he had also launched himself as a comic poet, with *A Book of Nonsense*, which comprised the illustrated verses that he had composed for Derby's children.

Lear had initially made his name as an ornithological draughtsman, in issuing *Illustrations of the Family of Psittacidae, or Parrots* in parts between 1830 and 1832. His work would continue to feature birds both serious and humorous, including a duck in his poem, 'The Duck and the Kangaroo' (circa 1865), and the limerick, 'D was a Duck' (from the comic alphabet, 'A was an Ant' of 1867), and a goose in 'G was a little old Goose' (from another comic alphabet, written in about 1880). The present fowl are more likely to be geese rather than ducks, as is indicated by the shape of their beaks and the length of their necks.

FRANKLIN LUSHINGTON

Sir Franklin Lushington, JP (1823-1901)

Franklin Lushington has gained lasting fame as a close friend of Edward Lear, indeed so close that they produced collaborative drawings. He had a distinguished legal career, initially as a judge to the Supreme Court of Justice in the Ionian Islands and later as a magistrate in London.

Nos 35-38 are by Edward Lear and Franklin Lushington.

Lear and Lushington in Greece in 1849

In 1848, Edward Lear left Italy, after a decade of living in that country. He did so partly to escape its increasingly unsettled political climate – despite being supportive of those driving reform – and partly to explore and record the eastern Mediterranean.

Lear was particularly excited at the prospect of visiting Greece, which had long impressed itself upon his imagination, whether in the form of classical myth or in Lord Byron's involvement in the Greek struggle for liberation from Turkish domination. Between Spring 1848 and Summer 1849, he undertook extensive travels in mainland Greece, including two trips, each shared with a younger friend. In June and July 1848, he travelled in the company of Charles Church, while, in March and April 1849, he travelled with Franklin Lushington. The four drawings included here were collaborations between Lear and Lushington that were made on the latter tour, and it is that which is the present focus.

While on Malta in Spring 1849, Edward Lear met Franklin Lushington through his elder brother, Henry Lushington, who was Chief Secretary to the government of the island, which was at that time ruled by a British military governor. At 26 years old – a decade younger than Lear – Franklin had recently become a Fellow of Trinity College, Cambridge, and was about to embark on a legal career as a student of the Inner Temple. Like his elder brothers, Edmund and Henry, he was a classical scholar; so, in agreeing to travel to Greece with Lear, he could contribute a deep knowledge of the ancient world that would complement Lear's experience and preparation. Lear would write to his sister, Ann, on 8 March, telling her that Franklin was 'a very amiable and talented man – to travel with whom is a great advantage to me as well as pleasure'.

Having left Malta on Saturday 3 March, Lear and Lushington arrived in Patrás on Wednesday 7, and two days later they began their exploration on horseback in the company of a dragoman, travelling eastwards. On 10 March, they arrived at the monastery of Megaspelion (Mega Spileo), which Lear described in a letter to his sister Ann, of 4 April, as 'a wondrous place containing 200 or 300 monks – in a large cave'. From there, they headed south to Kalavryta and into the mountainous heart of the Peloponnese. On their arrival at Lake Phonia (Feneos) on 13 March, Lear considered 'the scenery' to have 'more of a Swiss character – all black pines & snow mountains'. The following day, they reached Levidi, close to the ancient site of Orchomenos, and, the day after that, Tripoli, which had been almost destroyed during the recent war of independence.

On Friday 16 March, the small party turned westwards towards Karitaina, and on the following day reached **Andritzena** (Andritsaina), the subject of the earliest of the four collaborative drawings by Lear and Lushington that are presented here [36]. Lushington was an amateur artist, who was very happy to work alongside and learn from the professional, Lear. However, he had the opportunity to do more than that, as Fani-Maria Tsigakou has explained in her seminal article, 'Reassessing the Edward Lears at the Benaki Museum' (Μουσείο Μπενάκη, 2, 2020, pages 137-146), which makes public her discovery that the museum holds collaborative works by the two men that were formerly thought to be by Lear alone. Lear would make copies of some of his outline drawings, and then give one version to Lushington for him to elaborate and complete. So this view of Andritzena can be compared to a similar composition by Lear that is held in the collection of the Houghton Library, Harvard University (17 March 1849 (38)), as are many of the drawings made on this trip. The buildings silhouetted at top right are almost identical, and the other buildings and mountains similarly placed. The present drawing differs in such details as the figures and coloured washes, and these have clearly been added by Lushington. In passing, it is perhaps worth mentioning that another of Lear's drawings of Andritzena, made on the same day, which is held in the collection of the National Gallery of Canada, is inscribed with the first two lines of a limerick, 'There was an old man of Andritzena/Who possesses a sack – and he sits in her'. It shows how Lear's serious and comic work resonate more closely with each other than is sometimes realised.

Continues on page 34 ☞

35 Gorge of Taygetum near Sparta
Signed with initials, inscribed with title and '21', and dated 'March 24/49' by Franklin Lushington
Pen ink and watercolour with pencil
9 ¾ x 6 ¾ inches

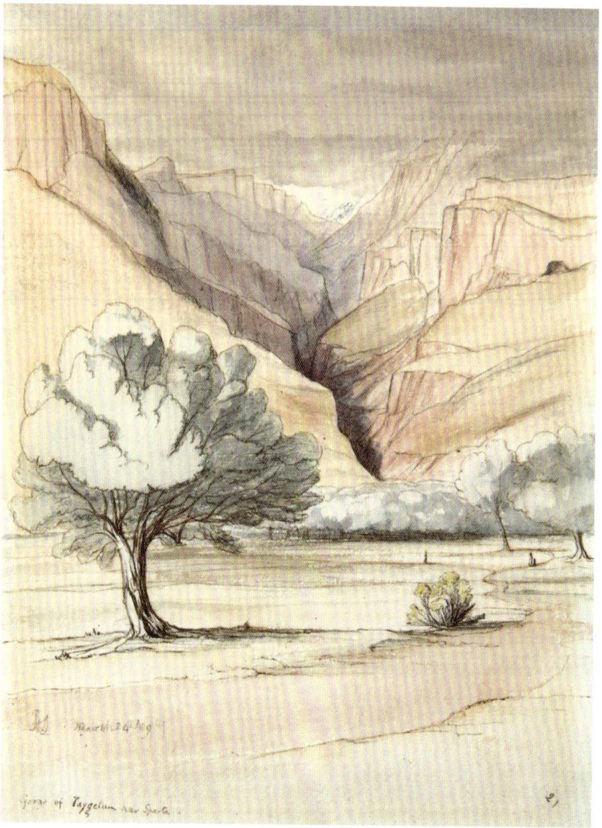

36 Andritzena (below)
Signed with initials, inscribed with title and '13', and dated 'March 17/49' by Franklin Lushington
Watercolour with pen and ink
6 ¾ x 9 ¾ inches

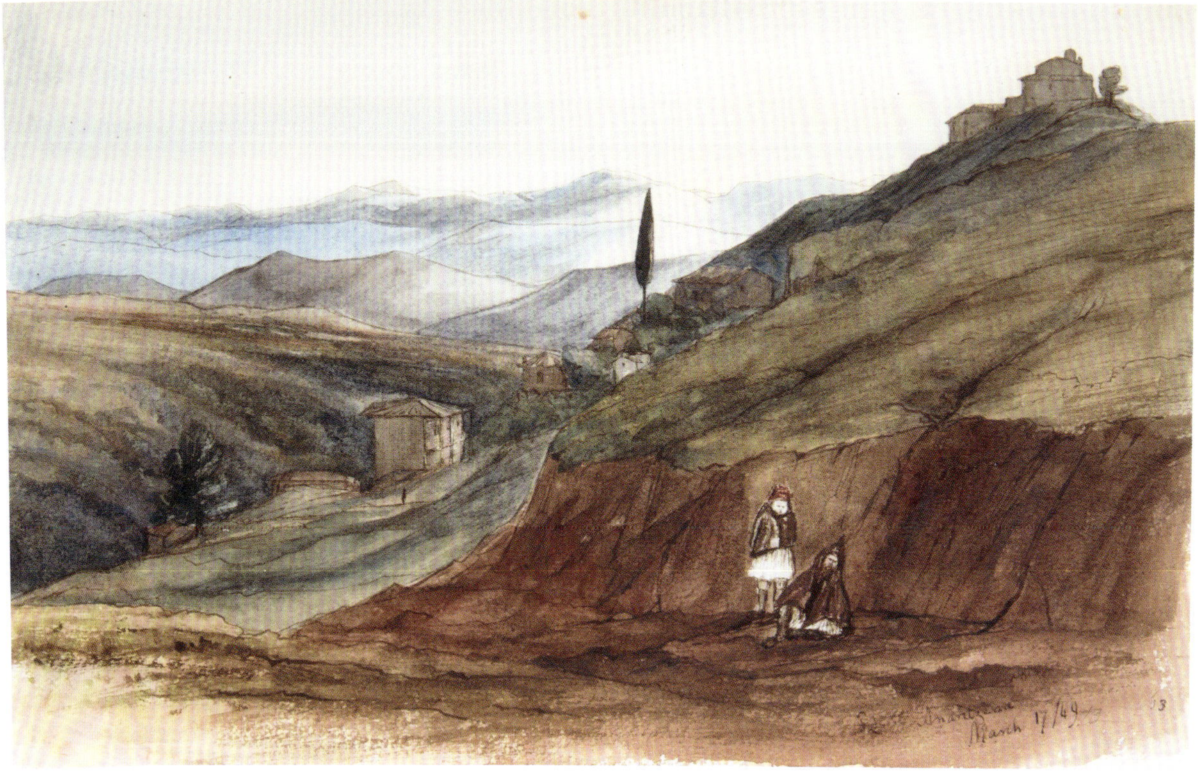

☞ On Sunday 18 March, the party arrived at Bassae, which, as Lear explained to his sister, Ann, is the site of a 'temple to Apollo – perhaps the finest Greek ruins after the Parthenon'. Though he 'never saw such a beautiful landscape', his attempts to capture it on paper were curtailed by a snowstorm. Nevertheless, he made a sufficient number of drawings to provide the basis of *The Temple of Apollo at Bassae*, a major oil of 1854-55 (The Fitzwilliam Museum, Cambridge).

By Tuesday 20 March, Lear and Lushington were led south by their dragoman to the village of Mavromati and the nearby ancient site of Messene, both of which sit in the shadow of Mount Ithome. From there, they went east, reaching Leontari on 22 March, and Sparta on the following day. In writing to Ann, Lear described 'the landscape of Sparta as extremely grand – a wide plain below tremendous mountains – always snow topped' and the modern town as 'one of the most stirring in Greece'. The site of ancient Sparta, as capital of Lacedaemon, was also likely to have been a highlight for both of the English travellers. On 24 March, they produced the second of the present drawings, Gorge of Taygetum near Sparta [35, see page 33], Lear providing the initial outline and Lushington working it up in pen and watercolour. It possibly shows the Caeadas chasm of the Taygetus mountains into which the Spartans threw criminals. While in the area, they also visited the monastery of Pantanassa in Mystras (24 March). On Sunday 25 March, the party headed north, via Vourlia and Kria Vrisi, towards Argos, where, as Lear reminded Ann, 'Agamemnon & all those people lived'. The response of Lear and Lushington to the beauty of the plain of Argos may be considered as epitomising both their shared experience of the trip and the friendship that was developing out of it. Lear explained to Ann that 'The ground had been literally covered with flowers' and that he and Lushington 'gather them all day like children'. On 30 March, they travelled north to Mycenae and Nemea, and on the following day arrived in Corinth.

From Corinth, Lear and his companions left the Peloponnese to travel east into Attica and onto Athens. Their time in Athens included a visit to Cape Colonna (Sounion) on Friday 6 April, to see the Temple of Minerva. On 10 April, they headed northwest to **Thebes**, in Boeotia, where Lear had been taken ill with malaria in the previous year, while on his trip with Charles Church. On the following day, he and Lushington produced the third of the present drawings [37], showing the mountains surrounding Thebes. The outline is very similar to a composition by Lear in the Houghton Library (11 April 1849 (156)), on which he notated a tune played by a shepherd on a bugle. From Thebes, they went, via Livadeia (13 April), to Mount Parnassus, the home of the gods (14 April), where Lear made a number of drawings that would provide the basis for oils.

Continuing west, Lear's party stayed at Arachova, on the night of Saturday 14 April, *en route* to **Delphi**, which in ancient times had been the home of Pythia, the famous Apollonian oracle. It provided a wealth of subjects for drawings during the days that were spent there, including *Delphi and Parnassus from Plain below Crissa* [38], the fourth of the present group of collaborations between Lear and Lushington, produced on 18 April. Again it is very similar in composition to a drawing in the Houghton Library (18 April 1849 (201)), and, though that is inscribed 'Near Amfissa: Scala di Salona', they clearly record the same place; Amfissa (or Salone as it was also known) lies to the northwest of Crissa (Chryso) and Delphi.

On the last five days of their tour together, Lear, Lushington and their dragoman journeyed along the coast of Locris towards Antirrio, so that they could cross the Gulf of Corinth at its narrowest point and thus return to Patrás. From there, Lushington went back to Malta, while Lear took the steamer north, to embark on the next stage of his travels, alone.

Lear remained a sufficiently close friend of Lushington to become godfather to his children and to make him his executor, leaving him his papers and a large collection of his work. However, they were never quite able to rekindle or develop their initial warmth. As Lushington pursued a distinguished legal career, he became increasingly reserved and more conventional.

The six weeks that Lear had spent with Lushington in Greece were among the happiest of his life. He had found this young man to be not only an exuberant travelling companion but also, potentially, an intimate friend. A number of Lear's biographers have considered his affection for Lushington to be the clearest sign of his homosexuality, and the weeks they spent in Greece to afford the greatest expression of that affection, however platonic its character.

37 **Thebes** (opposite above)
Signed with initials, inscribed with title and '16',
and dated 'April 11/49' by Franklin Lushington
Watercolour and pencil
9 ¼ x 12 ¼ inches

38 **Delphi and Parnassus from Plain below Crisoa**
(opposite below)
Signed with initials, inscribed with title and '22',
and dated 'April 18/49' by Franklin Lushington
Pen ink, watercolour and pencil
7 x 10 ¾ inches

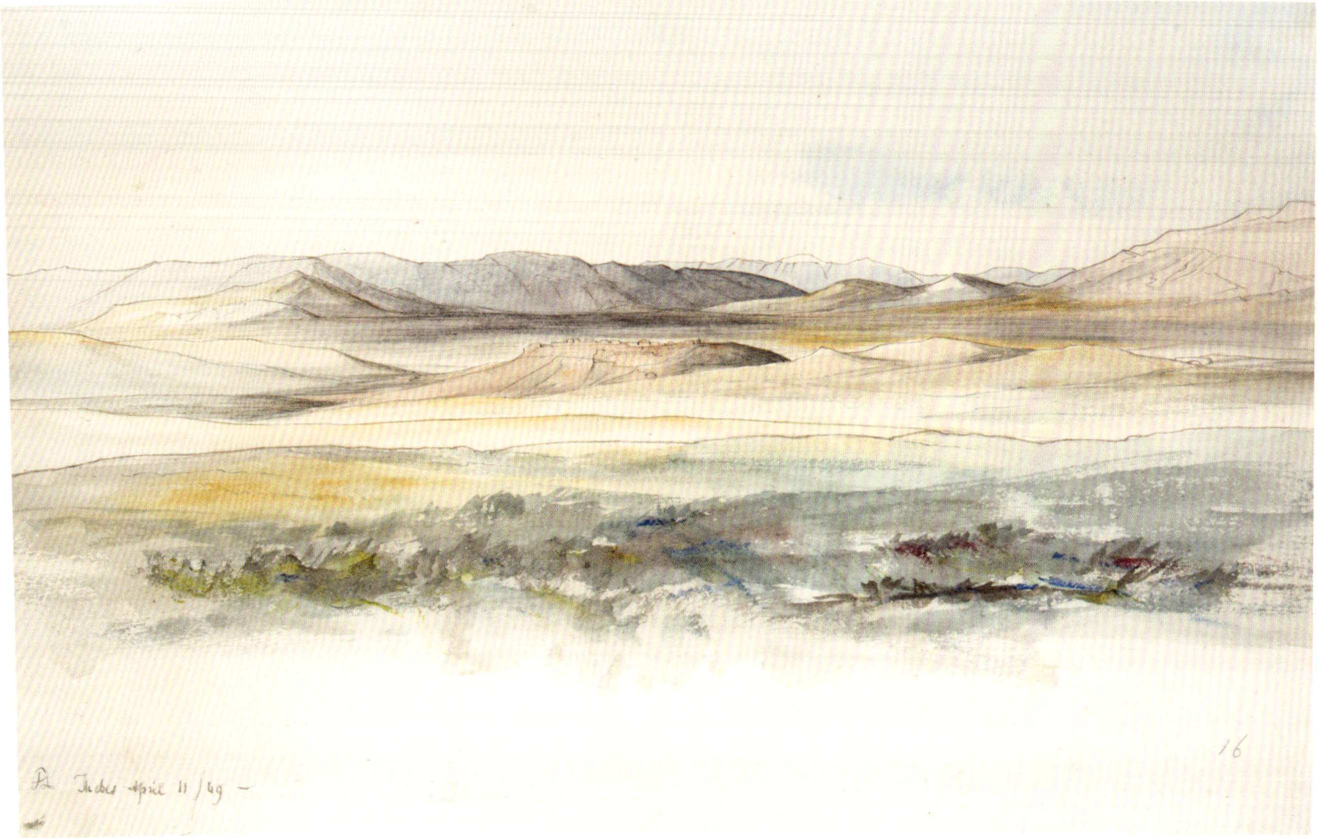
Thebes April 11/49 –
16

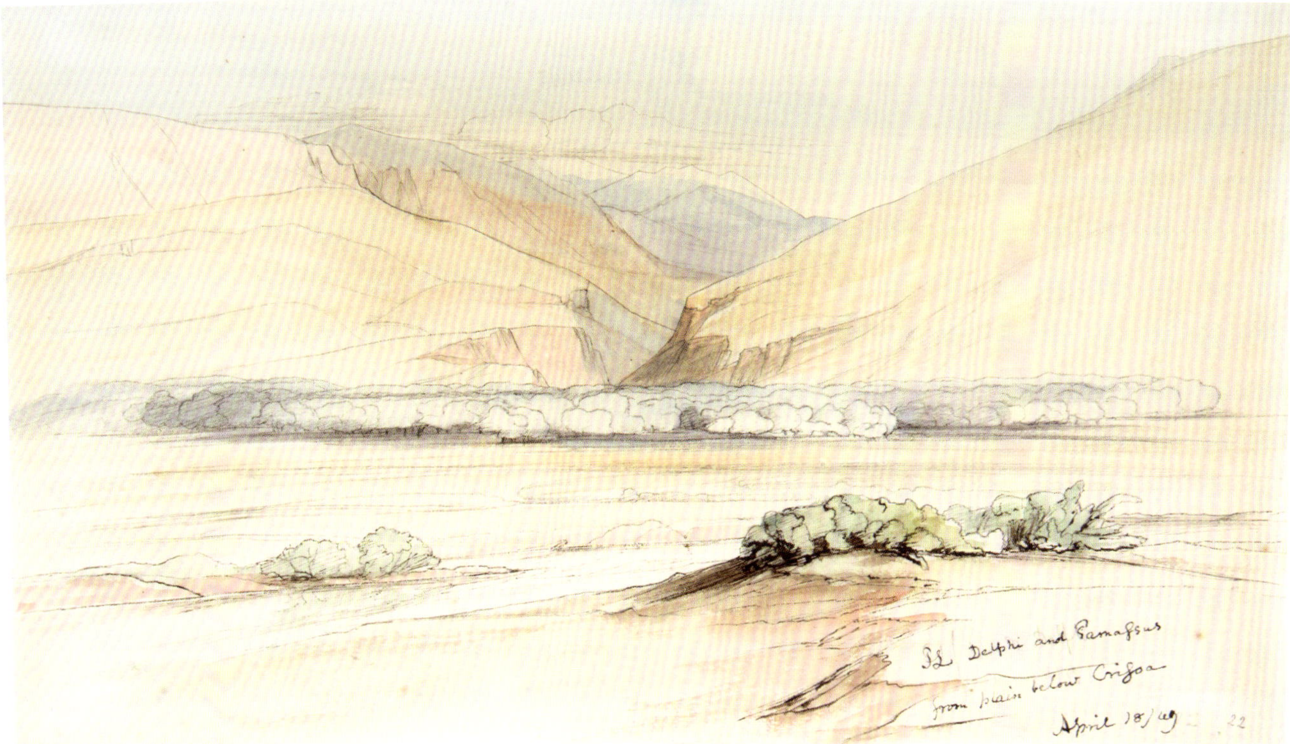
Delphi and Parnassus
from plain below Crissa
April 18/49
22

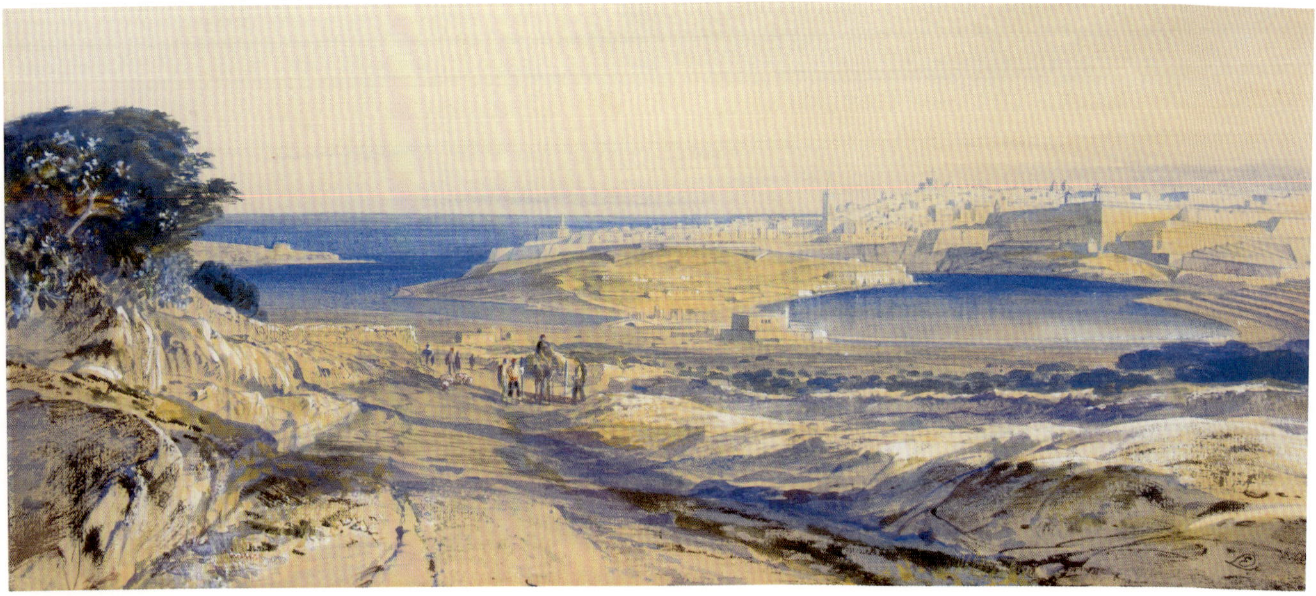

39 Valletta
Signed with monogram
Pen ink and watercolour with bodycolour
7 x 15 inches
Provenance: Probably Richard Bethell, 1st Baron Westbury (1800-1873) or his daughter the Hon Augusta Bethell, later Mrs Parker (1839-1931), and by descent

Valletta

The present panoramic watercolour of Valletta by Edward Lear is based on a study that he made while staying on Malta between December 1865 and April 1866, during the seventh of eight visits to the island. The study (which sold at a London auction in 2011) was, according to Lear's inscription, made on '7 Feby 1866' between '5 pm' and '5.30'. The view looks eastwards across Marsamxett Harbour to the Maltese capital, with, from left to right: Fort Tigné on Dragut Point; Manouel Island, with its hospital, in the harbour; and, in Valletta itself, the tall tower of the Anglican pro-cathedral of St Paul, and the shorter towers of the Roman Catholic cathedral of St John, the latter peaking above St Michael's bastion and its two (now demolished) windmills, which were used to grind gunpowder.

Lear made his first trip to Malta in 1848, when he made a brief stop on his way from Italy to Greece, while his last was in December 1866, when he stayed for an afternoon on his way to Egypt. From 1814, Malta had been ruled by a British military governor, and, in Spring 1849, Lear stayed with Henry Lushington, who was then Chief Secretary to the Government of Malta. Through him, Lear met his younger brother, Franklin, and with him 'established a lasting and important friendship' (Vivien Noakes, *Edward Lear 1812-1888*, London: Royal Academy of Arts, 1985, page 199). It is perhaps because of this friendship that he once described Malta as 'that much beloved place' (in a letter to Chichester Forstescue of 29 May 1862, published in Lady Strachey (ed), *The Letters of Edward Lear*, London: T Fisher Unwin, 1907, pages 243-44). [For more details on the friendship between Lear and Lushington, please see pages 32-35.]

In December 1865, Lear went to Malta 'largely to see' his friends 'Evelyn Baring [Lord Cromer] and Sir Henry Storks, who had been governor there since 1864, and was furious to find that they had left two days earlier' (Jenny Uglow, *Mr Lear: A Life of Art and Nonsense*, London: Faber & Faber, 2017, page 339). He took a house three miles from Valletta, at 9 Stradi Torri [Tower St], Sliema, with his servant, Giorgio Cocali, as his principal companion. Apart from a brief visit to Gozo, the second largest island in the Maltese archipelago, he remained on Malta for almost three months. While it proved to be such 'a sad and lonely winter' that 'the island ceased to have any charm for him' (Vivien Noakes, op cit, page 116), he worked as hard as ever, producing vividly detailed drawings that provided the basis for such scintillating watercolours as the present one.

GABRIELE CARELLI

Gabriele Mariano Nicolai Carelli (1820/21-1900), sometimes known as Gabriel Carelli

To the anglophone public, Gabriele Carelli is the best-known member of a dynasty of Italian landscape painters. First taken up by the Duke of Devonshire, he soon developed a distinguished clientele for his fresh topographical watercolours of Europe and the Middle East. From 1880, Queen Victoria became a great favourite of his work.

For a biography of Gabriele Carelli, please refer to *Chris Beetles Summer Show*, 2014, page 8.

40 **Cannes**
Inscribed with title
and dated 1879
6 ½ x 13 ¼ inches

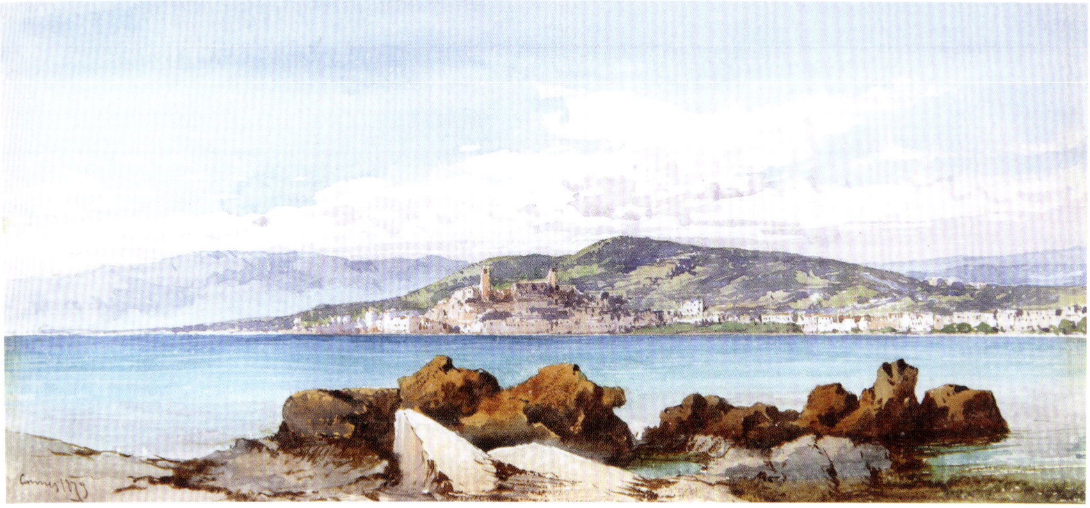

41 **The Albert Memorial**
Watercolour
9 x 17 inches

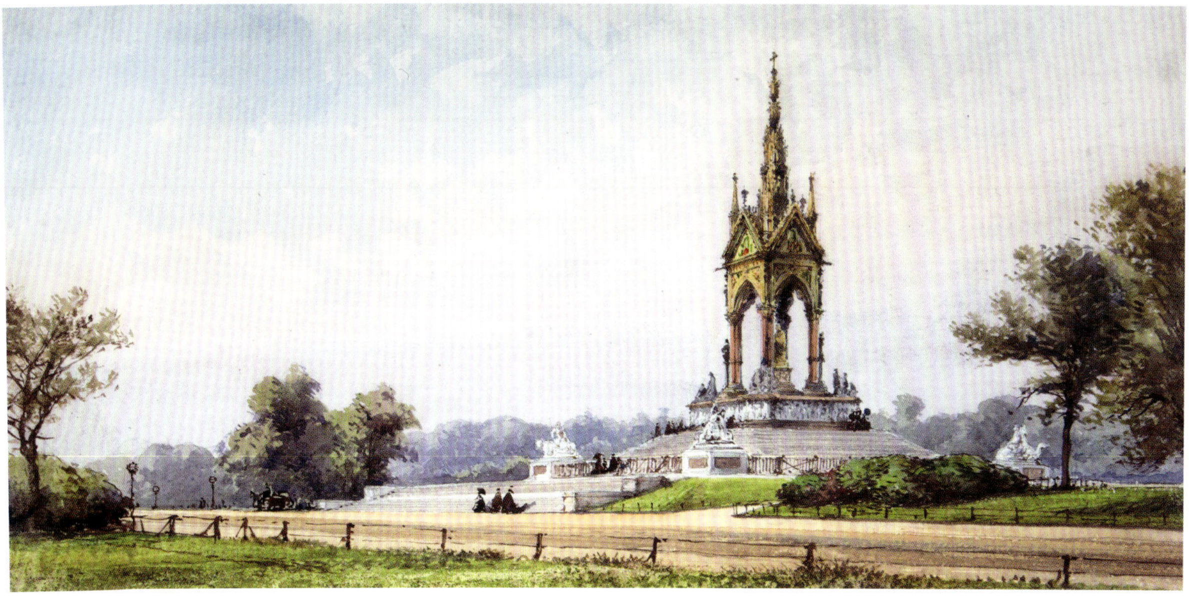

The Albert Memorial

Queen Victoria commissioned the Albert Memorial in memory of her beloved husband, Prince Albert, who died in 1861. Sir George Gilbert Scott designed it in the form of a Gothic ciborium, a freestanding structure consisting of a canopy supported by columns, which covers an altar or other revered object. As constructed in Kensington Gardens, London, it involved the talents of a number of craftsmen, mosaicists and sculptors. Most notable among these was John Henry Foley, who was responsible for the central gilt bronze statue of Albert, as well as *Asia*, one of the four allegorical sculptures representing the continents, which mark the outer corners of the sanctuary. Though the memorial was officially opened by Queen Victoria in July 1872, the statue of Albert was not installed until 1876, two years after Foley's death. In the following decade, Queen Victoria would become one the principal patrons of Gabriele Carelli, the artist of the present watercolour.

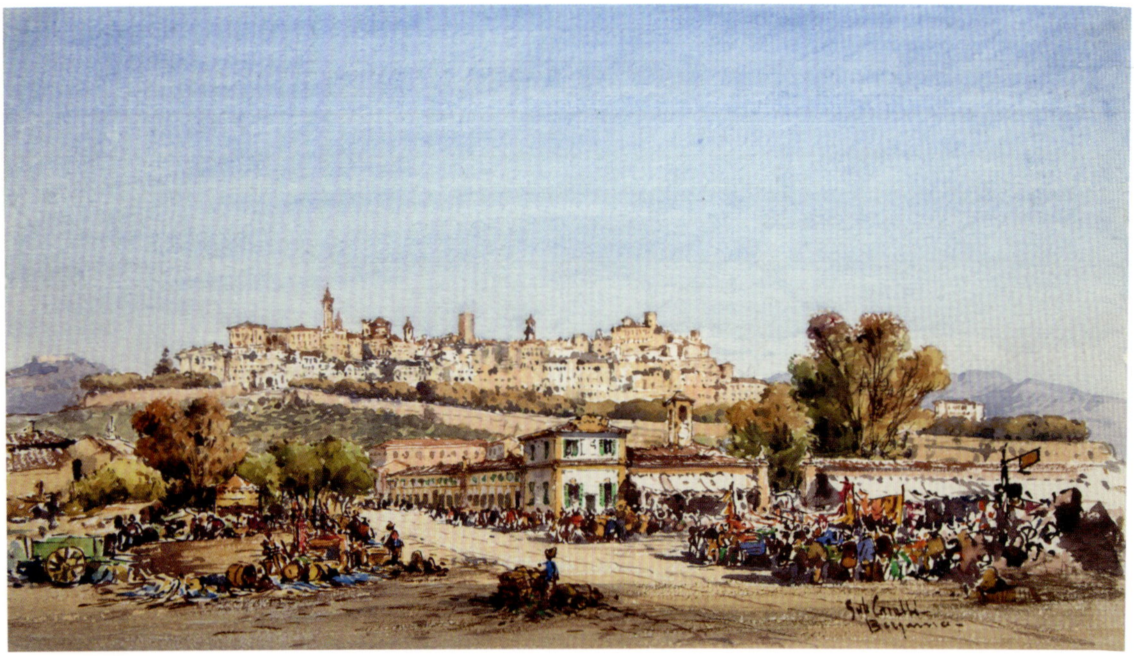

42 Bergamo (above)
Signed and inscribed with title
Watercolour
8 ½ x 13 ¾ inches

43 Squero di San Trovaso, Zattere, Venice (below)
Signed and inscribed 'Zattere'
Watercolour
9 ½ x 13 ½ inches

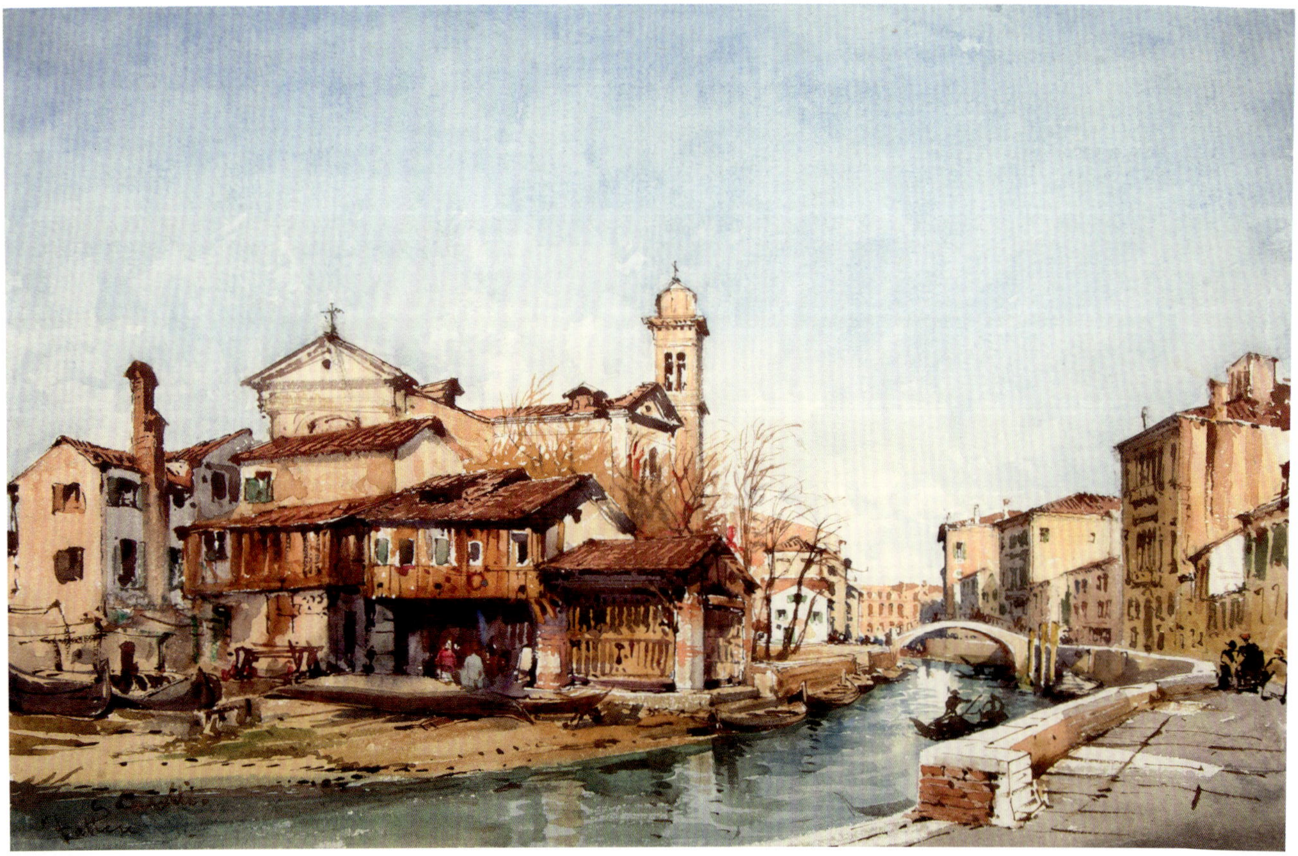

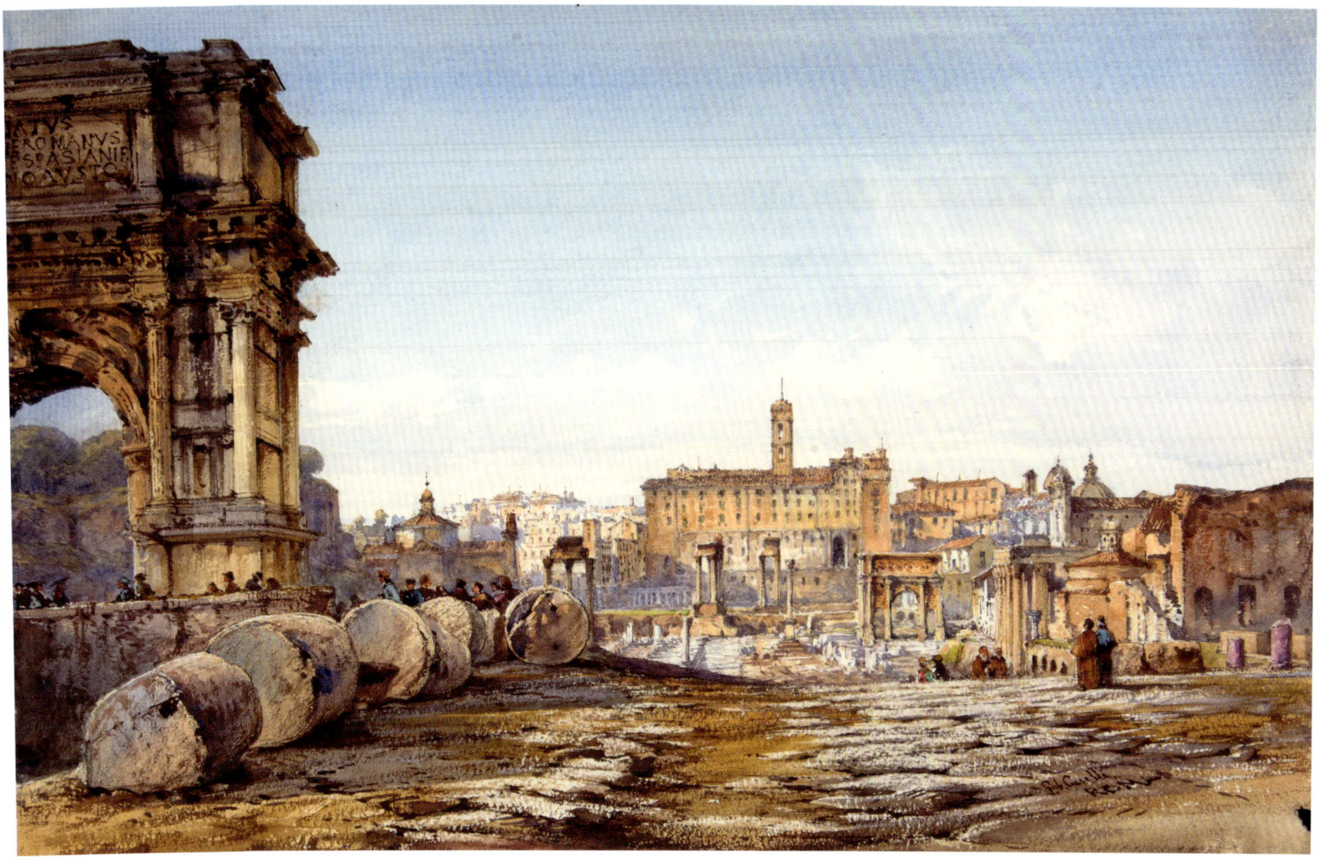

44 **The Forum, Rome**
Signed and inscribed 'Roma'
Watercolour
14 x 21 ¼ inches

Squero di San Trovaso, Zattere, Venice (opposite)
The Squero di San Trovaso is a small boatyard that is situated on the corner of the Rio dei Ognissanti and the Rio di San Trovaso. It is in the Dorsoduro district of Venice, and close to the quayside known as the Zattere. Established in the seventeenth century, it is the oldest of three remaining boatyards in the city producing traditional wooden gondolas. Behind it stands the church of San Trovaso, dedicated to the fraternal Saints Gervasius and Protasius, and also Saint Chrysogonus. The current church was probably designed by Palladio's pupil, Francesco Smeraldi, known as Il Fracà, following the collapse of the nave of the previous building in 1583.

For another view of this area of Venice, please see Hercules Brabazon Brabazon's *Zattere, Venice*, page 97 [100].

The Forum, Rome (above)
From a position just to the north of the first-century Arch of Titus (which appears on the left), Gabriele Carelli has composed an evocative panorama of the Roman Forum that includes the following historic structures:

Santa Maria Liberatrice, which was built in the early seventeenth century to a design by Onorio Longhi, but demolished around 1900 in order to excavate the fifth-century church, Santa Maria Antiqua;

Temple of Castor and Pollux (495 BC);

Temple of Saturn (497 BC) and the Temple of Vespasian and Titus (79 AD), behind which stands the mediaeval Palazzo Senatorio surmounting the Tabularium (78 BC), the archive of ancient Rome;

Arch of Septimus Severus (203 AD);

Santi Luca e Martina, completed to designs by Pietro da Cortona in 1664;

Temple of Antoninus and Faustina, which was built in 141 AD and converted into the church of San Lorenzo in Miranda, possibly as early as the seventh century, then remodelled in the sixteenth and seventeenth centuries;

Temple of Romulus, in front of the preceding building, which was built in the early fourth century and converted into the church of Santi Cosma e Damiano in 527;

Basilica of Maxentius and Constantine (308-312 AD).

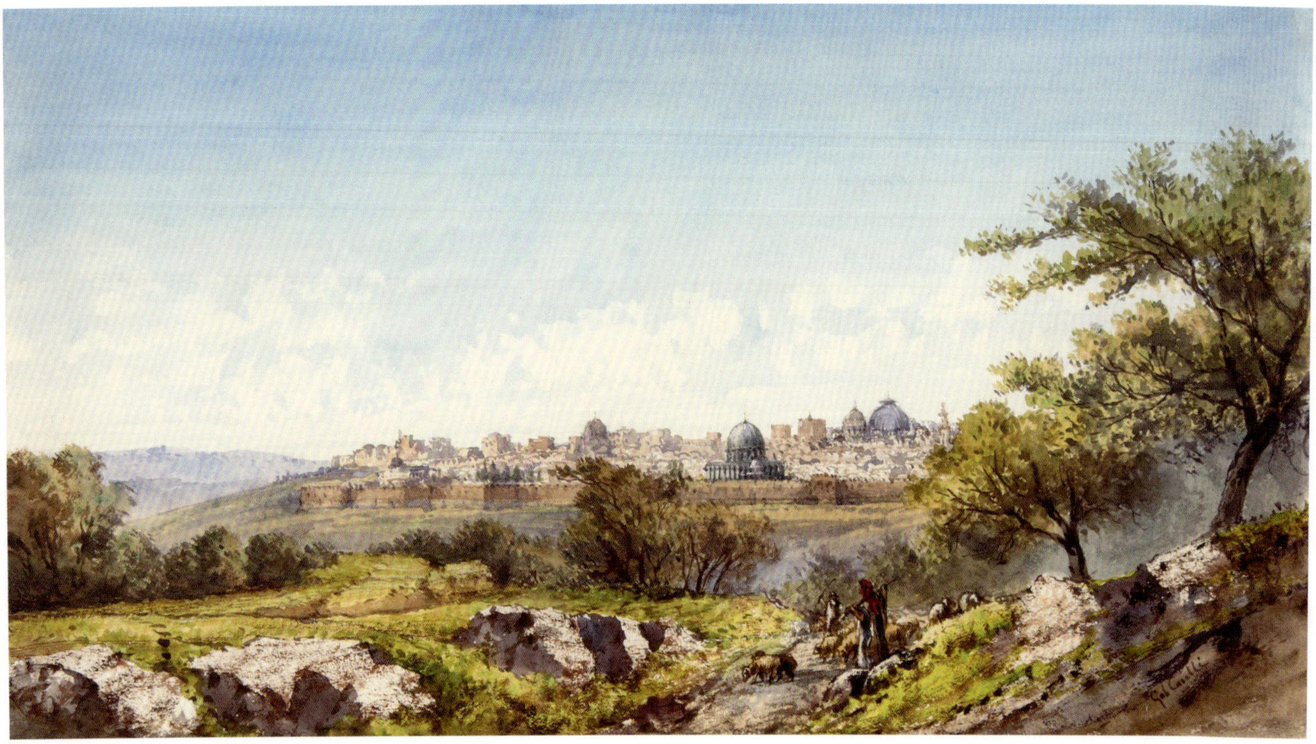

45 Palestine: View of Jerusalem with Mount Moriah, the Holy Sepulchre and Mount Zion across the Cedron (Kidron) Valley from the Mount of Olives (above)
Signed
Watercolour
12 x 21 ¼ inches

46 The Cotton Bazaar and Mosque of Sultan Al Ghuri, Cairo (opposite)
Signed and inscribed 'Cairo'
Watercolour
21 x 14 ¾ inches

Palestine: View of Jerusalem with Mount Moriah, the Holy Sepulchre and Mount Zion across the Cedron (Kidron) Valley from the Mount of Olives
This panoramic view is possibly even richer in resonance than that of *The Forum, Rome* [44]. It is taken from the Mount of Olives, the location of several key events in the life of Jesus, including his ascension into heaven; and looks across the Kidron Valley, which is mentioned in both the Old and New Testaments. Within the walls of Jerusalem, three domes stand out against the skyline. That to the left belongs to the Al-Aqsa Mosque, first established in 705 AD, and considered to be the third holiest site in Islam. That in the middle belongs to the Dome of the Rock, also of Islamic affiliation, which was originally built in the years 688-692 on the site of the Second Jewish Temple. Then the most outstanding of those to the right belongs to the Church of the Holy Sepulchre, which was consecrated in 335 AD, and contains the two holiest sites in Christianity: Golgotha or Calvary, the place where Jesus was crucified, and the tomb where he was buried and resurrected.

The Cotton Bazaar and the Mosque of Sultan Al Ghuri, Cairo
This watercolour of the historic heart of Cairo presents a view south through the old cotton bazaar towards the monumental complex of Sultan Qansuh al-Ghuri. Built between 1503 and 1505, the complex straddles both sides of al-Mu'izz Street in the Fahhamin quarter. On the eastern side (to the left of the image) stands the building housing the Sultan's mausoleum (identified by its dome), a khanqah (designed for the gathering of Sufis), a sabil (or water distribution kiosk) and a kuttab (Islamic primary school). On the western side (the right) stands the congregational mosque-madrasa (identified by its minaret). The projection of the sabil-kuttab at the north and of the minaret at the south together create a kind of square. This was rented to stallholders to provide an income to help maintain the complex. Despite such maintenance, the dome of the mausoleum proved unstable and was replaced by a flat wooden roof at the end of the nineteenth century. Today, the mosque-madrasa remains in use, while the khanqah-mausoleum is open to visitors as a historic site.

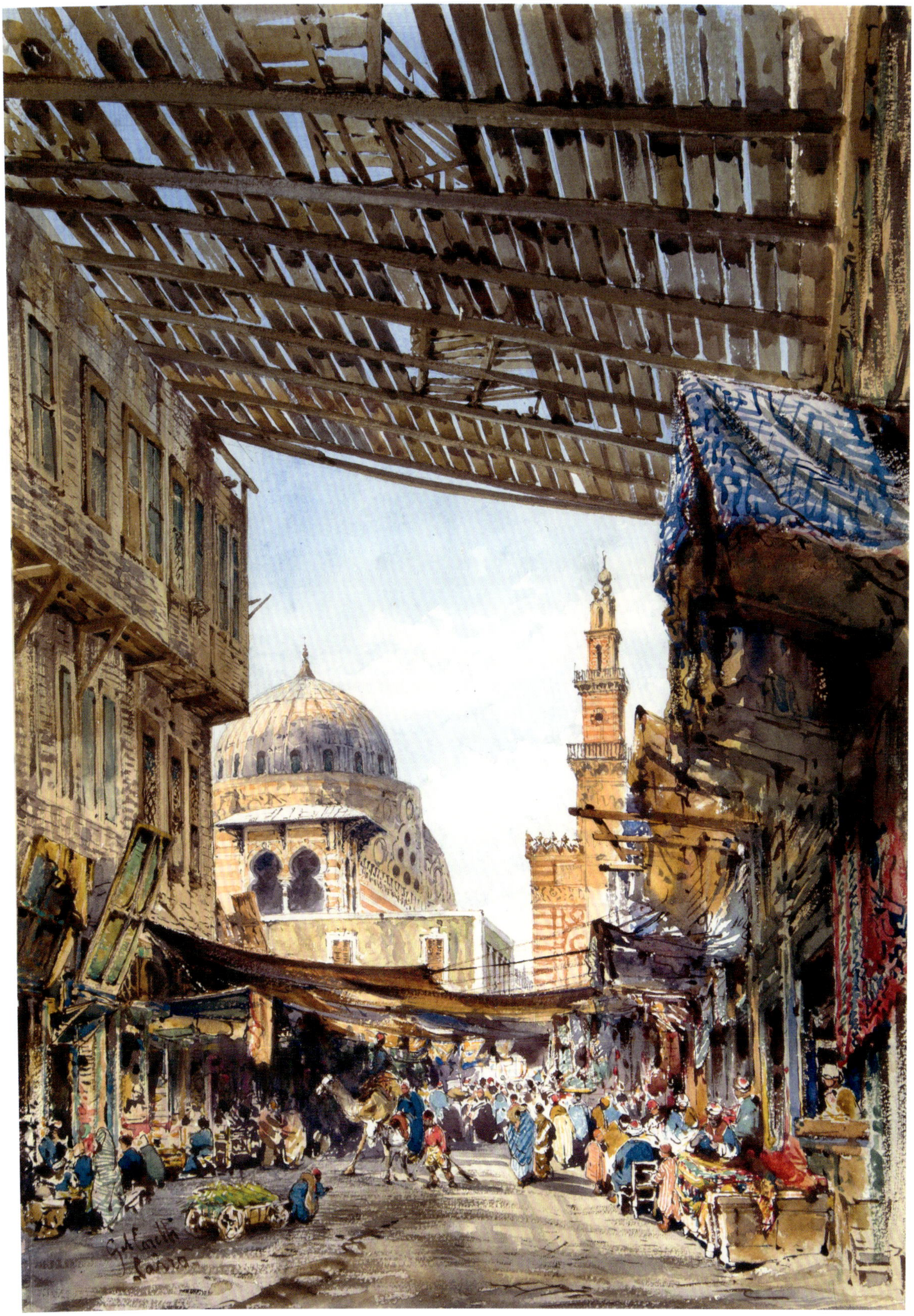

ALFRED JOSEPH WOOLMER

Alfred Joseph Woolmer, RBA (1805-1892)

The painter and sculptor, Alfred Joseph Woolmer, was best known for his distinctive genre subjects, and especially 'elegant courtship scenes in light dappled gardens and shady bowers' and 'sensuous, mildly erotic images of ladies at their *toilette*' (Robyn Asleson on her entry on Woolmer in the *Oxford Dictionary of National Biography*, 2018). While he sometimes illustrated specific episodes from literature, he focussed more often on the evocation of a poetic atmosphere through the fluid handling of a rich palette. Initially emulating 'the romantic historical costume pieces' (Asleson, op cit) that were popular in the 1820s and 30s, he gradually developed a personal approach through the assimilation of an eclectic range of influences that most notably included Watteau.

For a biography of Alfred Jospeh Woolmer, please refer to page 112.

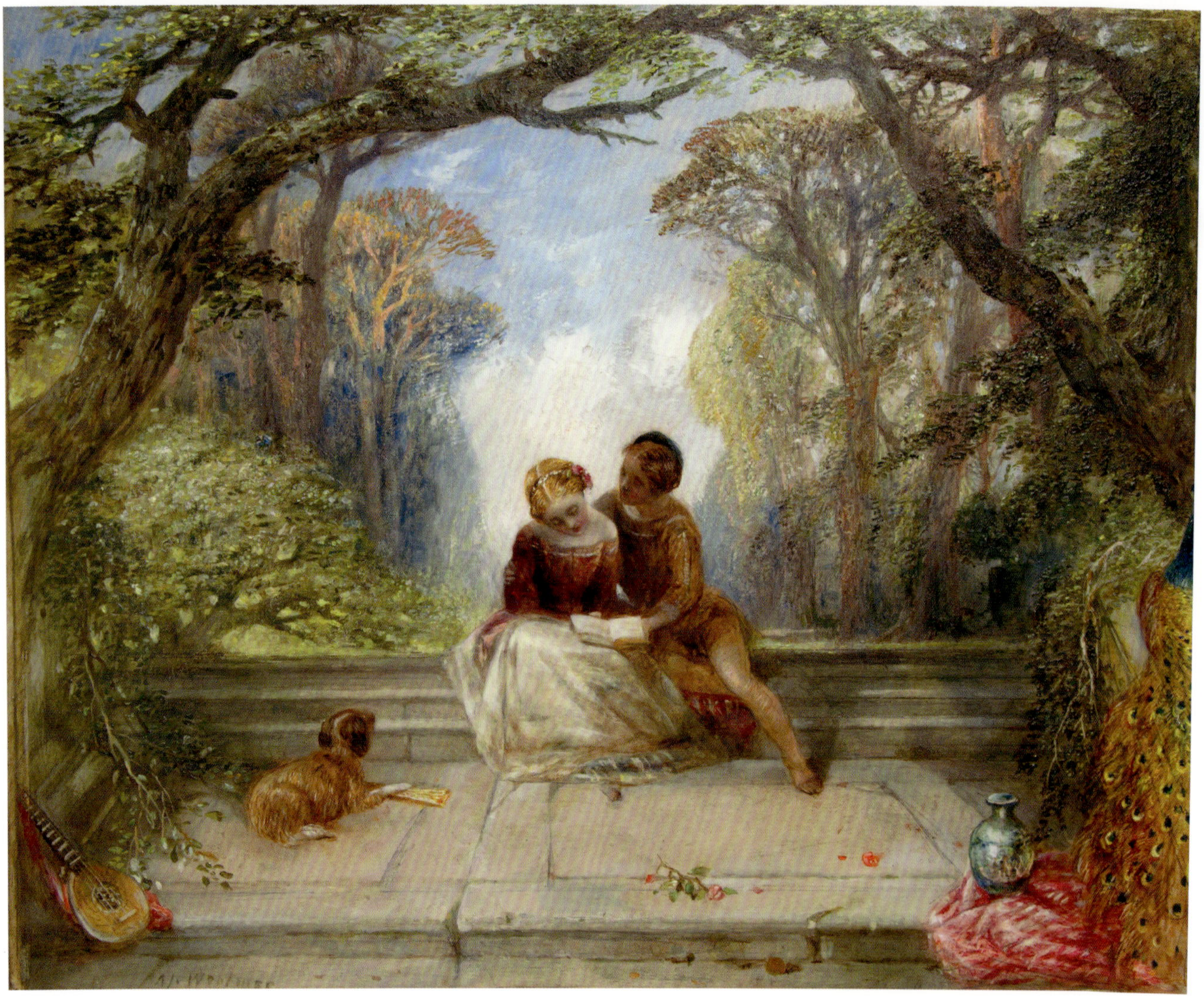

47 **Early Summer**
Signed
Signed and inscribed with title, 'No 3' and artist's address, 'The Limes, Dartmouth Park Avenue, Upper Holloway', on label on reverse
Oil on board
13 ¾ x 17 inches

GEORGE FREDERIC WATTS

George Frederic Watts, OM RA (1817-1904)

By the end his long career, George Frederic Watts had become the most revered figure in British art, and was one of first to hold the Order of Merit, when it was instituted in 1902. Inspired by the example of the Renaissance masters, he attempted to revive the tradition of history painting by producing ambitious allegories that promoted a moral message, stating that 'I paint ideas, not things'. The allusive, often expressive results reveal an association with the Continental Symbolist movement. In addition, he was a distinctive and penetrating portraitist, and an occasional, but invariably impressive sculptor.

For further information on George Frederic Watts, please refer to page 112.

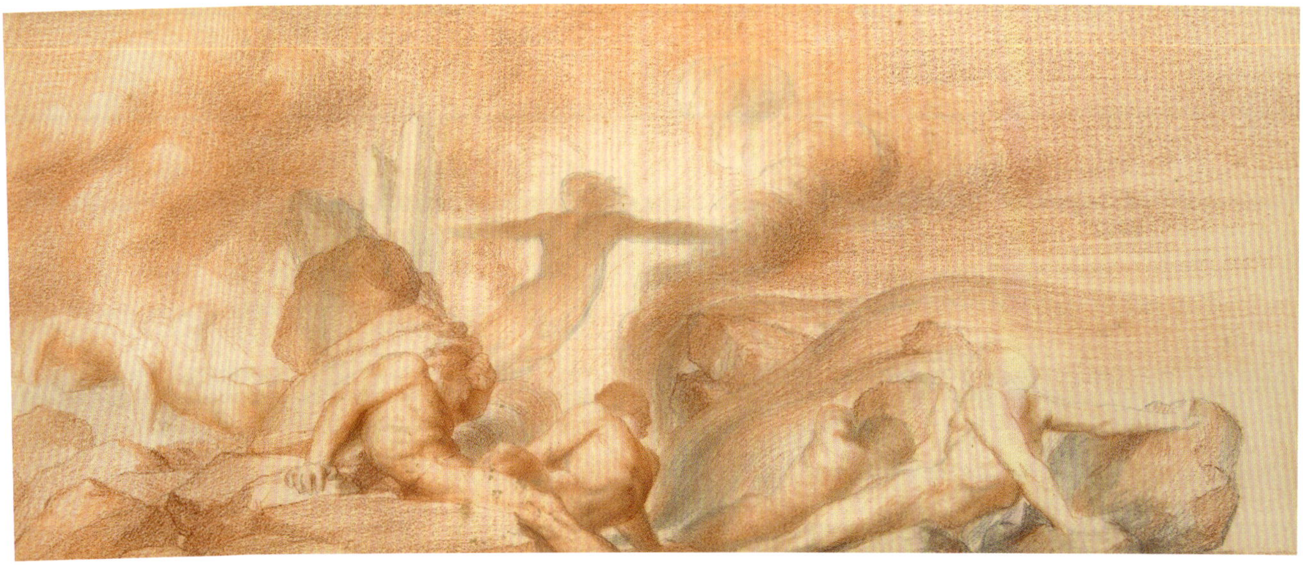

48 **Chaos**
Crayon with pencil; 5 ¾ x 12 ¼ inches

Chaos

The present drawing by George Frederic Watts is a preliminary study for *Chaos*, one of a projected cycle of murals that would gain the overarching title of 'The House of Life'.

During an extended stay in Italy, between 1843 and 1847, Watts visited the Sistine Chapel, in the Vatican City, in 1845, to see Michelangelo's frescos. These inspired him, through the late 1840s, to conceive a plan to decorate the interior of a vast building with a cycle of allegorical paintings. This would represent the progress of the cosmos and the spiritual development of mankind. From 1860, he actually set to work, and produced preliminary drawings, sculptural maquettes and large-scale paintings, only some of which he completed, sometimes in collaboration with assistants. He began to explain his conception to the public in the catalogue to the exhibition of his work held in 1884 at the Metropolitan Museum of Art, New York. However, he never brought the cycle to complete fruition. After his death, his widow would describe it as 'the ambition of one half of his life and the regret of the other half' (Mary Seton Watts, *George Frederic Watts: The Annals of an Artist's Life*, London: Macmillan & Co, 1912, vol 1, page 100).

Chaos was intended to be the first work in the cycle and to be painted on the ceiling of the large interior. The complete composition of *Chaos* exists in two large-scale versions, painted in oil on canvas, one in the Watts Gallery, Compton, and the other, more highly finished, in the Tate, both being approximately dated to the years 1875-82. The right-hand side of the composition is based on Watts's finished oil on panel, *The Titans*, of 1869-75, which is also in the Watts Gallery.

The present red chalk drawing is a preliminary study for the left-hand side of *Chaos*, in which giants, representing primeval confusion, struggle to release themselves from fire and vapour. In the middle of the complete composition (not shown in this drawing), a single figure emerges from the sea, marking the beginning of time. On the right of the composition (again not shown in this drawing), a chain of female figures signals the establishment of measurable time and space, while above them powerful giants lie oblivious, typifying the mountains formed during the making of the earth. Watts developed this original mythology from a variety of sources, including the classical poetry of Hesiod's *Theogony* and Ovid's *Metamorphoses*, and also John Milton's *Paradise Lost*. He was also affected by the contemporary evolutionary theories of Charles Darwin. According to Barbara Bryant, 'Later Watts wished he had called [the composition] *Cosmos* or *Chaos Passing to Cosmos*' (Mark Bills and Barbara Bryant, *G F Watts: Victorian Visionary*, New Haven/London: Yale University Press/Watts Gallery Compton, 2008, Page 190).

Plaster maquettes of some figures in this drawing are in the collection of the Watts Gallery, while other drawings for *Chaos* are in the collections of the British Museum and the Royal Academy of Arts.

JOSEPH NOEL PATON

Sir Joseph Noel Paton, RSA (1821-1901)

Joseph Noel Paton was the leading Scottish artist of the Victorian period to specialise in imaginative figure subjects, and notably fairies. In producing such masterpieces as *The Quarrel of Oberon and Titania*, he capitalised on his mimetic skills in order to represent the supernatural with great conviction.

For a biography of Joseph Noel Paton, please refer to page 113.

The Islesman at Home

The Islesman at Home is a powerfully concentrated example of the products of Celtic Revivalism, a network of movements that, through the nineteenth and twentieth centuries, encouraged a revival of interest in Celtic culture.

From an early age, growing up in Dunfermline, Joseph Noel Paton was inspired by his father's collection and his own reading to establish interests as an antiquary and folklorist, and he developed a wide knowledge of Celtic romance and legend, as well as an expertise in, particularly, historic arms and armour. Both he and his father became Fellows of the Society of Antiquaries of Scotland, and, when he inherited and expanded his father's collection, he sometimes lent items from it to exhibitions. Inevitably – and intentionally – his knowledge and expertise informed his paintings, including the present one, with its panoply of jewellery, weapons and other distinctive objects.

The Islesman at Home is unlikely to depict a specific individual or event. (For Paton tended to clarify the subjects of his paintings through the precision of his titles, as he did with *Dawn – Luther at Erfurt*, which he produced in the same year, 1861.) Rather, it provides a potent mixture of history and myth and, in its focus on the family, encourages a positively emotive response to ancient Scottish forebears. The title suggests that the protagonist is a ruler or warrior from the 'Kingdom of the Isles', a country that existed from the ninth to the thirteenth centuries, and comprised the Hebrides, the islands of the Firth of Clyde and the Isle of Man. Paton was certainly acquainted with the first two of these places, and especially Arran, in the Firth of Clyde, where he and his family often spent summer holidays. He may therefore have woven a specifically personal strand through the wider implications of his composition.

Detail of **49**

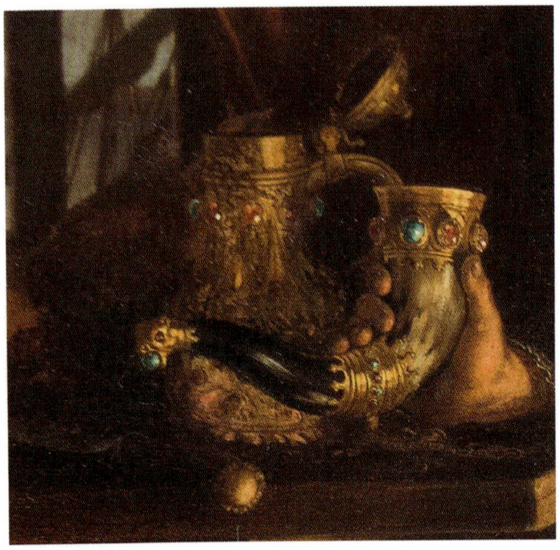

49 The Islesman at Home
Signed with monogram
Oil on paper laid on panel
22 ¼ x 27 ½ inches
Exhibited: Royal Scottish Academy, 1861, No 332;
Midland Counties Art Museum, Nottingham Castle

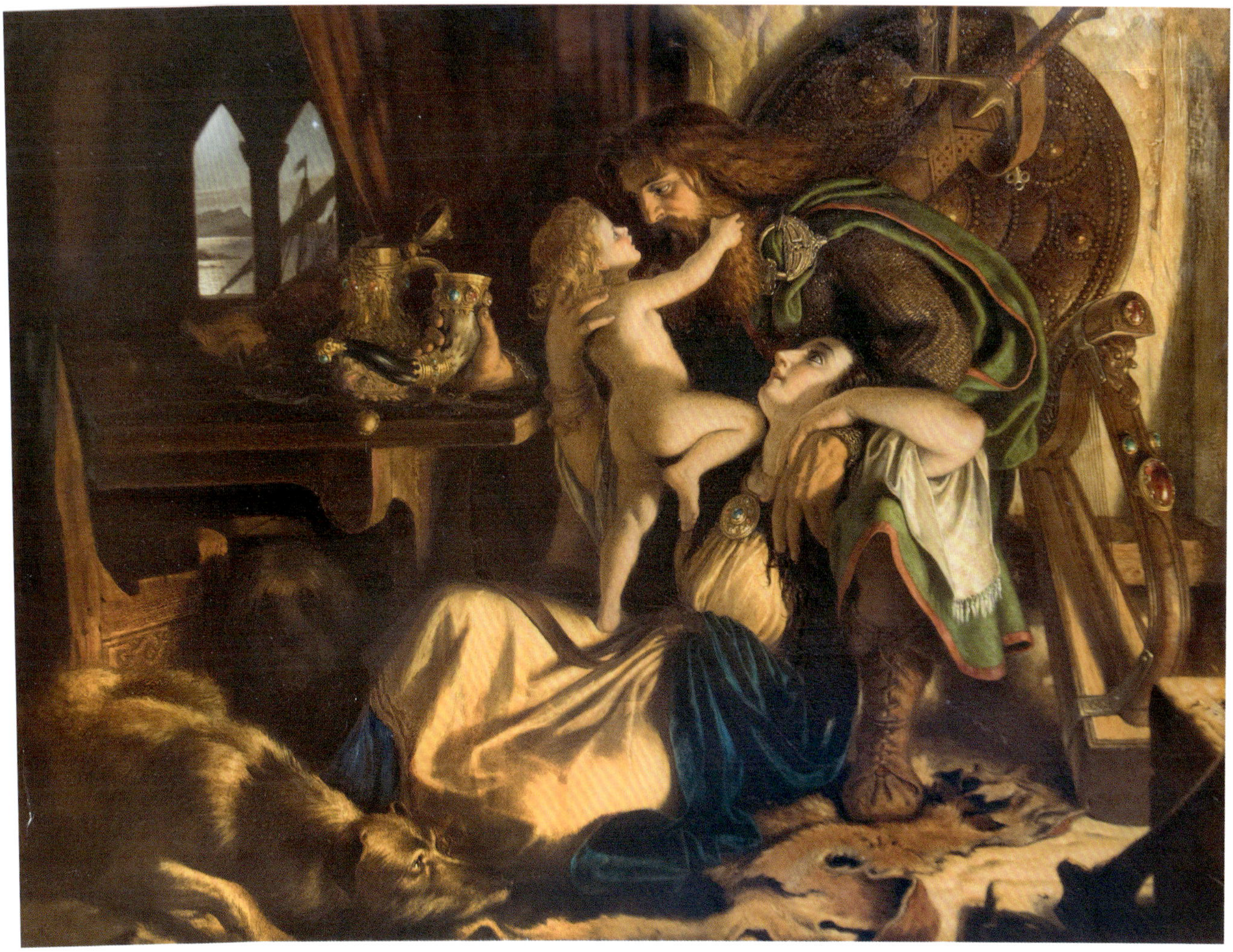

CHARLES GREEN

Charles Green, RI (1840-1898)

Charles Green was a painter and illustrator of genre and historical subjects. He is now best remembered for images illustrating, or inspired by, the work of Charles Dickens.

For a biography of Charles Green, please refer to page 114.

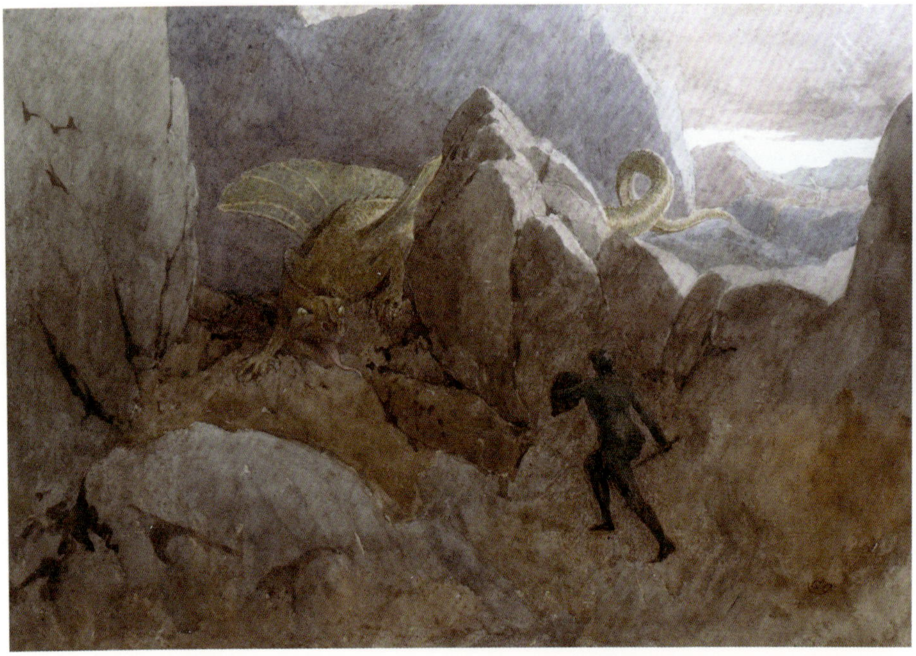

50 St George and the Dragon
Signed with initials
Watercolour
9 ½ x 13 ¾ inches

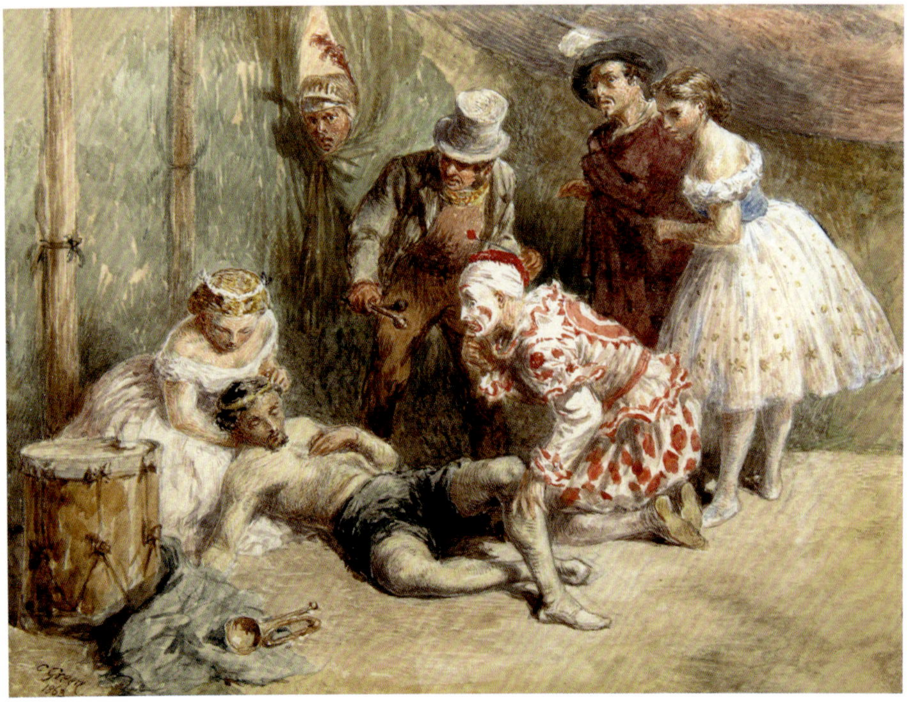

51 Backstage
Signed and dated 1863
Watercolour
5 ¾ x 7 inches
Exhibited: Fine Art Society, January 1901

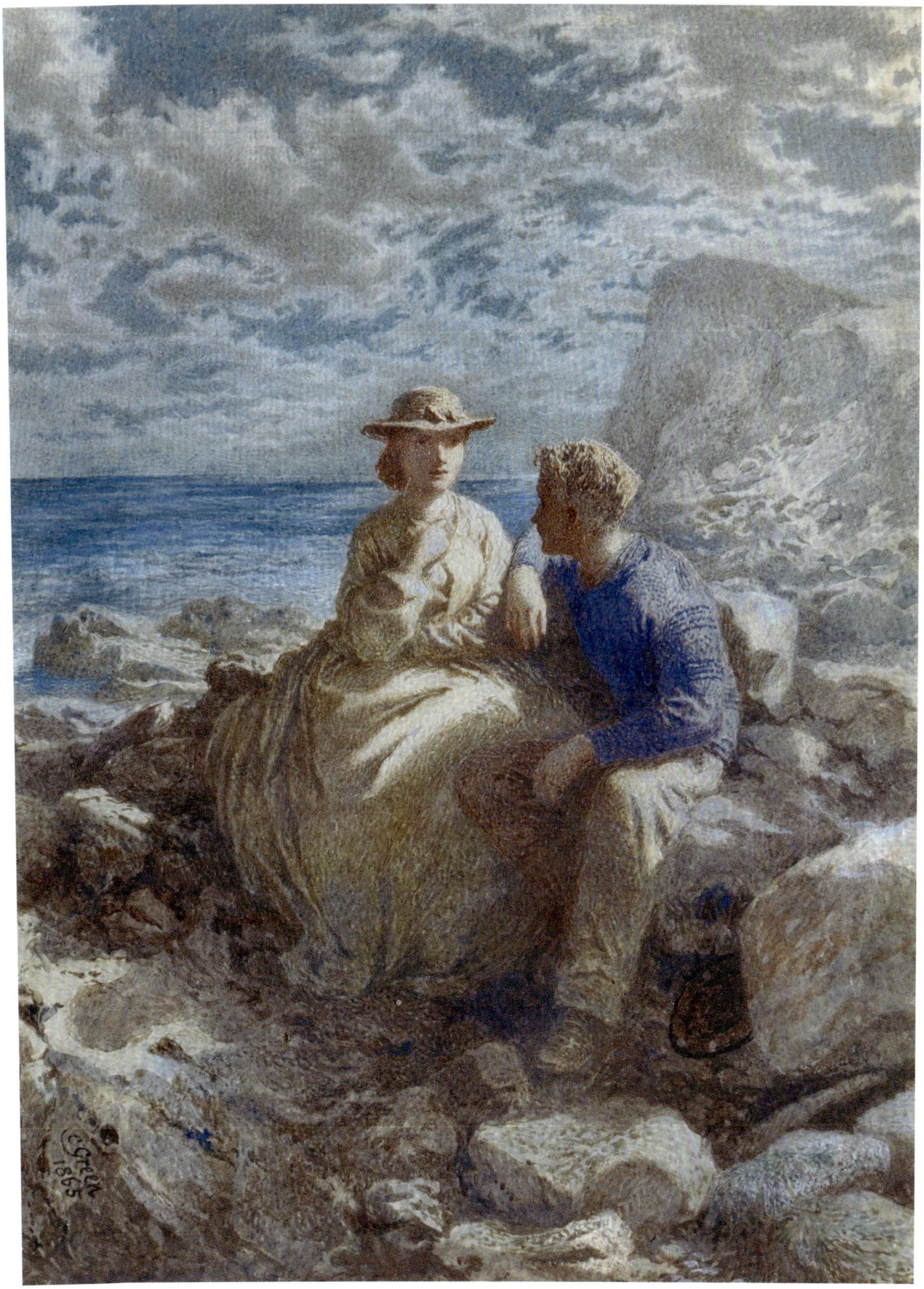

52 **By the Sea**
Signed and dated 1865
Watercolour with bodycolour
8 x 5 ¾ inches

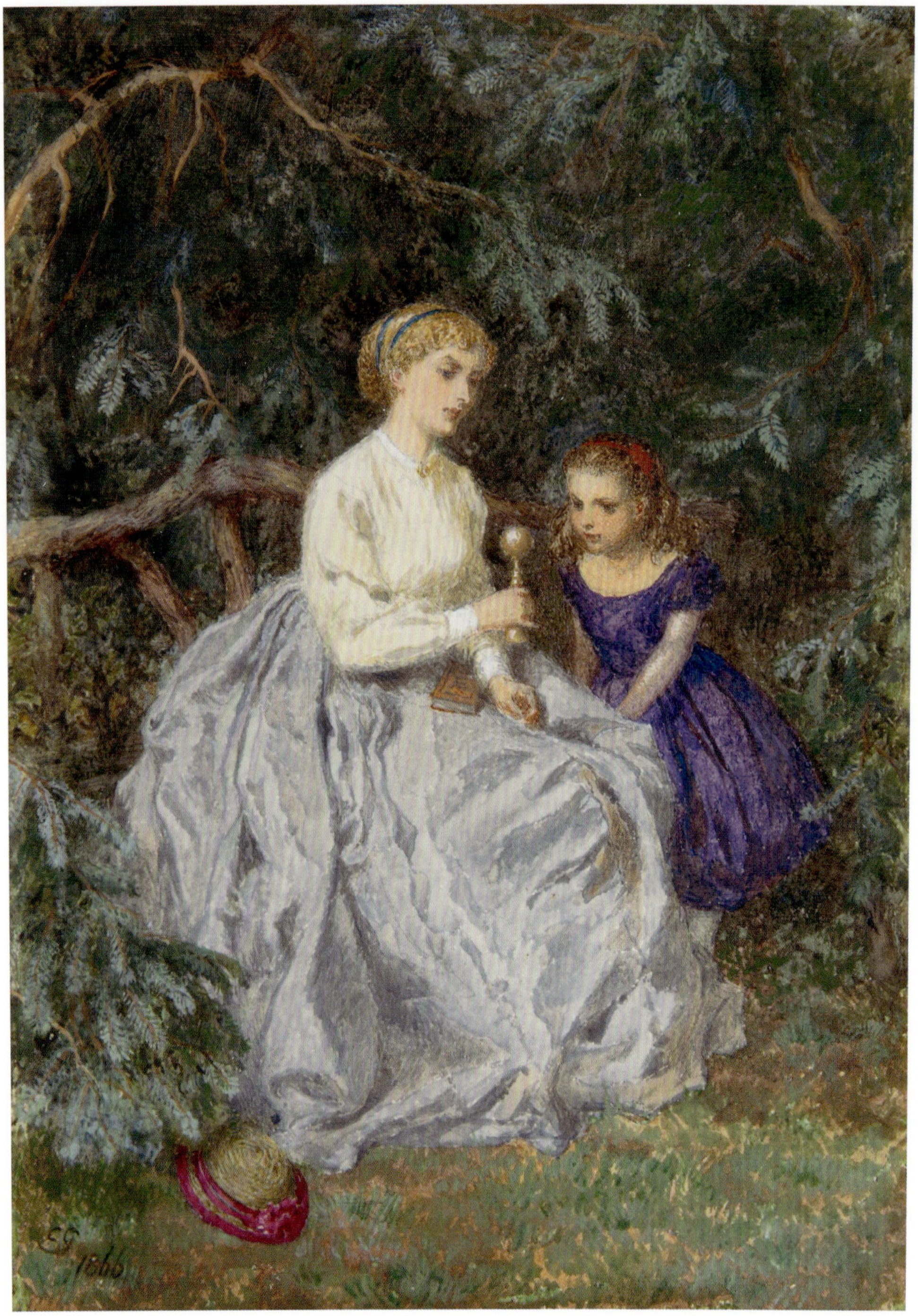

53 A Lesson Outdoors
Signed with initials and dated 1866
Watercolour with bodycolour, ink and pencil
6 ½ x 4 ½ inches

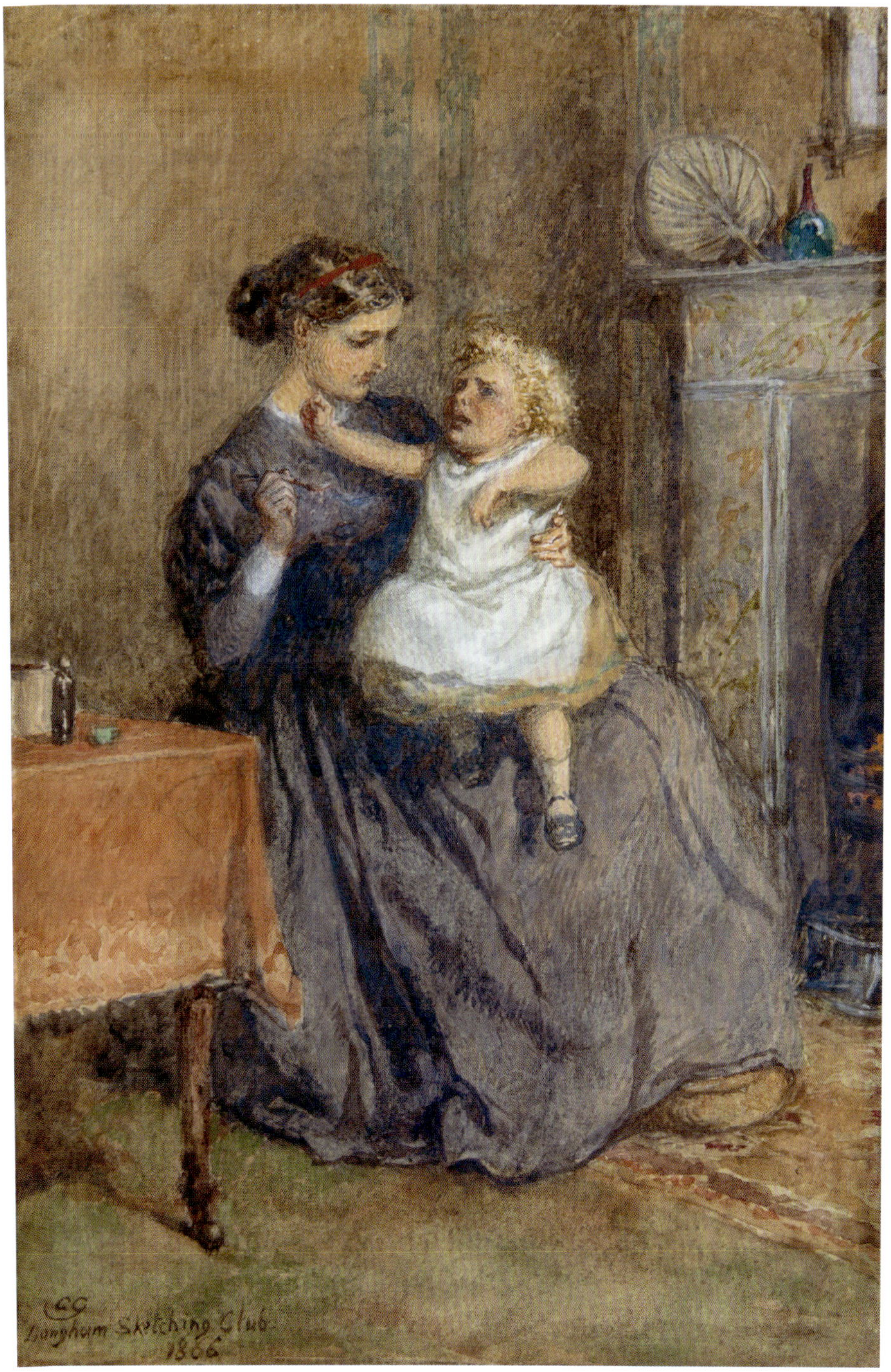

54 A Spoonful of Medicine
Signed with initials, inscribed 'Langham Sketching Club' and dated 1866
Watercolour with bodycolour
6 ¾ x 4 ½ inches

JOHN DAWSON WATSON

John Dawson Watson, RWS RBA (1832-1892)

As both painter and illustrator, John Dawson Watson absorbed the influence of the Pre-Raphaelites in general, and of John Everett Millais in particular. This he displayed in the clarity of draughtsmanship, the accuracy of detail and the intensity of colour of his concentrated genre scenes, both contemporary and historical.

For a biography of John Dawson Watson, please refer to *Chris Beetles Summer Show*, 2017, page 62.

Robinson Crusoe

John Dawson Watson had a strong attachment to Daniel Defoe's novel, *The Life and Adventures of Robinson Crusoe* (1719), and may even have identified with the titular character. Indeed, photographs of the artist suggest that the present painting is, to a degree, a self-portrait. He seems to have been particularly fond of the episodes that describe Crusoe's ideal island life, exhibiting two works inspired by them at the Royal Academy of Arts: *Robinson Crusoe: 'It would have made a stoic smile to see me and my little family'* (1855, No 185) and *Robinson Crusoe teaching his parrot to talk* (1863, No 92). Both these oils and other watercolours informed his preparations for an illustrated edition of the novel, which was published by Routledge, Warne, and Routledge in 1864. His illustrations have been described as 'characterized by the fineness of line and the clarity of execution' (David Blewett, *The Illustrations of Robinson Crusoe, 1719-1920*, Gerrards Cross: Colin Smythe, 1995, page 109). Both the present oil and a similar, exactly contemporary, watercolour – once in the collection of David Daniels and Steven Beck Baloga – demonstrate that Watson's interest in the subject was sustained rather than exhausted by this illustrative project. A description of that watercolour applies equally well to this oil:

> Daniel Defoe's hero Robinson Crusoe [is] making baskets, accompanied by his faithful dog and the parrot that he tamed and taught to speak. Crusoe had tried to make baskets from twigs and tree branches, but finding them too brittle, had looked for alternative materials. Remembering the way basket makers he had observed in his childhood had used wicker, he experimented with the shoots that grew from the cut stakes with which he had fortified his hut. These he dried and then carried to his cave where 'during the next season, I employed myself in making, as well as I could, a great many baskets, both to carry earth, or to carry or lay up any thing as I had occasion; and tho' I did not finish them very handsomely, yet I made them sufficiently serviceable for my purpose'.

(Christopher Newall, *English Realist Watercolors, 1830-1915: a collection assembled by David Daniels and Stevan Beck Baloga*, New York: Shepherd Gallery, 1997)

55 Robinson Crusoe
Signed with initials and dated 1866
Oil on panel
11 ¾ x 15 inches

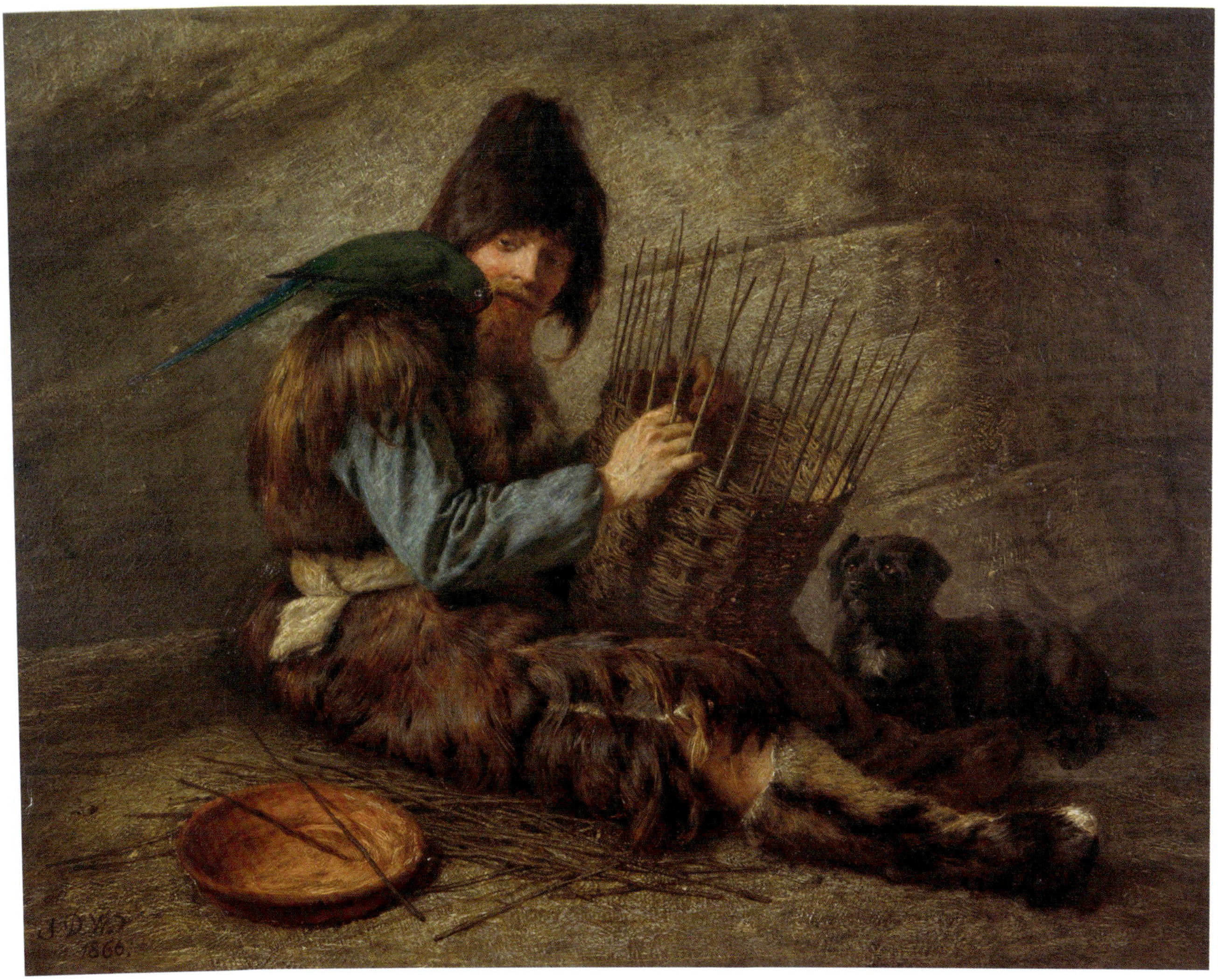
1866.

FRANK WILLIAM WARWICK TOPHAM

Francis William Warwick Topham, RI ROI (1838-1924)

Frank William Warwick Topham was best known as a painter of charming genre scenes in oil and watercolour, especially those with Italian settings. In addition, he produced a number of portraits.

For a biography of Frank William Warwick Topham, please refer to page 115.

56 Primrose Day
Signed and dated 1891
Signed letter, on paper headed 'Garden Chambers, 32 Great Ormond Street' attached to reverse
Oil on canvas
20 x 14 inches
Provenance: Mrs Bernhard-Smith
Exhibited: Summer Exhibition, New Gallery, London, May 1892, No 196

The letter on reverse reads as follows:

9 Augt 92'
Dear Mrs Bernhard-Smith
The New Gallery closed on Saturday, so I now have the pleasure of sending you your little picture "Primrose Day" and am very glad it has such a good home.
Hoping you are all well.
Very truly yours
Frank W W Topham

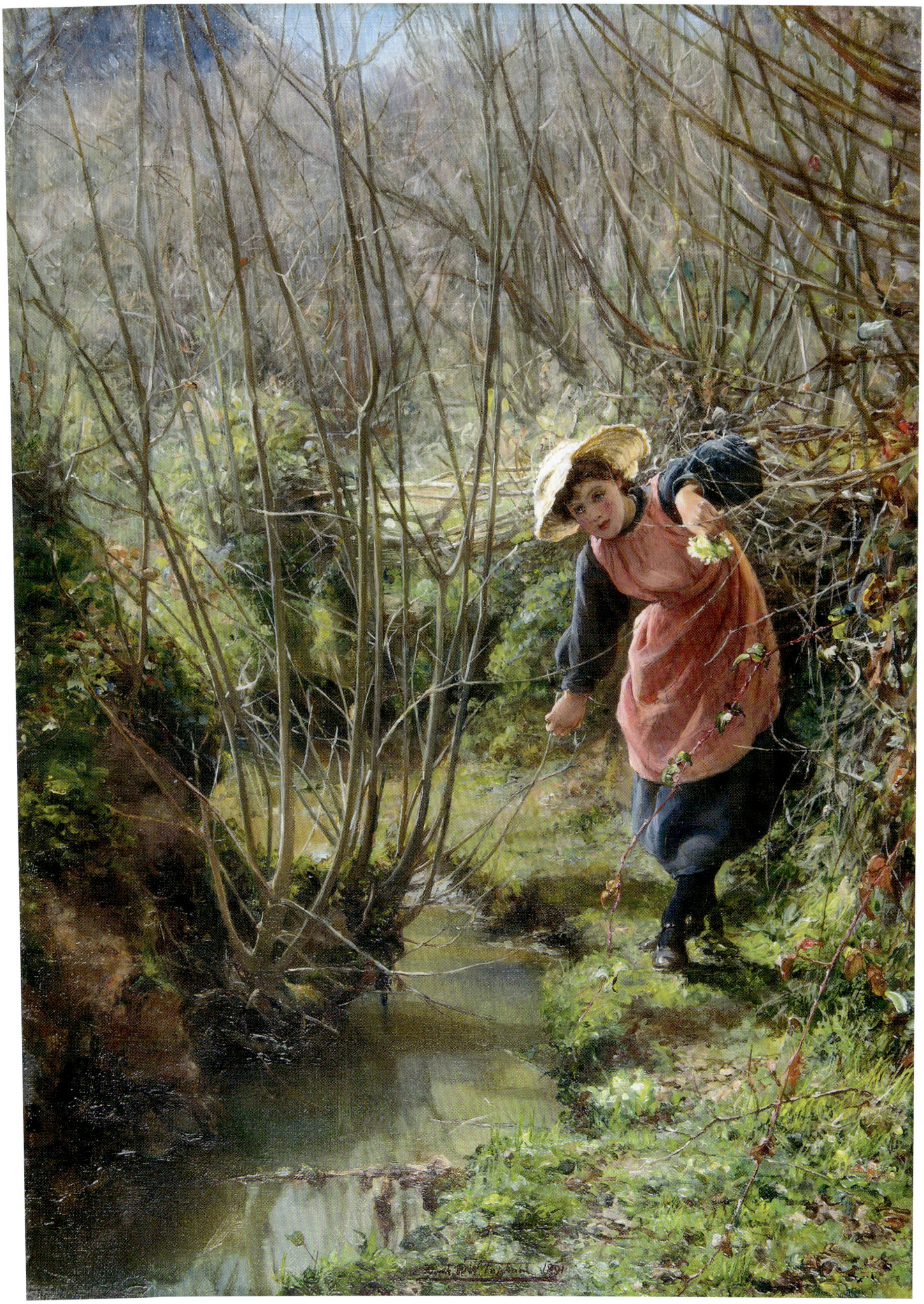

BEATRICE HEWITT

Beatrice Marion Hewitt (1859-1908)

Beatrice Hewitt is best known as a painter of sensitive miniature portraits. However, her early watercolours of flowers and the present impressive figure study in oil demonstrate that she was an artist of range as well as skill.

For a biography of Beatrice Hewitt, please refer to page 116.

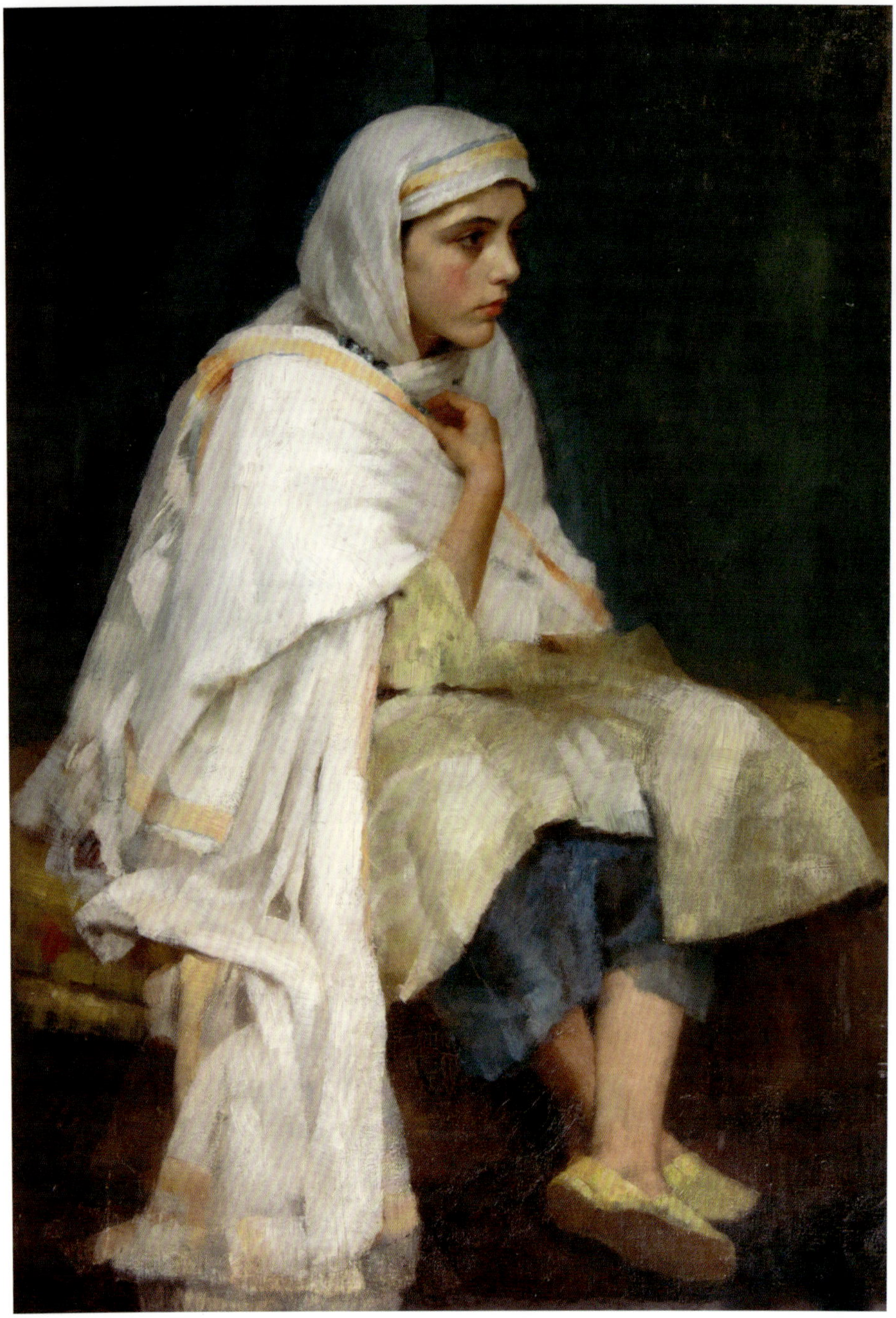

57 **An Academy Model**
Signed with initials
Signed on reverse
Oil on canvas
29 ¾ x 20 inches

ALICE MARY CHAMBERS

Alice Mary Chambers (1854/55-1920)

Alice Mary Chambers was a significant figure in British artistic circles of the late nineteenth century, and in was particular a valued friend of the infamous artists' agent, Charles Augustus Howell. Her beautiful drawings and watercolours reveal a debt to both Pre-Raphaelitism and Aestheticism, and especially to the work of Dante Gabriel Rossetti.

For a biography of Alice Mary Chambers, please refer to page 117.

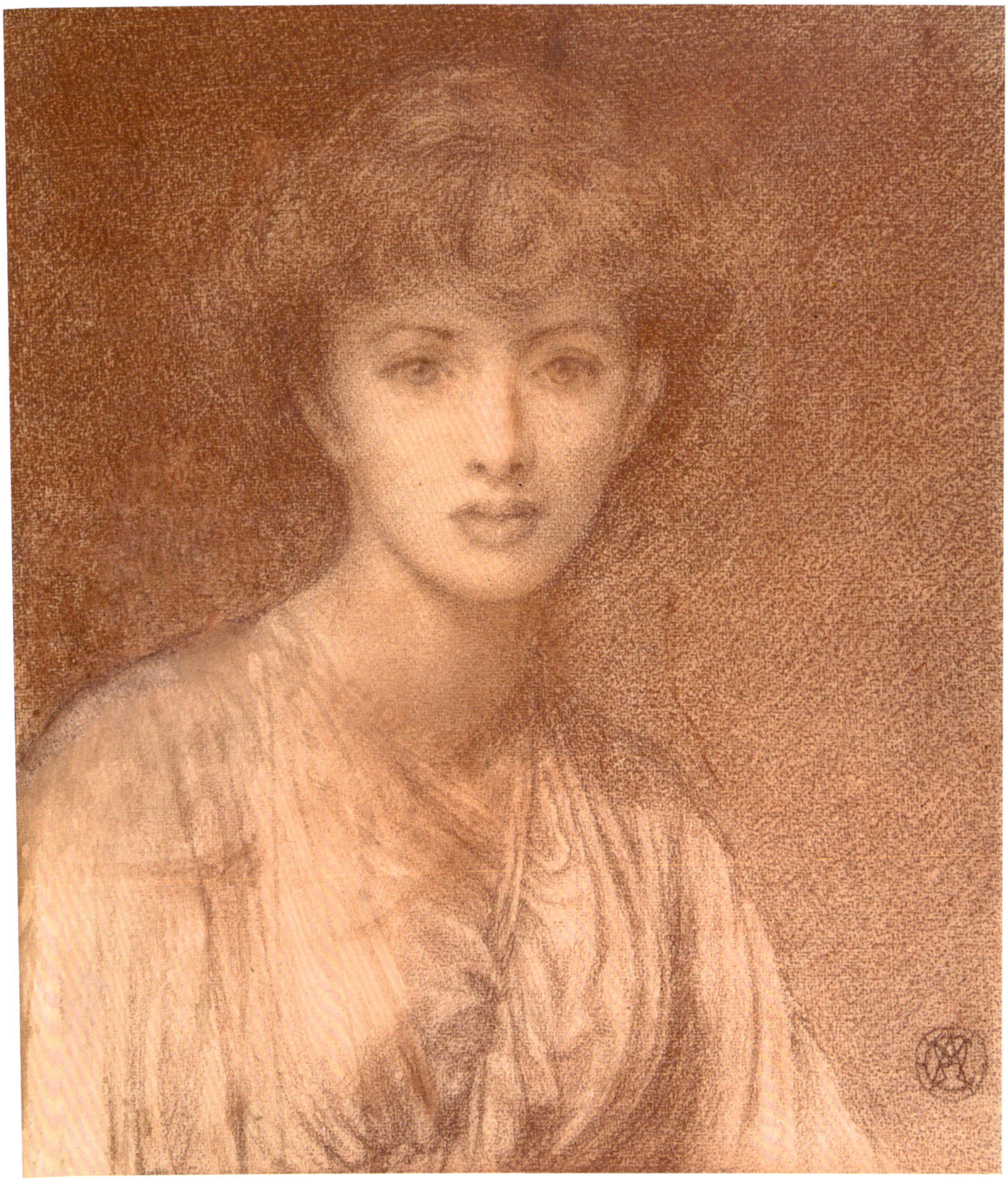

58 **Portrait of a Young Lady**
Signed with monogram
Chalk
16 x 13 ½ inches

ALBERT CHEVALLIER TAYLER

Albert Chevallier Tayler, RBA RBC ROI NEAC
(1862-1925)

Albert Chevallier Tayler painted a variety of figure subjects, both contemporary and historical. He became best known for his interior scenes, including dinner parties and domestic celebrations, and was admired for the high finish of his canvases. Absorbing Continental influences through study in Paris, he established himself as a member of the Newlyn School by producing social realist scenes *en plein air*. Then, following his conversion to Catholicism in 1887, and his move to London in 1895, he focussed increasingly on religious imagery, middle class settings and portraiture.

For a biography of Albert Chevallier Tayler, please refer to page 118.

The Dining Room

In 1890, the year in which he produced the present work, Albert Chevallier Tayler received a commission from the Fine Art Society to visit Boulogne-sur-Mer, in order to paint the ceremony of the blessing of the sea. The best known result of the trip was *The Departure of the Fishing Fleet, Boulogne*, which was exhibited at the Royal Academy in 1891 as *La Vie Boulonnaise*, and bought by the private collector, Richard Payne, for presentation to Birmingham Museum & Art Gallery (where it still resides).

Given that *The Dining Room* was produced during the same period, it is at least possible that it represents lunch in a Boulonnaise restaurant or hotel dining room, and perhaps the hotel at which Tayler stayed. Certainly the artist beautifully captures a sense of light suggestive of a coastal location; it penetrates semi-transparent curtains, illuminates the whiteness of cloth and napkin, and reflects off the polished surfaces of china, glass and metal, the linoleum floor and even the shoes of the most prominent diner. At once precise and atmospheric, the work appears to emulate such French realist interiors as Gustave Caillebotte's *Le Dejeuner* of 1876. Though much smaller than *The Departure of the Fishing Fleet, Boulogne*, it acts as a counterpart to it in encapsulating a clean, calm middle-class interior that is the very opposite of the bustling working-class quayside.

59 **The Dining Room**
Signed and dated 1890
Oil on canvas
17 ¾ x 21 ½ inches

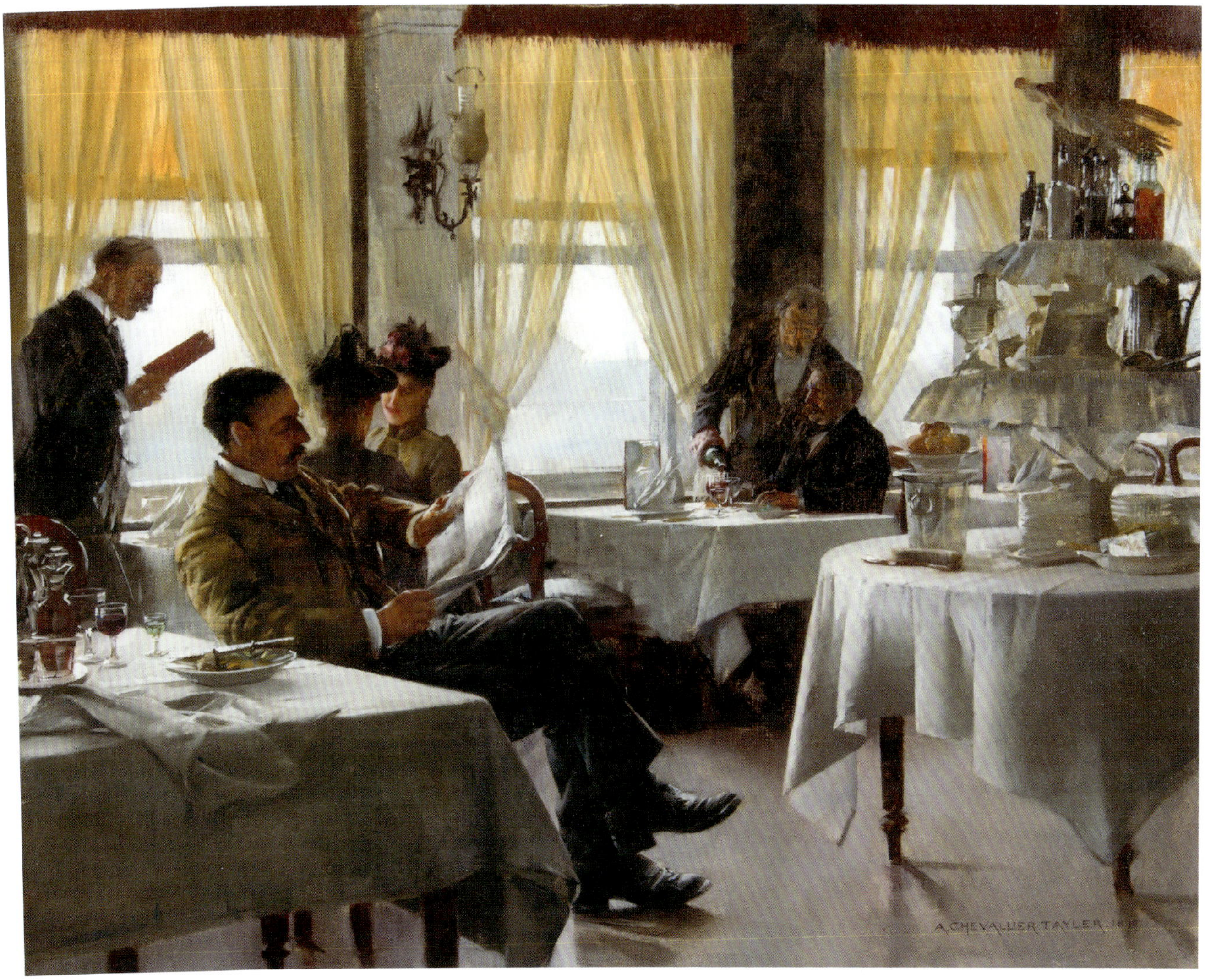
A. CHEVALLIER TAYLER

ROBERT WALKER MACBETH

Robert Walker Macbeth, RA RWS RE RI (1848-1910)

Robert Walker Macbeth was a painter and etcher who developed a distinctive vein of rural genre, in which the figures are treated with a touch of nobility.

For a biography of Robert Walker Macbeth, please refer to *Chris Beetles Summer Show*, 2005, page 15.

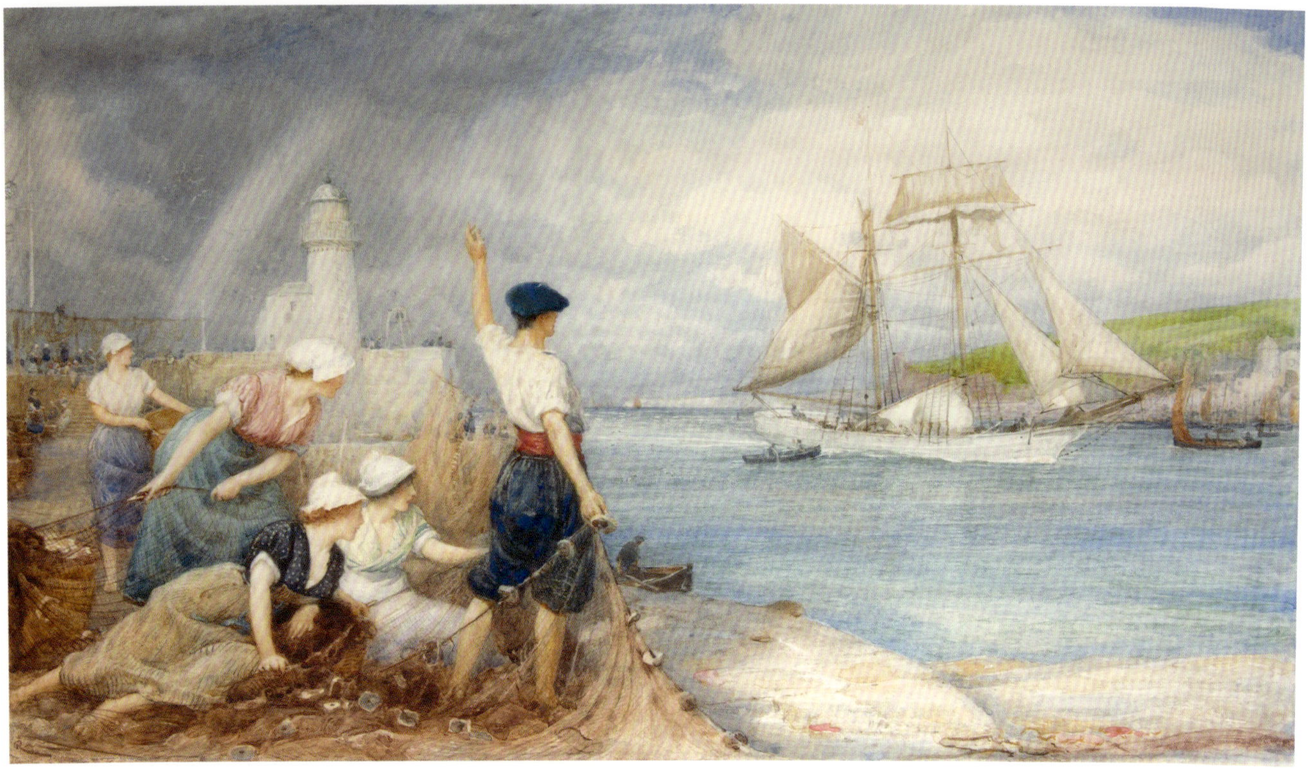

60 The Return of a Whaler
Signed with initials
Watercolour with ink and pencil on board
12 ¾ x 21 inches

HUBERT VON HERKOMER

Sir Hubert von Herkomer, CVO RA VPRWS RE RI (1849-1914)

Bavarian-born Hubert von Herkomer was a leading and sometimes controversial figure in the cultural life of Victorian Britain. He first made his name as a Social Realist, with wood-engraved illustrations for *The Graphic* and paintings exhibited at the Royal Academy of Arts. Broadening both his methods and his subject matter, he became particularly well known as a portraitist. He set up his own school of art in Bushey in 1883 and, two years later, was appointed Slade Professor of Fine Art at Oxford University. Ever energetic and forward thinking, he produced 'pictorial-music-plays' in his own theatre and, at the end of his life, became a pioneering film-maker.

For further information on Hubert von Herkomer, please refer to page 119.

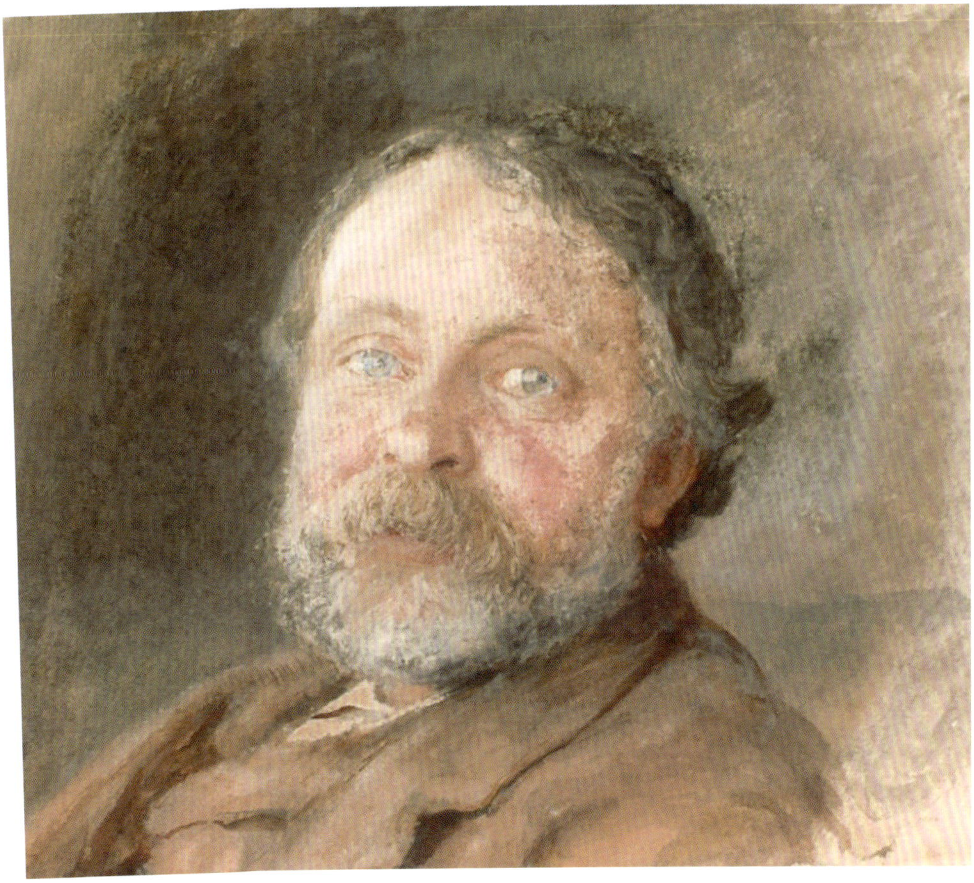

61 Portrait of J W North
Watercolour
4 ½ x 5 inches
Literature: Randall Davies (ed), *The Old Water-Colour Society's Club, Fifth Annual Volume*, 1927-1928, facing page 35

Portrait of J W North

In 1892, Hubert von Herkomer moved to Lodge House, Old Cleeve, west Somerset, in order to be close to J W North, who was living a little to the south in Beggearn Huish House. He hoped to learn from North as much as he could about the tradition that had been established by North's friend and fellow artist, Frederick Walker, who had died prematurely in 1875. However, he soon discovered that North had become a more original painter than Walker, and had perfected a unique painting technique. As a result, Herkomer revolutionised his own approach to painting, and promoted North in various ways, so encouraging his election as an associate of the Royal Academy in 1893. While in Somerset, Herkomer painted the present watercolour portrait of North, and another of the artist, Robert Walker Macbeth (which is in the collection of the Royal Academy). The friendship between North and Herkomer came to an abrupt end in 1897 when Herkomer found that North had opposed his election to the position of President of the Royal Society of Painters in Water-Colours.

CARLTON ALFRED SMITH

Carlton Alfred Smith, RBA RI ROI (1853-1946)

Carlton Alfred Smith was a painter, mainly in watercolour, of gentle rural genre scenes, including many of mothers and daughters.

For a biography of Carlton Alfred Smith, please refer to page 119.

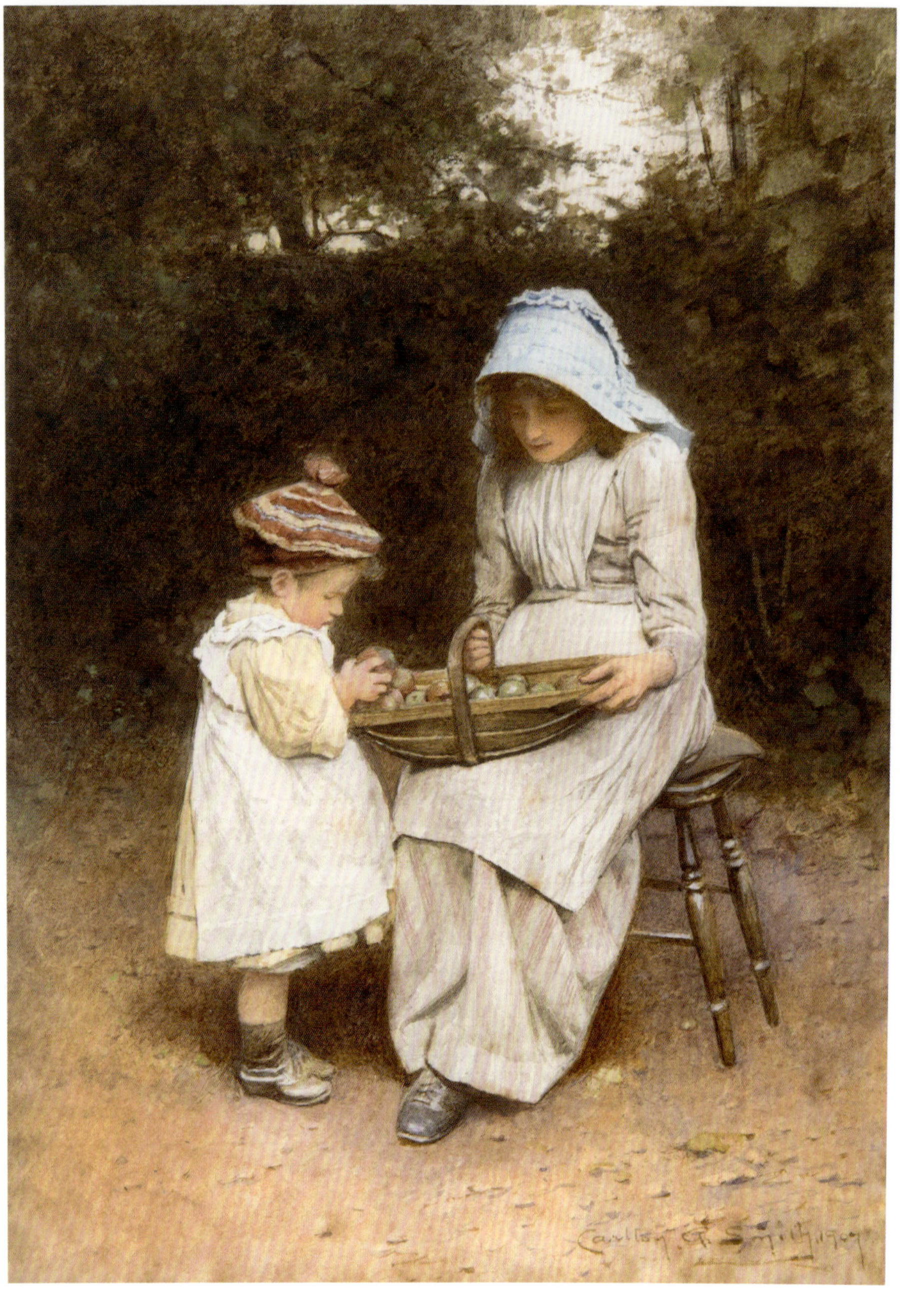

62 **Nearly Ripe**
Signed and dated 1907
Watercolour
10 ½ x 7 ½ inches

BIRKET FOSTER

Myles Birket Foster, RWS (1825-1899)

Myles Birket Foster was one of the most popular artists of the Victorian period, achieving success first as an illustrator and then as an exhibition watercolourist. In both disciplines, he conveyed a gentle naturalism through mastery of technique.

For a biography of Birket Foster, please refer to *Chris Beetles Summer Show*, 2017, page 65.

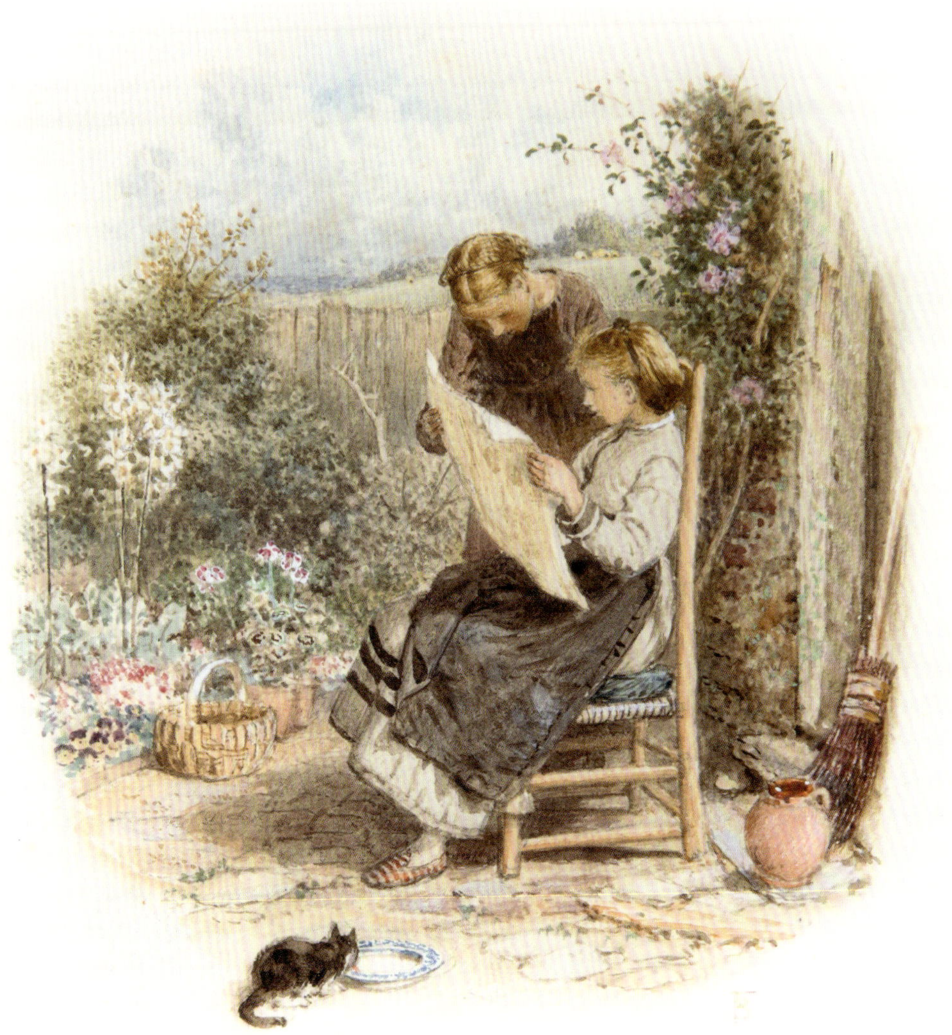

63 **Morning News**
Signed with monogram
Watercolour with bodycolour
6 x 5 inches

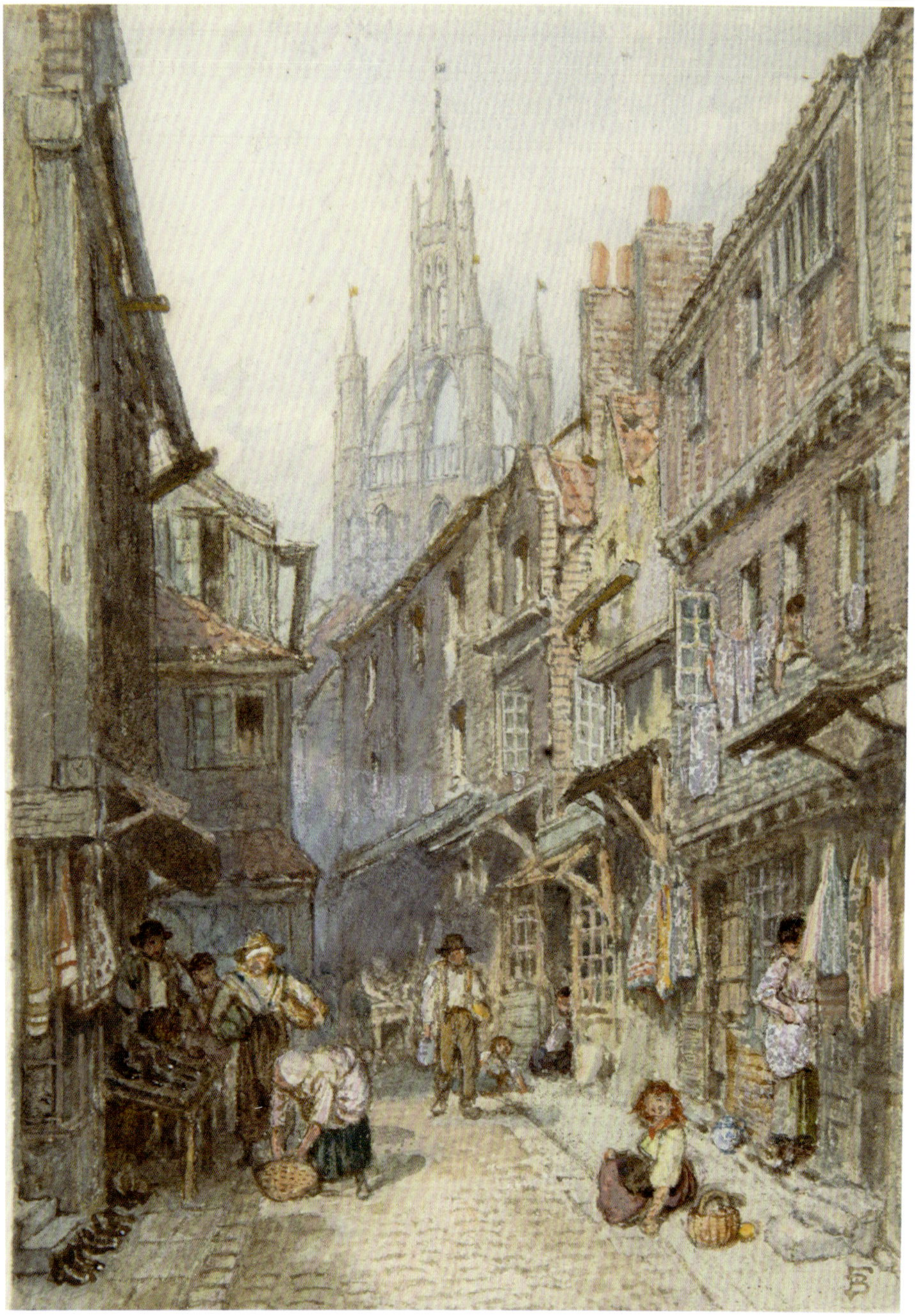

64 Castle Garth, Old Newcastle
Signed with initials
Watercolour with pencil
5 ½ x 4 inches

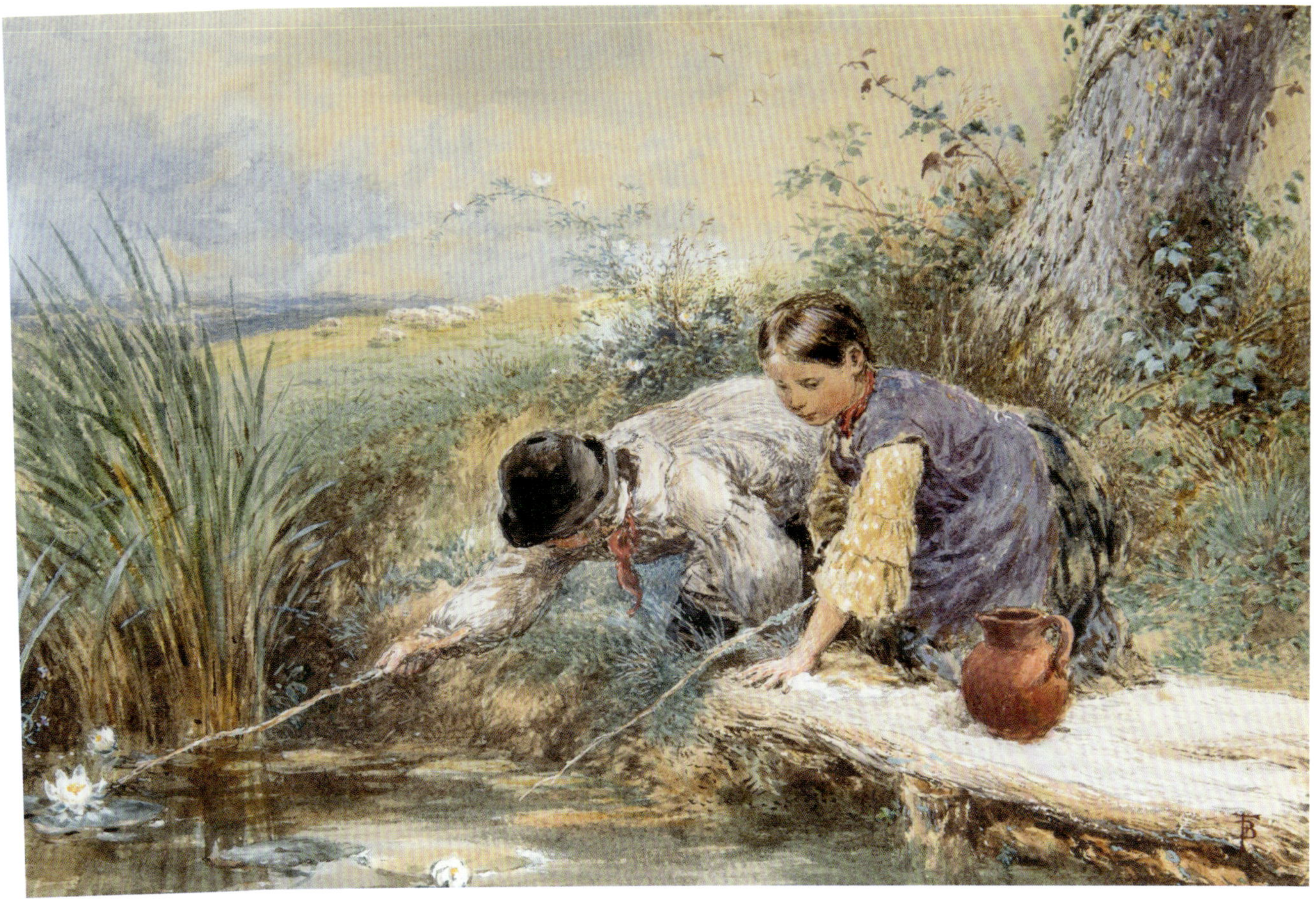

65 Water Lilies
Signed with monogram
Watercolour with bodycolour
5 x 7 inches

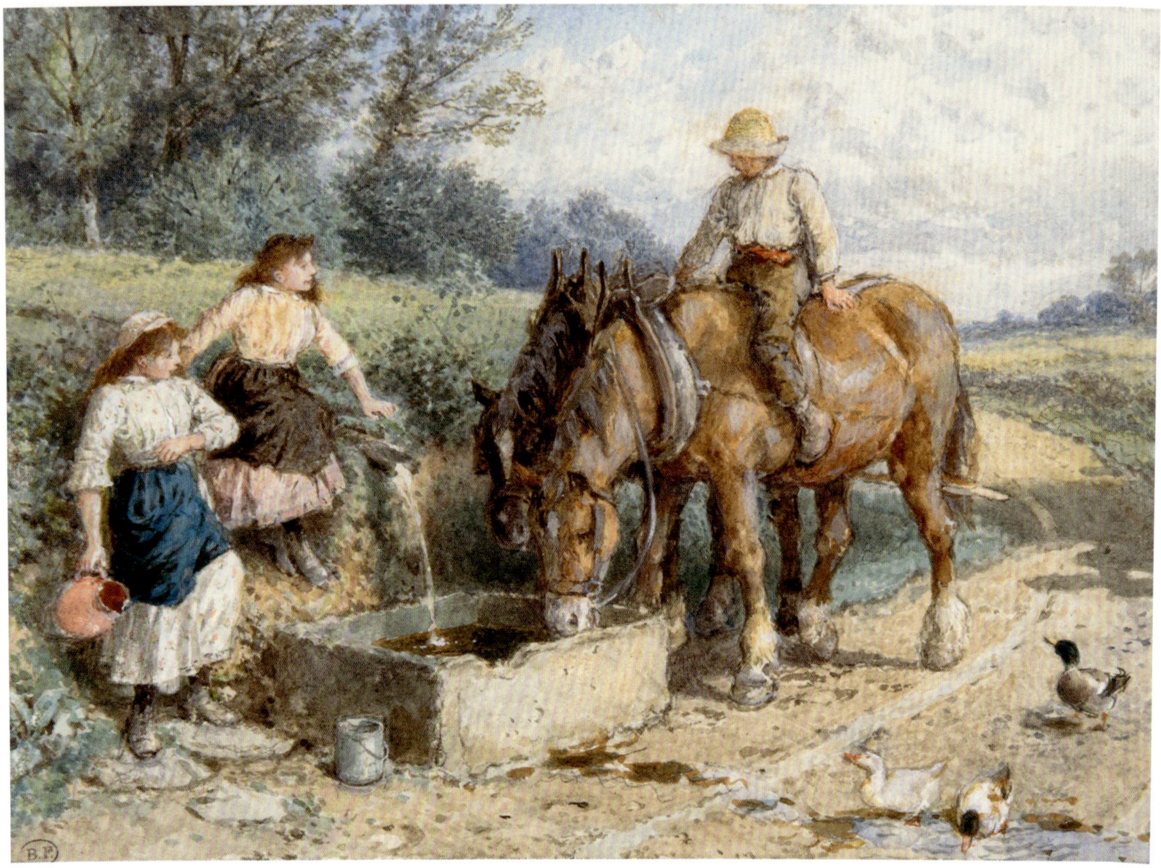

66 The Drinking Trough
Stamped with Birket Foster studio stamp
Inscribed with title on card attached to backboard
Watercolour with bodycolour
6 x 8 inches
Provenance: Thomas Agnew & Sons

ROBERT THORNE WAITE

Robert Thorne Waite, RWS RBC ROI (1843-1935)

Robert Thorne Waite was a painter, mostly in watercolour, of bright and airy landscapes and pastoral scenes. He was particularly fond of the corn and hay fields of the South Downs.

For a biography of Robert Thorne Waite, please refer to page 120.

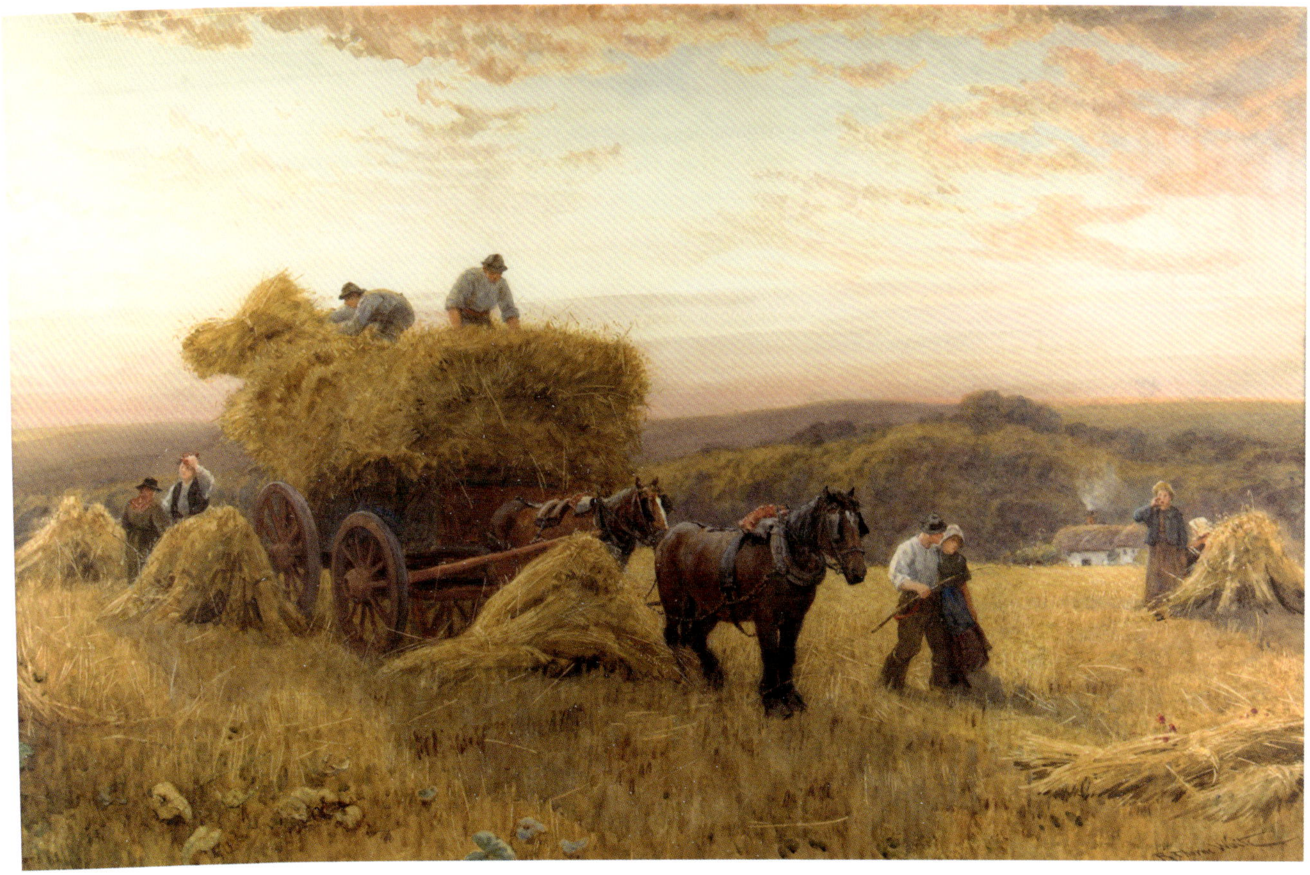

67 **The Last Load**
Signed
Watercolour with bodycolour
26 x 40 inches
Provenance: Hewson & Forster, Fine Art Dealers, 16 Church Street, Sheffield

ALFRED PARSONS

Alfred William Parsons, RA RSW PRWS RI HRMS ROI NEAC (1847-1920)

Alfred Parsons became an expert in various branches of the art of the garden. He used watercolour to produce fresh portraits of gardens and accurate illustrations of botanical specimens. Having collaborated on books with the famous gardener, William Robinson, he went on to become a designer of gardens in Britain and the United States. His transatlantic connections were strengthened through his membership of the Anglo-American 'Broadway Group' of artists and writers that included Henry James and John Singer Sargent. He further broadened his horizons and deepened his knowledge through trips to Japan in the period 1892-94.

For a biography of Alfred Parsons, please refer to *Chris Beetles Summer Show*, 2016, page 21.

69 **A Summer Garden** (opposite)
Oil on canvas
19 x 13 inches

68 **The Duck Pen**
Signed
Watercolour on paper laid on board
13 ½ x 19 ¾ inches

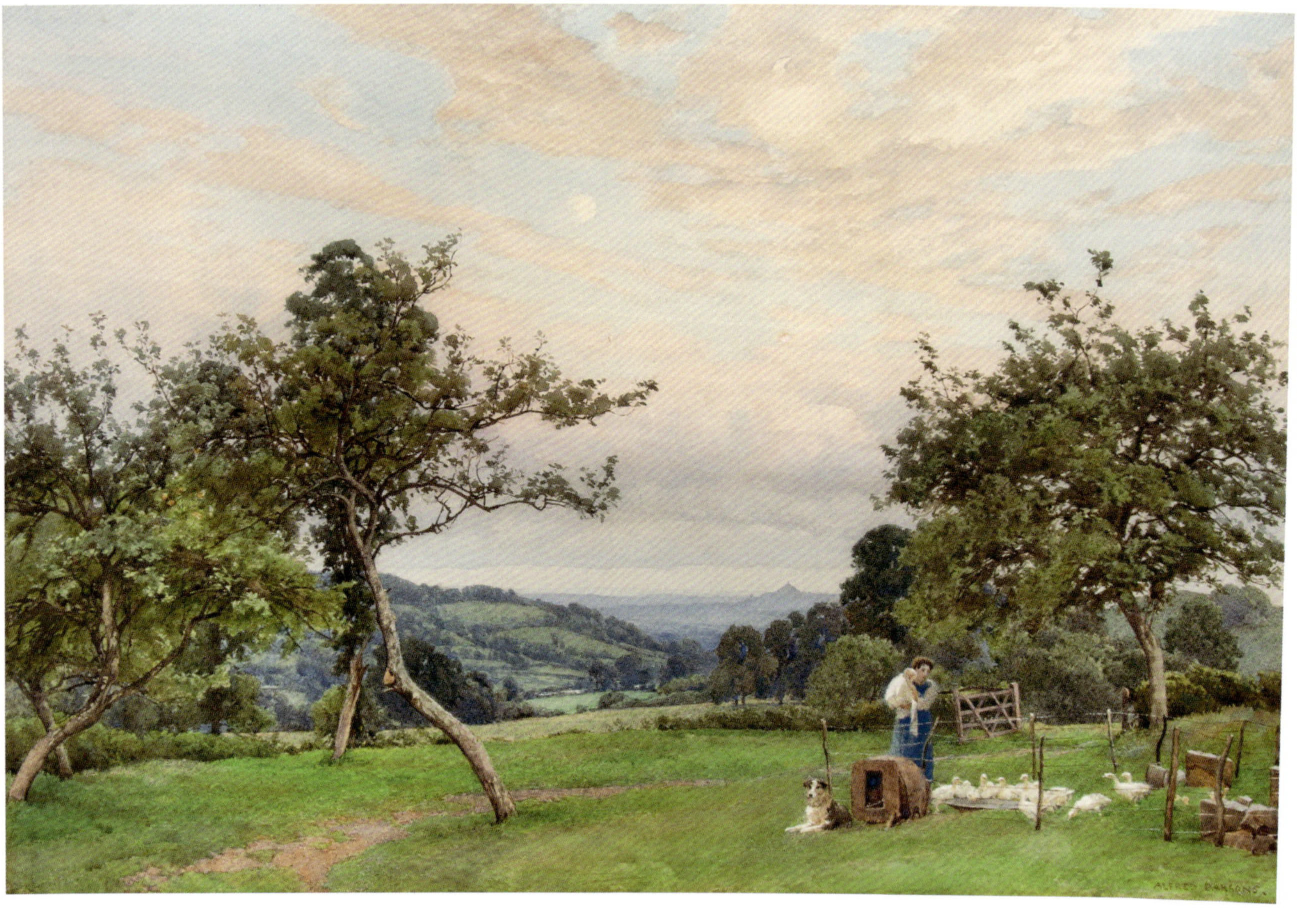

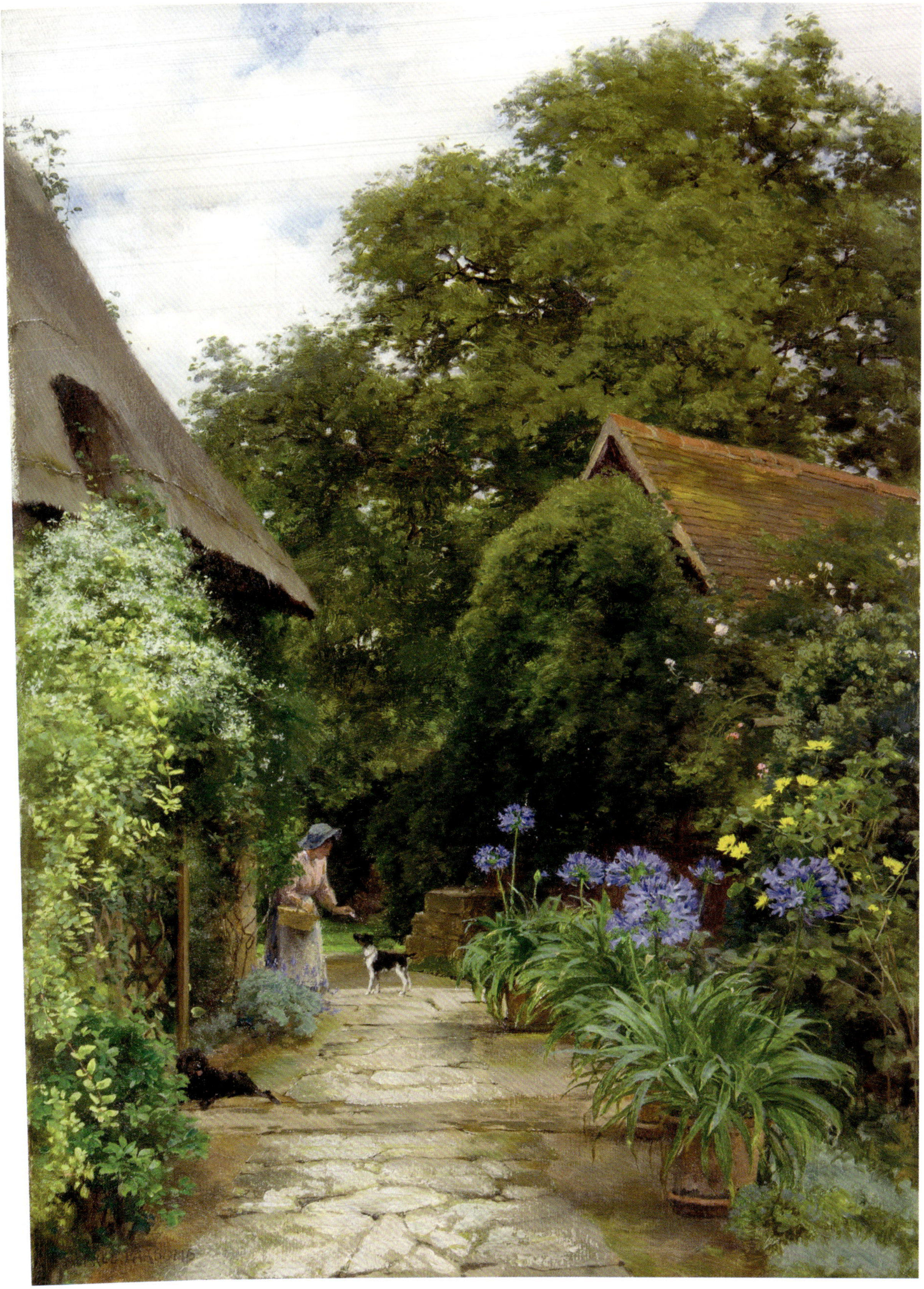

70 By the Sundial, Early Summer
Signed
Watercolour with bodycolour
13 x 9 inches

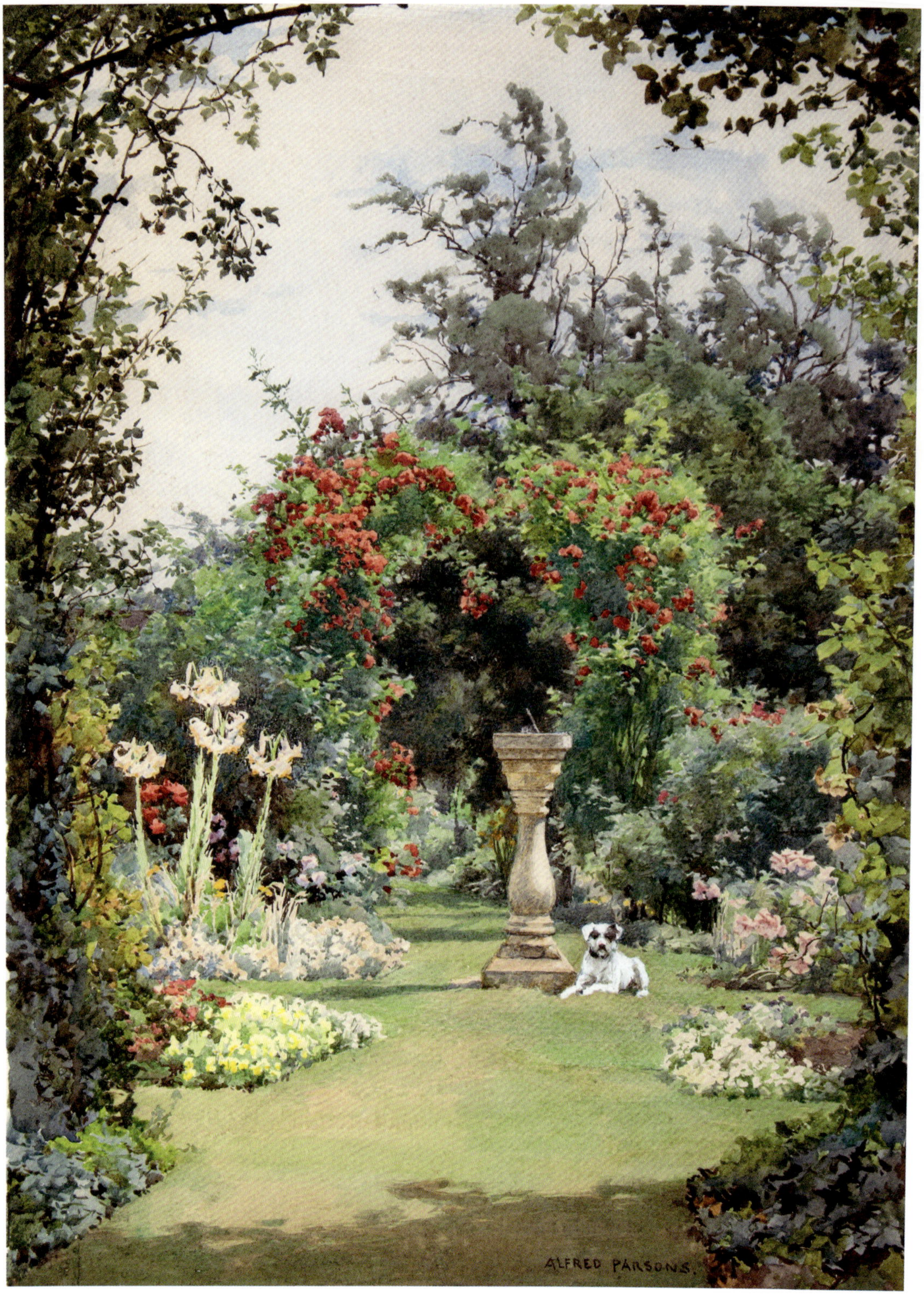

HELEN ALLINGHAM

Helen Mary Elizabeth Allingham (née Paterson), RWS (1848-1926)

One of the most successful women artists of the Victorian age, Helen Allingham produced archetypal watercolour images of cottages and gardens.

For a biography of Helen Allingham, please refer to *Chris Beetles Summer Show*, 2016, page 18.

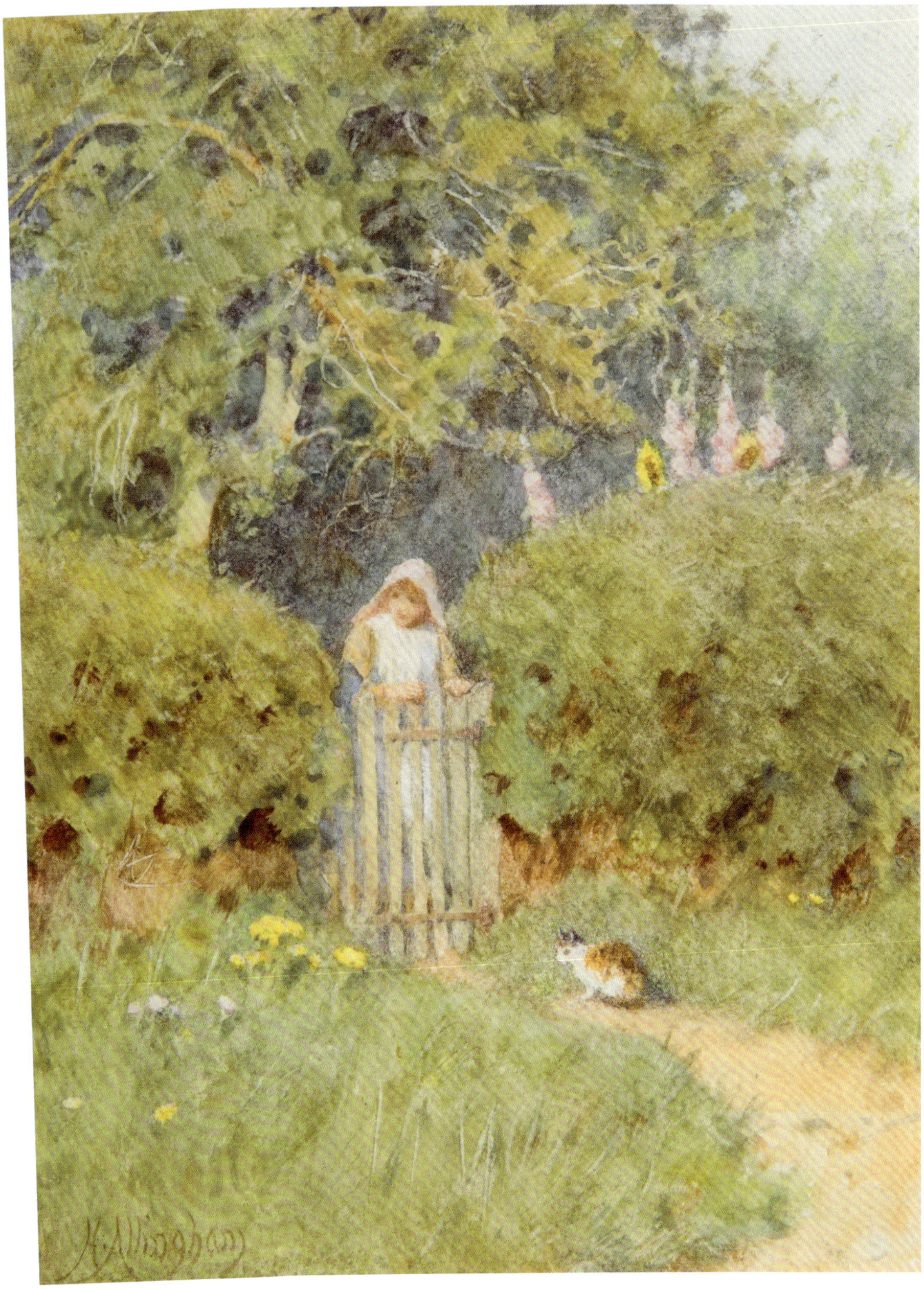

71 At a Cottage Gate
Signed
Watercolour with bodycolour
6 ½ x 4 ½ inches

HELEN ALLINGHAM

72 **A Wiltshire Cottage**
Signed
Watercolour with bodycolour; 10 ¼ x 7 ¾ inches
Exhibited: Royal Society of Painters in Water-Colours,
Winter 1920, No 246

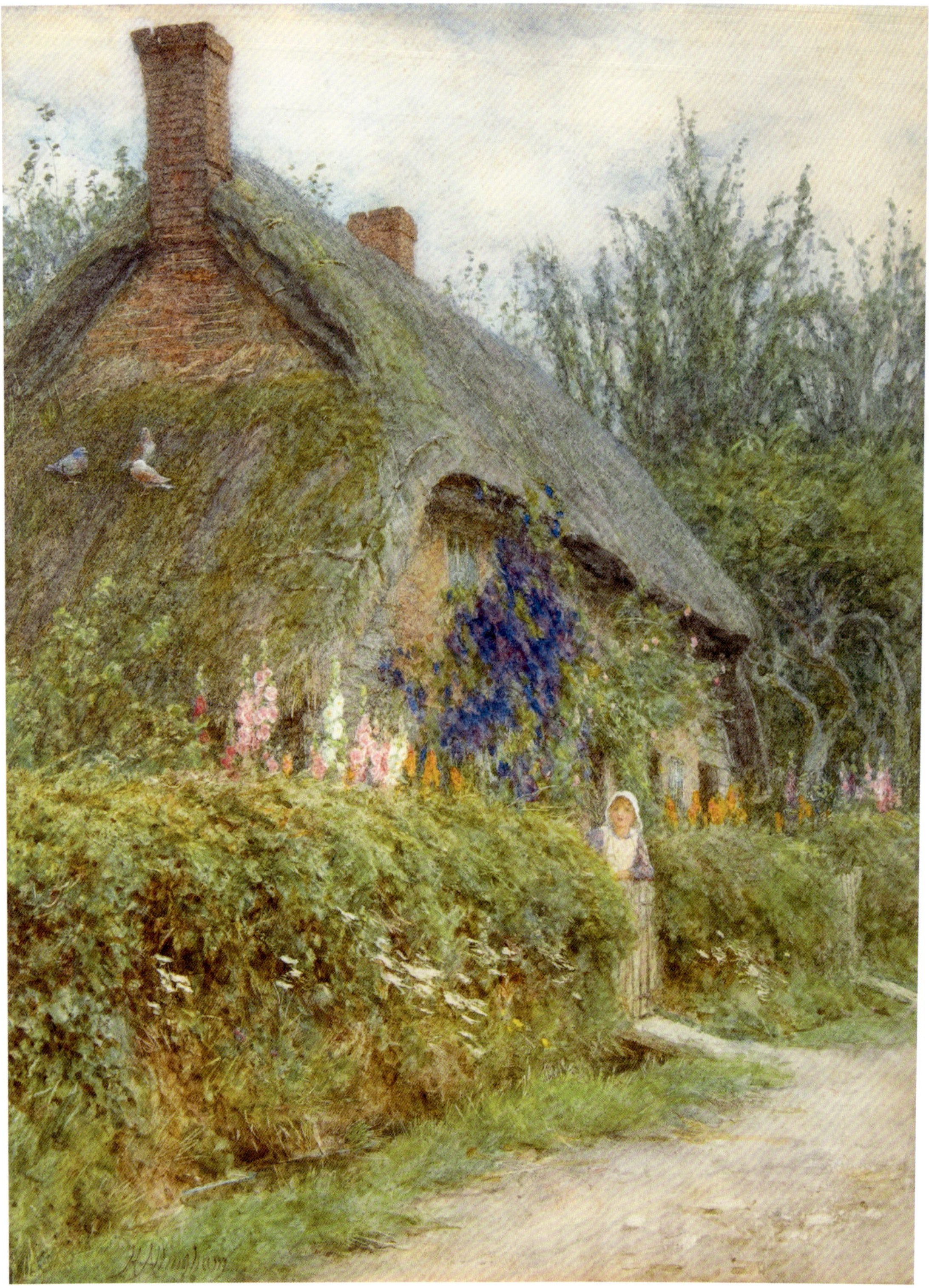

GEORGE MARKS

George Marks (1857-1938)

Working in oil and watercolour, George Marks produced landscapes that imbued many of the secluded places of Southern England with a quiet poetry, be they gorse bushes on the downs or primrose patches in the dells.

For a biography of George Marks, please refer to page 120.

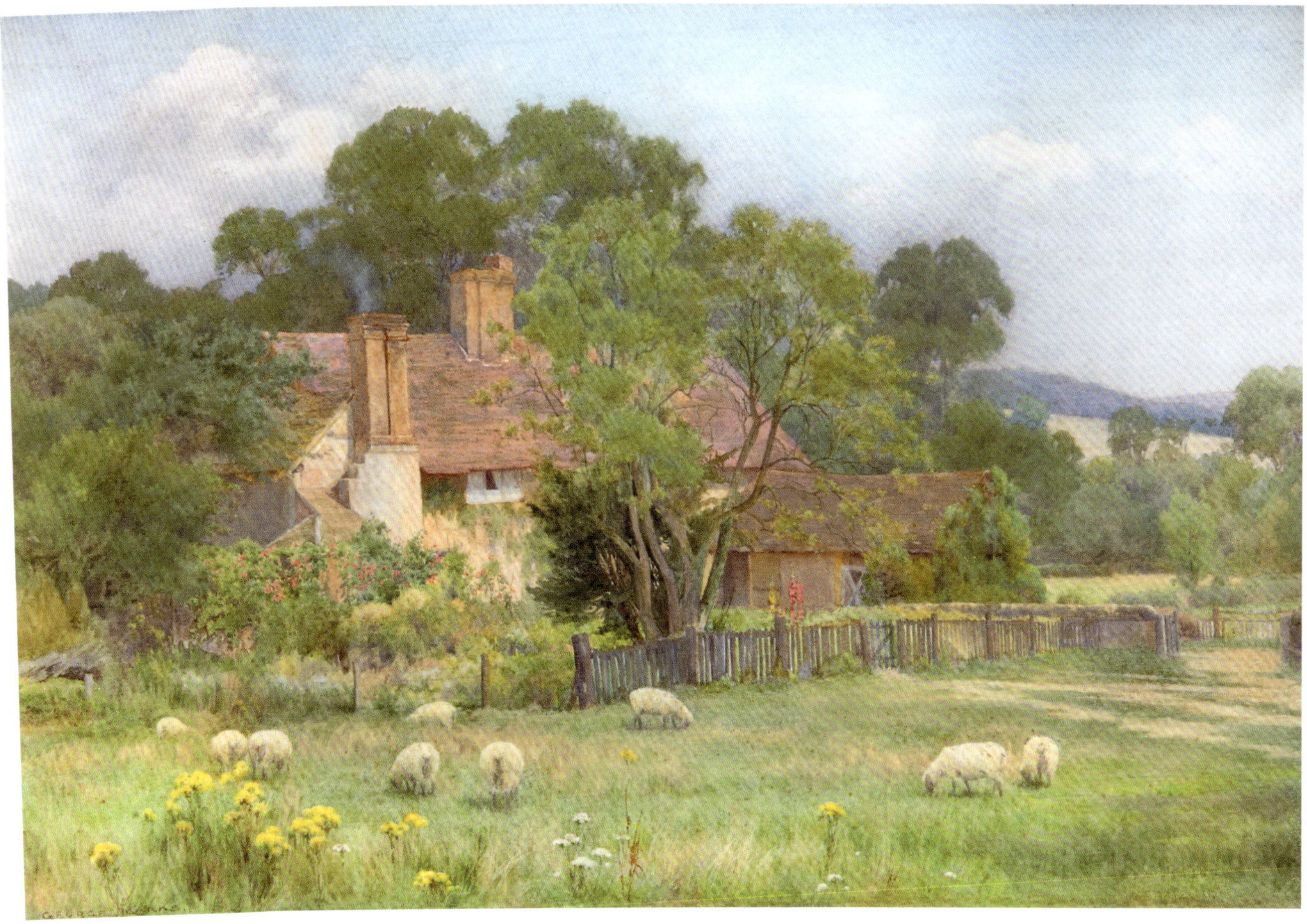

73 **The Edge of a Sussex Common**
Signed
Inscribed with title on reverse
Watercolour with bodycolour on board
10 ½ x 15 inches

SAMUEL READ

Samuel Read, RWS (1815-1883)

Samuel Read was a painter and illustrator, specialising in architectural subjects and, to a lesser extent, coastal views. He was particularly fond of producing images of the interiors and exteriors of cathedrals, many of which were reproduced in *The Illustrated London News*, for which he worked as its first Special Artist (a visual journalist sent to record major news stories for illustrated publications).

For a biography of Samuel Read, please refer to page 121.

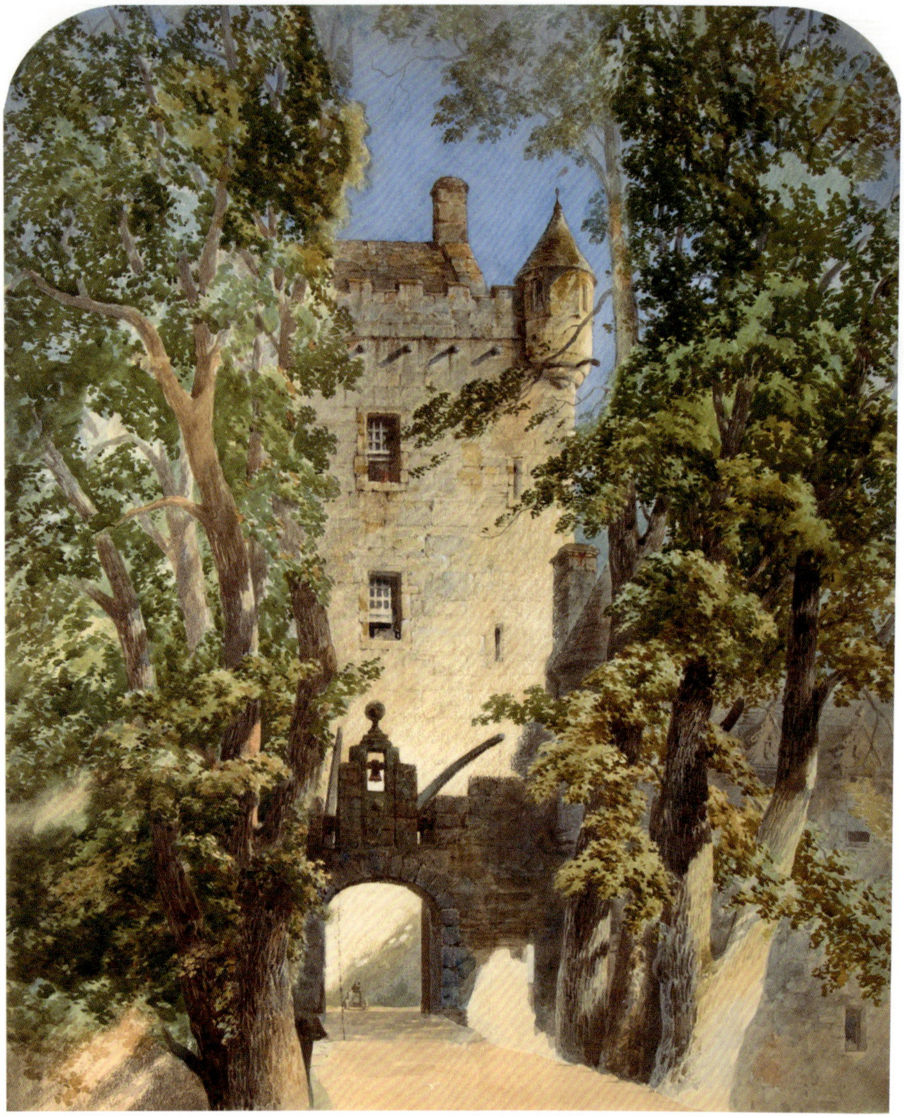

74 Cawdor Castle
Watercolour
with pencil
21 ¾ x 18 ½ inches

Cawdor Castle

Samuel Read visited Cawdor Castle in order to illustrate an article that appeared in *The Illustrated London News* on 22 February 1868. The article begins as follows:

> This old Scottish baronial residence, the family seat of the Earls of Cawdor, is pleasantly situated amidst woods and water, at the base of a far-stretching range of hills, in the county of Nairn … It is a bold castellated mansion of the fifteenth century, to which additions have been made from time to time. We still enter by the ancient drawbridge, within which is an open paved court, roomy enough to accommodate a strong body of defenders; and if they were driven to retreat, there are loopholes in the massive tower behind from which to harass the enemy and protect the entrance.

GILBERT BAIRD FRASER

Gilbert Baird Fraser (1865-1947)

The watercolours of Baird Fraser tend to be both looser and warmer than those of his brothers.

For a biography of Gilbert Baird Fraser, please refer to page 121.

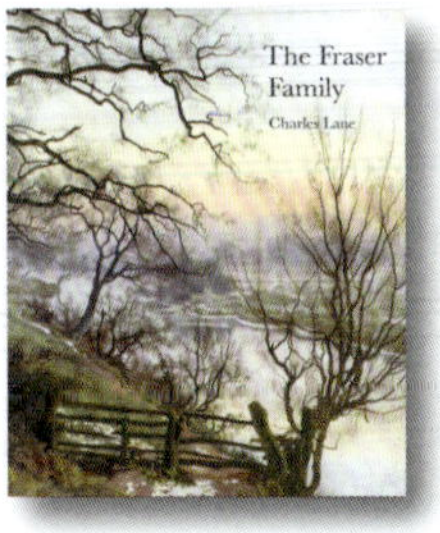

Charles Lane's *The Fraser Family*
The Chris Beetles Gallery has regularly shown a range of works by members of the Fraser family that has been significant in both number and quality. In 2010, it built on its experience by publishing Charles Lane's *The Fraser Family*, the first substantial publication devoted to the artists.

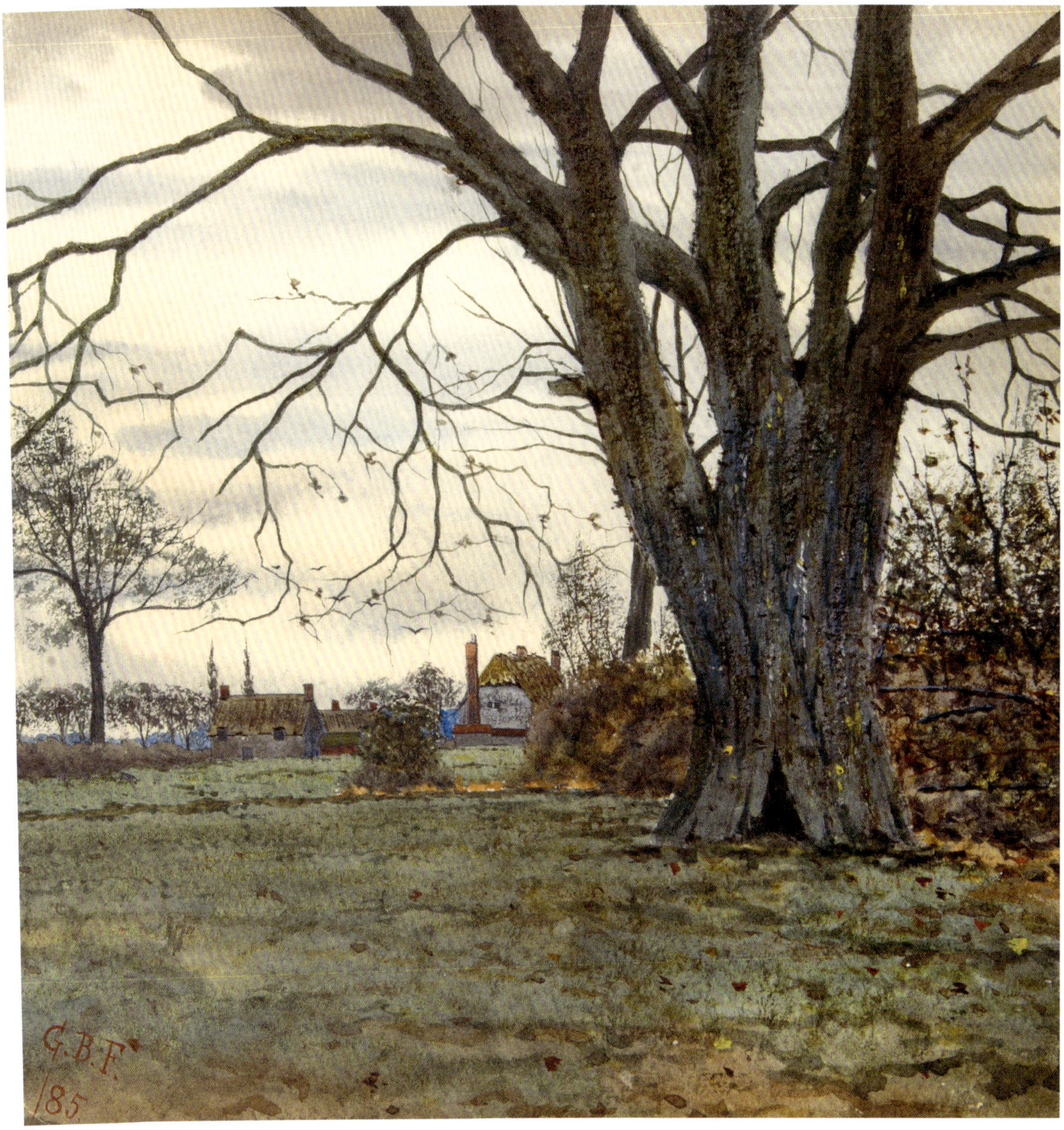

75 **The Ancient Tree**
Signed with initials and dated /85
Watercolour with pen and ink
8 ¼ x 8 inches

CONSTANCE FREDERICA GORDON-CUMMING

Constance Frederica Gordon-Cumming (1837-1924)

Constance Frederica Gordon-Cumming was one of the most intrepid and enterprising women travellers of the Victorian period, who also had the skill and industry to record her journeys in word and image. Encouraged by her many distinguished connections, during the height of the British Empire, she visited India, Ceylon and many of the countries of the Pacific Rim, between 1868 and 1880. The extent of her achievement is still in the process of evaluation.

For a biography of Constance Frederica Gordon-Cumming, please refer to *Chris Beetles Summer Show*, 2014, page 13.

Constance Frederica Gordon-Cumming in Ceylon
In the autumn of 1872, Constance Frederica Gordon-Cumming accepted an invitation from the Reverend Hugh Jermyn, formerly the parson of her birthplace of Altyre, in Morayshire, and latterly the Bishop of Colombo, to visit him and his daughter in Ceylon. She arrived in Colombo in February 1873 and stayed until the following summer, arriving back in London in July 1874. Her experiences formed the basis of her book, *Two Happy Years in Ceylon*, published almost 20 years later in 1892.

Ceylon was granted independence from Britain in 1948, and became a republic within the Commonwealth in 1972, when its name was changed to Sri Lanka.

The notes on the works by Constance Frederica Gordon-Cumming are written by Alexander Beetles.

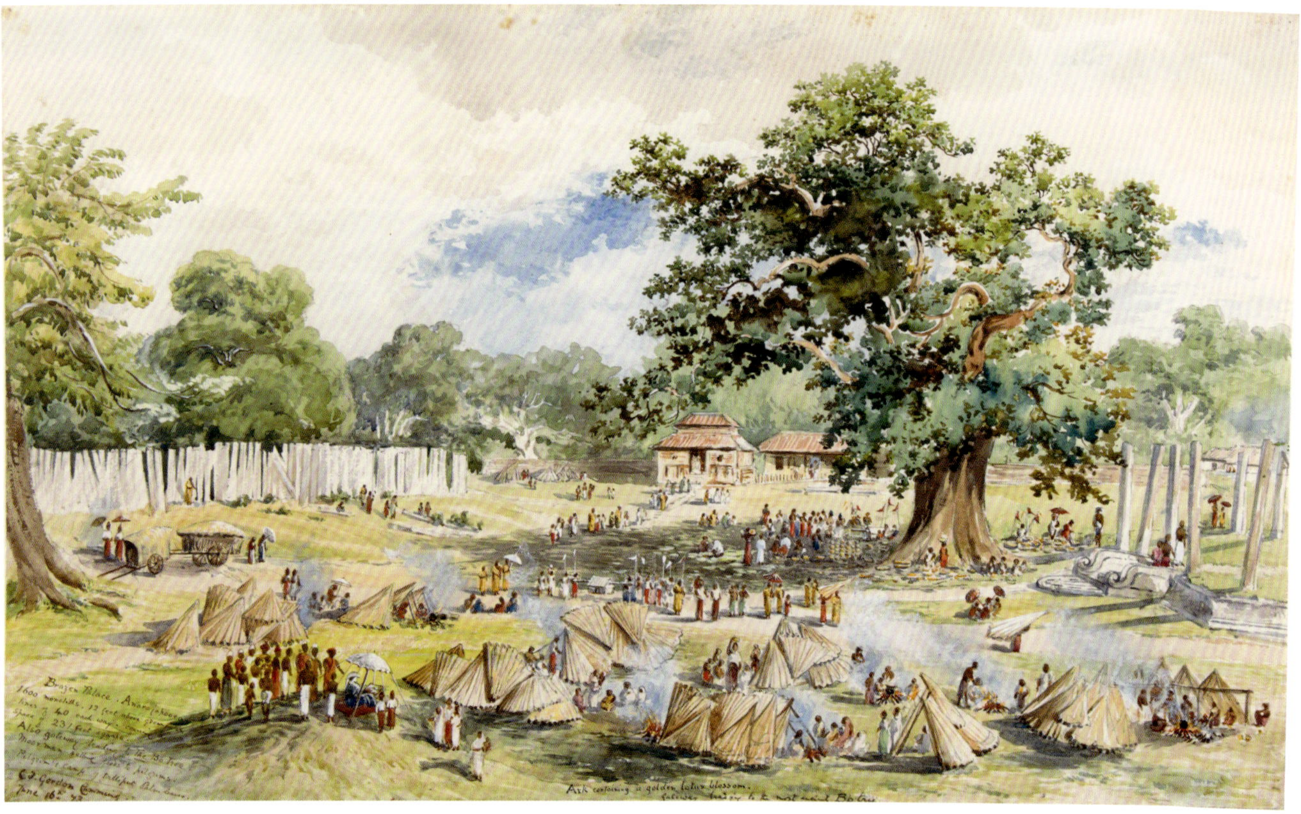

76 **The Brazen Palace, Anuradhapura (Sri Lanka)**
Signed, inscribed 'Brazen Palace. Anarajapoora. 1600 monoliths. 12 feet above ground in lines of 40 each way. Covering a space of 231 feet square. Also gateway leading to the Bo Tree. Moor men selling goods to pilgrims. Pilgrim's camp of Talliput Palm leaves.' and 'Ark containing a golden lotus blossom. Gateway leading to the most ancient Bo tree.', and dated 'June 16th 73'
Watercolour with bodycolour and pencil
15 ¾ x 24 ½ inches

77 **The Kuttam Pokuna or twin bathing tanks near the Jetawanarama Dagoba – Anaraiapura** (opposite)
Signed, inscribed with title and dated 'June 73'
Watercolour with bodycolour and pencil
18 ¾ x 29 inches

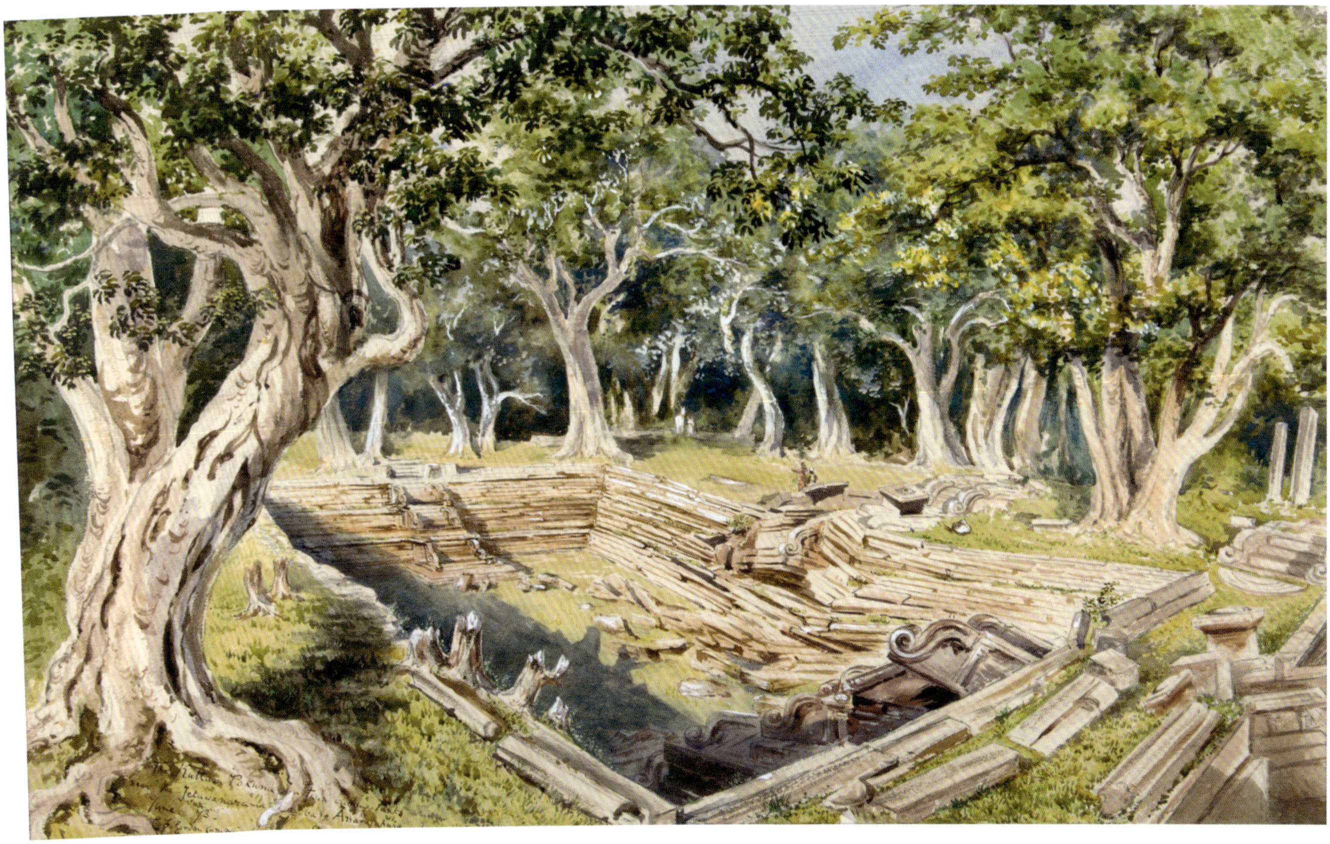

77 The Kuttam Pokuna or twin bathing tanks near the Jetawanarama Dagoba – Anaraiapura

The Brazen Palace (opposite)
Located 127 miles north of Colombo in Sri Lanka's North Central Province, Anuradhapura was Ceylon's capital city and heart of Theravada Buddhism for over 1,400 years. Though the city fell to the South Indian kingdom of Pandya in the ninth century AD and its great many buildings, monuments and relics ransacked and destroyed, it has remained a sacred site and important place of pilgrimage for Buddhists.

The 'Brazen Palace', or Lovamhapaya, was an ancient monastery which stood during the city's glorious past. It was described as being nine stories high, with each side being 400 feet long. The palace was bedecked in corals and jewels, with a roof covered in copper-bronze plates, which gave it its name. Each storey was said to contain 1,000 rooms, and the whole structure sat upon 40 rows of 40 copper-wrapped stone pillars. Though the palace was destroyed in a fire in the first century BC, it was rebuilt, demolished and rebuilt again multiple times, before its final destruction during the city's fall. The stone pillars which supported the building and appear in Constance Gordon-Cumming's watercolour were raised again in the twelfth century and still stand to this day. The small building seen in the centre was a later construction that served as a chapter house for Maha Vihara Buddhists.

Gordon-Cumming's visit to Anuradhapura in June 1873 was likely to have been linked to early attempts to survey the area, as official British interest in the area had only been registered in 1871. She was one of the earliest British recorders of Anuradhapura, as planned excavations of the site did not begin until 1890.

The Kuttam Pokuna (above)
During her visit to Anuradhapura in June 1873, Constance Gordon-Cumming came across the Kuttam Pokuna, or 'twin pools', in the gardens of the Abhayagiri Monastery. She described them as 'two beautifully constructed tanks, lined with great stones laid in terraces, and flights of steps, with handsome balustrade descending from every side to where water once was'. She was certainly impressed by this 'strange ruin of ancient luxury', declaring it 'as remarkable a scene as any in the jungle city' (*Happy Years*, page 427). Constructed as bathing pools for the Buddhist monks, possibly during the sixth century AD, the Kuttam Pokuna was a remarkable feat of hydrological engineering, as the water was supplied through a series of underground pipes and filters before entering the pools. When Gordon-Cumming visited the site, one pool (presumably unseen to the right of the present image) had been restored as a bathing-place, while the other had been left as an archaeological study.

Gordon-Cumming records the pools as being near the Jetawanarama Dagoba, a Buddhist 'stupa', or monument, that had been the tallest of its kind and the third tallest structure in the world on its completion in the third century AD, standing at 400 feet high. It fell into disrepair following the fall of Anuradhapura in the eleventh century, before being rebuilt in the following century at 233 feet, the height it stands today. Approximately 93.3 million bricks were used in its construction, enough, according to Gordon-Cumming, to 'construct a town the size of Ipswich or Coventry, or form a wall one foot in thickness and two feet in height, reaching from London to Edinburgh!' (op cit, page 386).

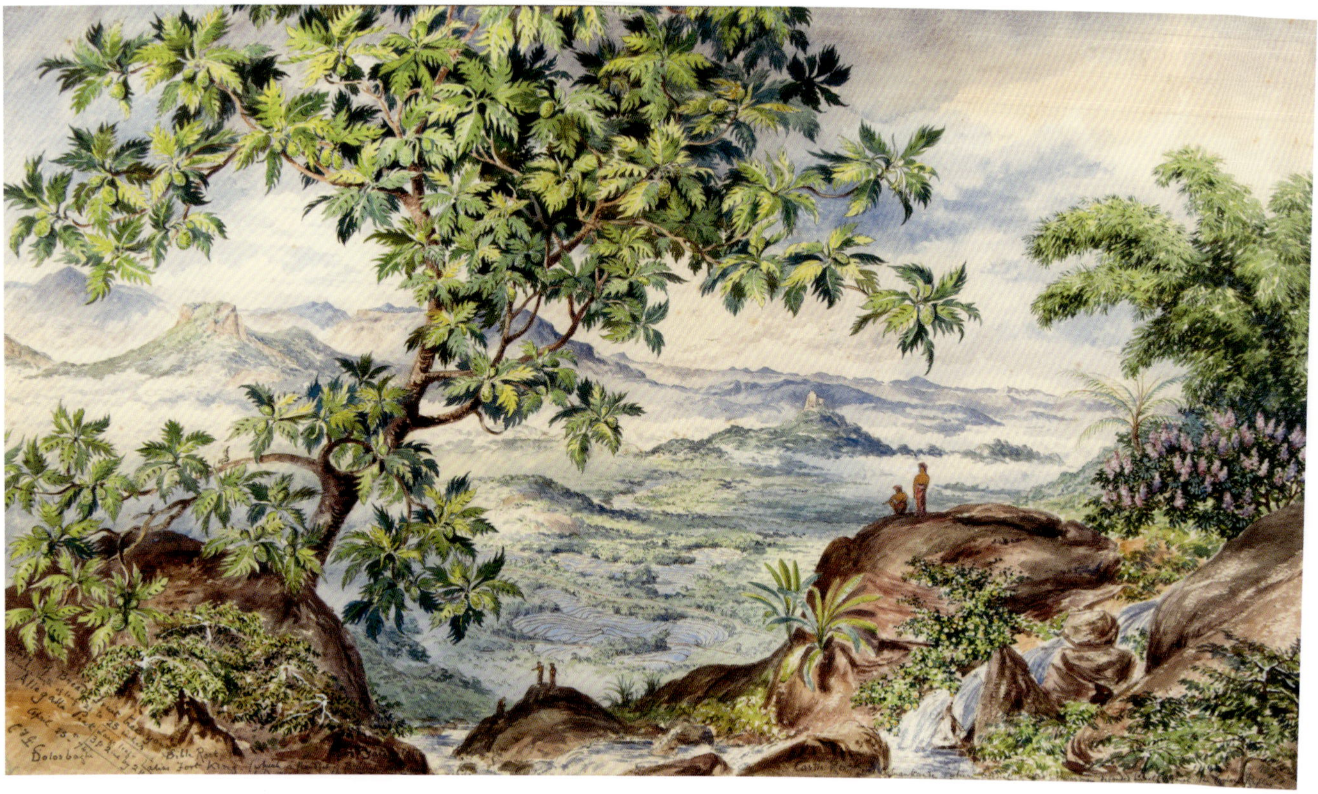

78 Study of Bread Fruit Tree, Allegalla Peak
Signed with initials, inscribed with title and 'Young', 'Average length of leaf 21 to 25 inches', 'Large leaf – 3 ft 2 inch by 2 ft 4 inch', 'Dolosbaghi', 'Bible Rock alias Fort King. / which a handful British soldiers held against a large body of Kandian rebels.', 'Yattiantotte' and 'Castle Rock alias Ootnankande – where Sardiel a noted highwayman defended himself against the Ceylon Rifles.', and dated 'April 25th – 74'
Watercolour with pencil
15 ¼ x 24 ¼ inches

Study of Bread Fruit Tree, Allegalla Peak

Alagalla Peak is the highest point of the Alagalla Mountain Range, located on the rail route from Colombo to Kandy, and standing at almost 4,000 feet. Constance Gordon-Cumming took this train line in the spring of 1874 and spent some time staying in the area before moving onwards to Kandy, enjoying 'happy days and weeks spent exploring many a lovely corner in that vast panorama'. She recalled with particular fondness a stay 'perched at the base of the mighty crag which crowns Allagalla Peak … in a sheltered nook embosomed in fruit-trees, and overlooking such a magnificent view as we may sometimes obtain for a few moments by climbing some mighty Alp, but which few homes can claim as their perpetual outlook' (*Happy Years*, page 159). It is likely that this vantage point was the inspiration for the present watercolour.

Gordon-Cumming's annotations to this work record much of the surrounding area. 'Dolosbaghi' (Dolosbage) and 'Yattiantotte' (Yatiyantota) were local villages and tea estates, where Gordon-Cumming may have stayed during her exploration of the area. The flat-topped rock seen on the left of the image is 'Bible Rock', or Bathalegala, so named because it is said to resemble an open book. On the right of the image is 'Castle Rock, alias Ootnankande' (Uthuwankanda), a rock formation in the shape of an ancient castle. Gordon-Cumming also refers to the famous Ceylonese highwayman and bandit Sardiel, who operated in the area until his eventual capture and execution in 1864. Sardiel has become a heroic figure in Sri Lankan lore thanks to his insurgency against British colonial rule. He was known to distribute much of what he stole amongst the poor, giving him the nickname the 'Robin Hood of Sri Lanka'.

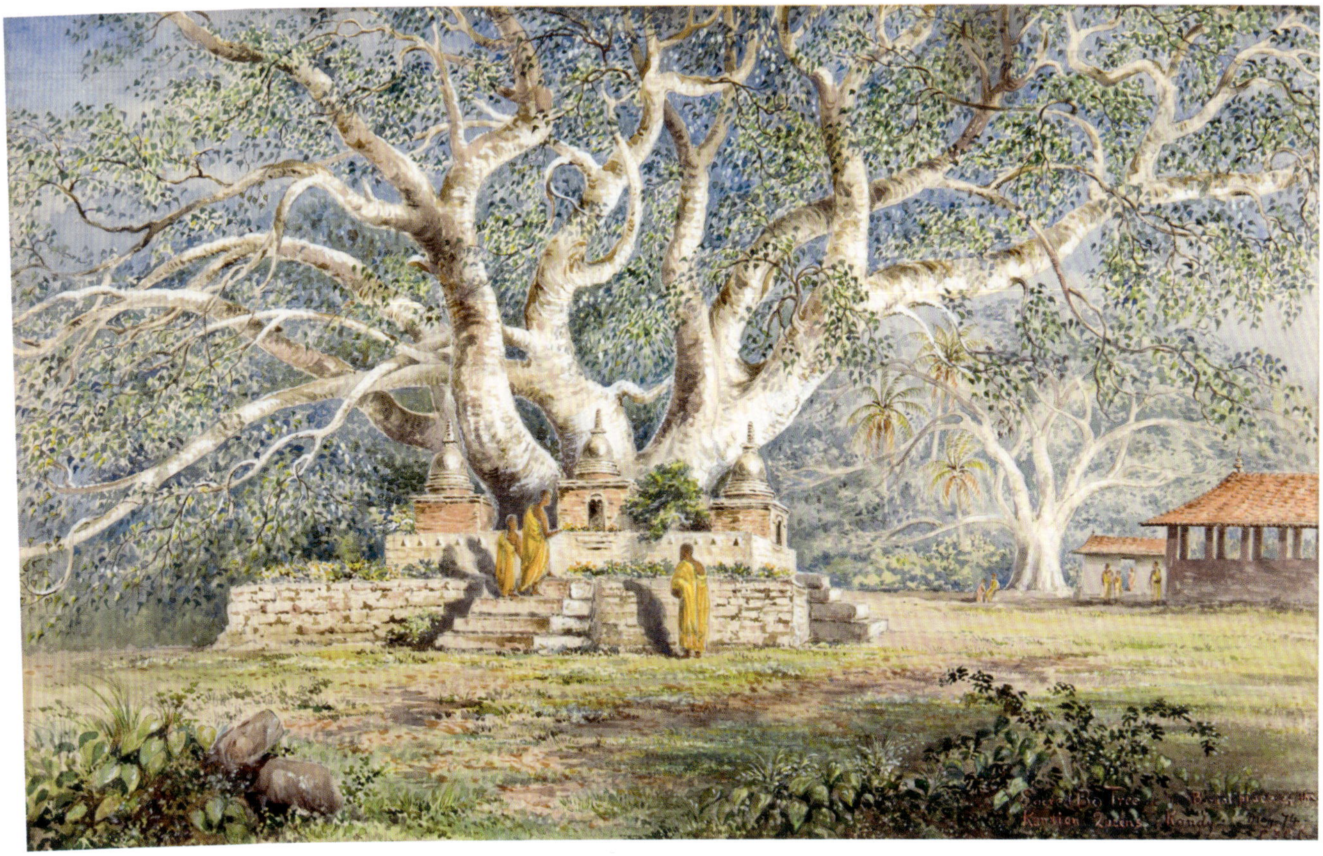

79 Sacred Bo Tree at the Burial place of the Kandian Queens, Kandy
Signed with initials, inscribed with title and dated 'May 74'
Watercolour with bodycolour and pencil
13 ¾ x 20 inches

Sacred Bo Tree at the Burial Place of the Kandian Queens, Kandy

Constance Gordon-Cumming is likely to have arrived in Kandy in late April or early May 1874, having spent a week with Bishop Hugh Jermyn at Pallagolla, before taking a coach to Gampola and onwards by rail. She described Kandy as 'a beautifully situated little town' where 'the vegetation of the hills meets that of the plains, and all the lovely varieties of foliage peculiar to each mingle in rank luxuriance' (*Happy Years*, page 243).

The Burial Place referenced here is the Asgiri Maha Viharaya, one of two fourteenth-century Buddhist monasteries in Kandy, which contain in their grounds the Sri Dalada Maligawa, or Temple of the Tooth, which houses a sacred relic said to be a tooth of the Buddha. The Asgiri had served as a royal crematorium and burial ground since the late fourteenth century, a tradition that started when Queen Chandravati, mother of the Kandyan King Sena Sammatha Vikramabahu, was cremated and buried there. However, in 1880, the royal burial ground and funerary dagobas were destroyed by the British to make way for a railway line to Matale.

The Bo Tree, or Bodhi Tree, is a species of fig tree considered sacred in the Buddhist religion. It is believed that the Buddha achieved spiritual enlightenment while sitting beneath such a tree in Bodh Gaya, India. A part of this tree was later transported to Ceylon and planted at Anuradhapura in 288 BC. This tree still lives today, making it the oldest living human-planted tree in the world with a known planting date. It is referenced in the annotations to *The Brazen Palace* [76]. The Bo Tree depicted here, as with all sacred Bo Trees in Ceylon, was said to have been grown from a part of the ancient tree from Anuradhapura. Within the enclosure that surrounds the tree, Gordon-Cumming notes that 'the priests or their attendants have kept tame cobras', remarking that 'these gentle pets are fed at regular hours, and it is suspected that the protection afforded them is not unmingled with some feeling of reverence' (op cit, page 413).

HERBERT MENZIES MARSHALL

Herbert Menzies Marshall, VPRWS RE ARIBA ROI (1841-1913)

'His special aim [is] to show how beautiful and mysterious is the common life of the streets and on the river when seen under the atmospheric effects which are found only in London.'

(Victor G Plarr, *Men and Women of the Time. A Dictionary of Contemporaries*, London: George Routledge, 1895, page 570)

Originally training as an architect, Herbert Menzies Marshall became one of the most atmospheric of the Edwardian painters of urban topography. While travelling widely on the Continent, he retained a special affinity for England and especially London.

For a biography of Herbert Menzies Marshall, please refer to *Chris Beetles Summer Show*, 2014, page 34.

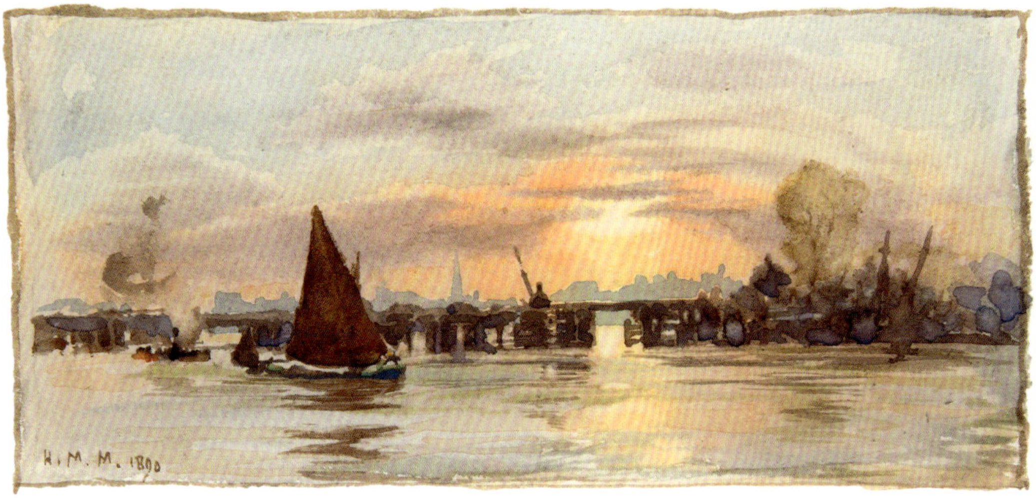

80 **Sunset on the Thames**
Signed with initials and dated 1890
Signed below mount
Watercolour
3 ¼ x 7 ½ inches
Provenance: Ernest Brown of the Leicester Galleries, and by descent

The Embankment with Old Scotland Yard and the Clock Tower of the Palace of Westminster Beyond (opposite)
Living close to the Palace of Westminster, at 1 Victoria Mansions, Victoria Street, for about a decade of the late nineteenth century, Herbert Menzies Marshall produced many iconic images of the building and its surroundings, of which the present oil on canvas is particularly outstanding.

This work is probably based on the drawing, *The Embankment, Westminster* (which illustrated Marshall's article, 'London as a Sketching Ground' in *The Studio* in 1894), and the watercolour, *On the Embankment* (once in the stock of the Chris Beetles Gallery). All three show the Embankment on a winter afternoon, and specifically during one of the severe winters of the early 1890s, at the end of what has become known as the 'Little Ice Age'. However, the oil omits the hansom cabs and affluent pedestrians included in the studies in order to convey a beautifully spare, and even melancholic atmosphere, in which there is a palpable chill in the air and a sparkle of reflected light in the snowmelt of the cart tracks. The result is a fascinatingly complex image which represents the centre of Imperial government at the highpoint of its history but also at the quietest time of the year.

The work's symbolic weight adds interest to its provenance. In October 1914, Matthew Murray (1857-1920) received the painting from the North East Coast Shiprepairers' Association 'in grateful recognition for his valuable services as Treasurer'. Born in Wallsend, on Tyneside, Murray spent most of his career as Secretary of the Wallsend Slipway and Engineering Company, a highly successful company of marine engineers and ship repairers, which, among other undertakings, provided parts to the Royal Navy for its warships. An important figure in the local community, he was active as a mason and served as Mayor of Wallsend (1905-7) and a Justice of the Peace. In 1919, he was presented with the Freedom of the Borough of Wallsend.

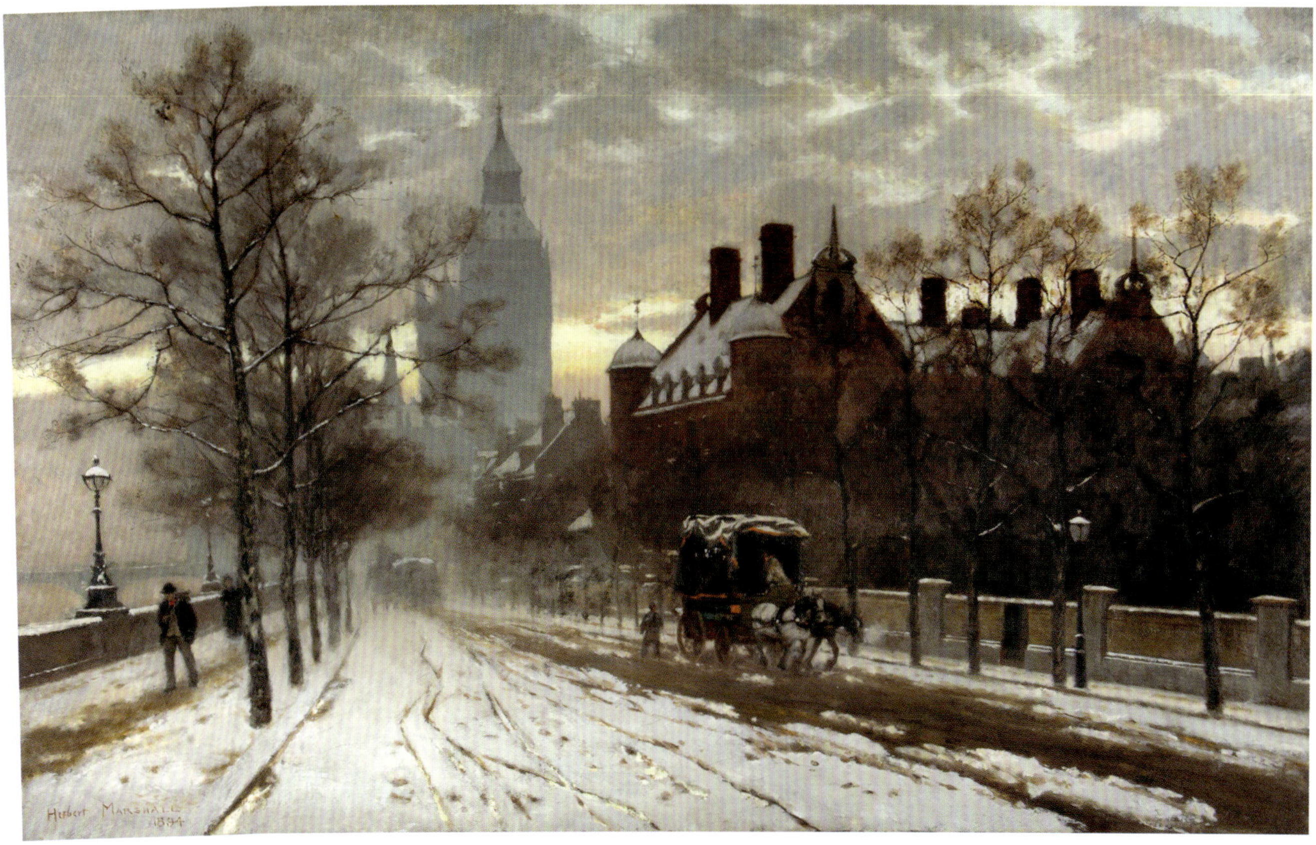

81 The Embankment with Old Scotland Yard and the Clock Tower of the Palace of Westminster Beyond

Signed and dated 1894

Oil on canvas

30 x 45 ½ inches

Provenance: Presented to Matthew Murray Esq JP by the North East Coast Shiprepairers' Association in grateful recognition of his valuable services as Treasurer, October 1914; and by descent

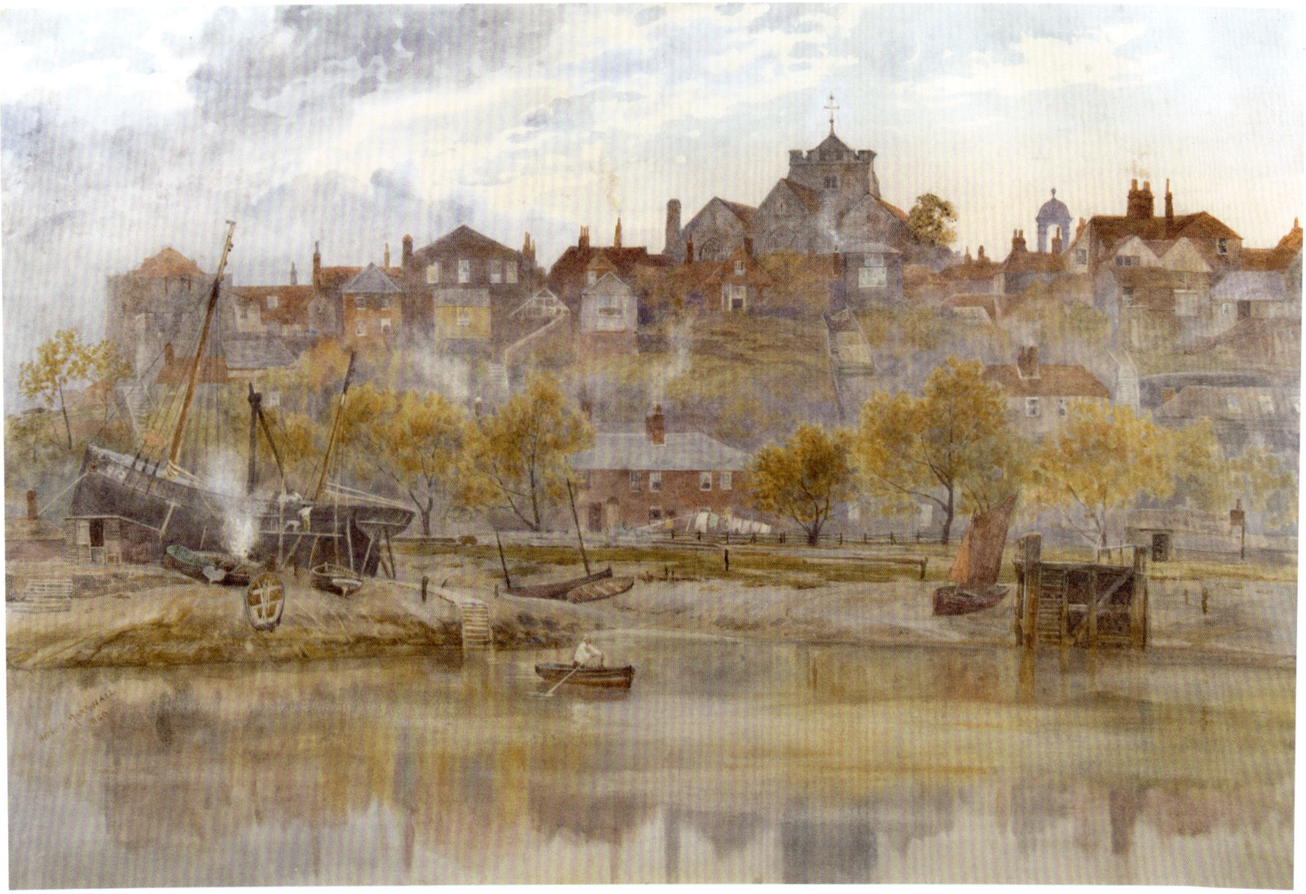

82 **Rye from the Harbour**
Signed and dated 1860
Watercolour
21 ½ x 30 ¾ inches

ALBERT GOODWIN

Albert Frederick Goodwin, RWS (1845-1932)

In synthesising the influences of J M W Turner and the Pre-Raphaelites, Albert Goodwin may be considered one of the most Ruskinian of Victorian landscape painters. Indeed, he was taken up by John Ruskin and, in 1872, given the opportunity to travel with him on an intensive tour of Italy and Switzerland. This set the pattern for many further and extensive travels. Like Ruskin, Goodwin responded to landscape with a religious fervour and understanding; but he interpreted it with even greater eclecticism than did his mentor, even experimenting with the style of James McNeill Whistler, Ruskin's adversary in the field of aesthetics.

For a biography of Albert Goodwin, please refer to *Chris Beetles Summer Show*, 2014, page 26.

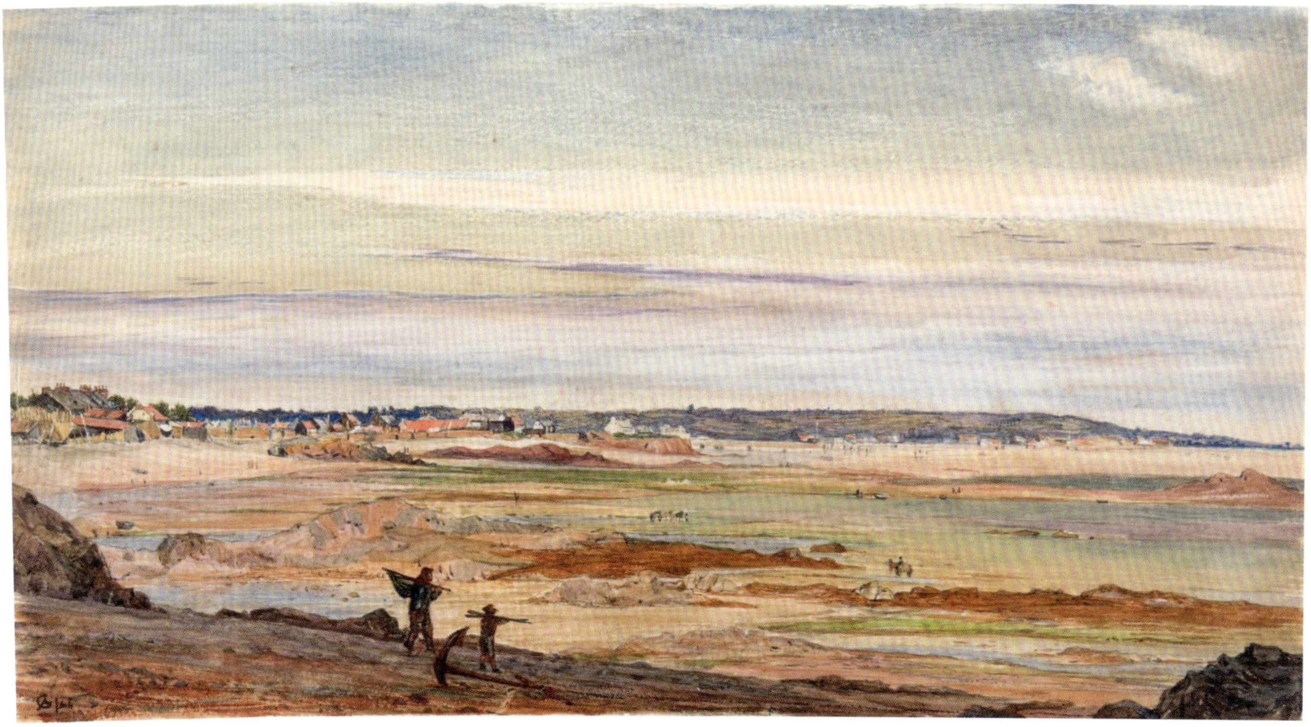

'Excellent sea-bathing may be had in St Clement's Bay, the sand of which is hard and fine. There are numerous bathing machines, and an extensive establishment for hot sea-water baths.'

(*A Guide to the Healthiest and Most Beautiful Watering Places in the British Islands*, Edinburgh: Adam and Charles Black, 1864, page 37)

83 **St Clement's Bay, Jersey**
Signed with monogram and dated /64
Watercolour with bodycolour and pencil
7 ¾ x 13 ¾ inches
Provenance: H Virtue Jebbs;
His sale, London, Christie's, 3 October 1900, Lot 10, bought Davis (5gns);
Christie's, 26 February 1985, Lot 136;
Sotheby's, 12 June 1997, Lot 107;
Private collection, Channel Islands

St Clement's Bay, Jersey

In 1864, Albert Goodwin made his first visits overseas, going to Holland and, in the summer, Jersey. While on Jersey, he produced a number of scintillating watercolours that display the influence of artists of the Pre-Raphaelite circle into which he had entered, including Arthur Hughes, William Holman Hunt, Ford Madox Brown and George Price Boyce. Exhibits at the Society of Painters in Water Colours in 1873 and 1874 suggest that he may have made a second visit to the island about a decade after the first.

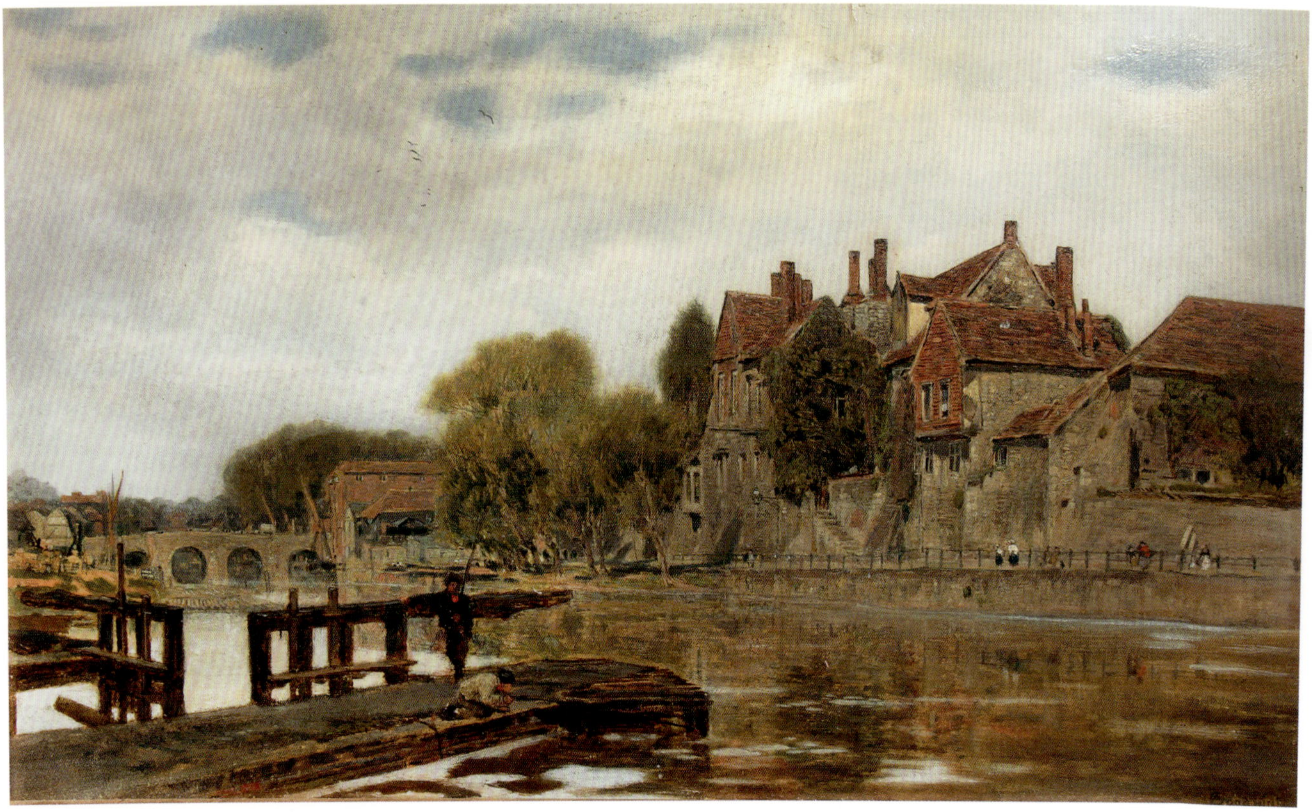

Albert Goodwin in Maidstone in 1871

Albert Goodwin remained attached to his birthplace of Maidstone in Kent, and often returned there both to visit his family and to paint. He was inevitably drawn to the impressive panorama that is laid out along the north bank of the River Medway and centres on the historic Archbishop's Palace (dating to the fourteenth and sixteenth centuries) and All Saints Church (built in the late fourteenth century as part of the College of All Saints newly founded by Archbishop Courtenay). In 1871, he painted these two oils with slightly different emphases from the same viewpoint. The smaller one focuses on the palace, while the larger also takes in the impressive church. In 1885, Goodwin's brother, Harry, would paint a more distant view, which shows that the land south of the river remained as fields.

84 **The Archbishop's Palace in Maidstone**
Signed and dated 71
Oil on board
11 ½ x 17 ½ inches

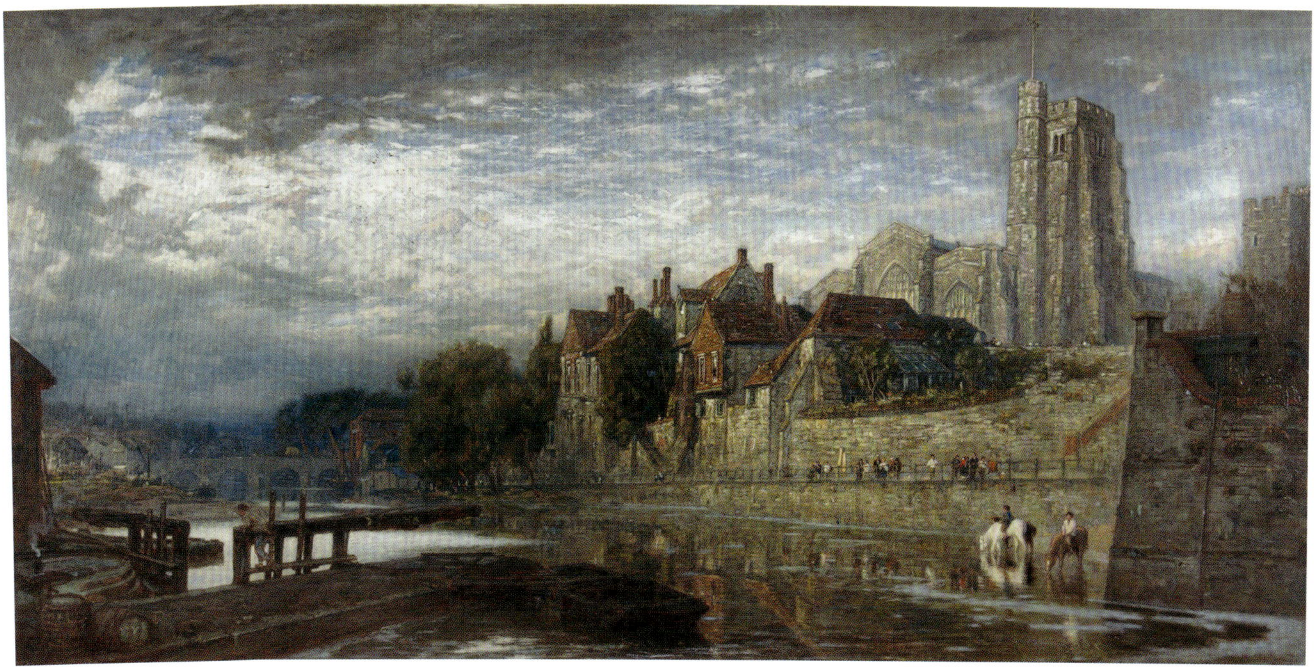

Detail of 85

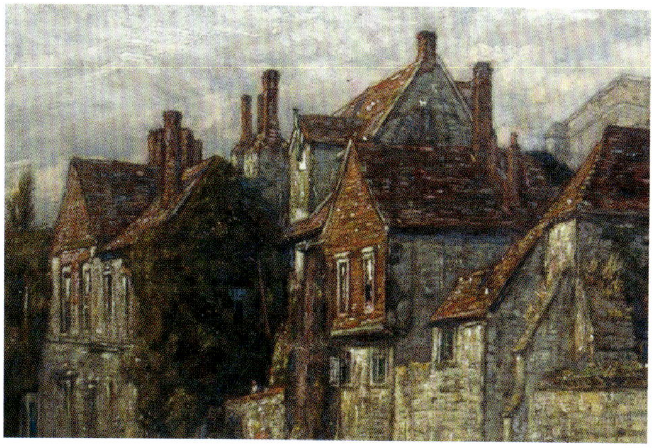

85 The Medway at Maidstone
Signed and dated /71
Oil on canvas
26 ½ x 52 inches
Exhibited: Royal Academy, Summer Exhibition, 1871, No 398;
'In Search of Sun and Shadow. The Art of Albert Goodwin (1845-1932)', Chris Beetles Gallery, October-November 2019, No 4

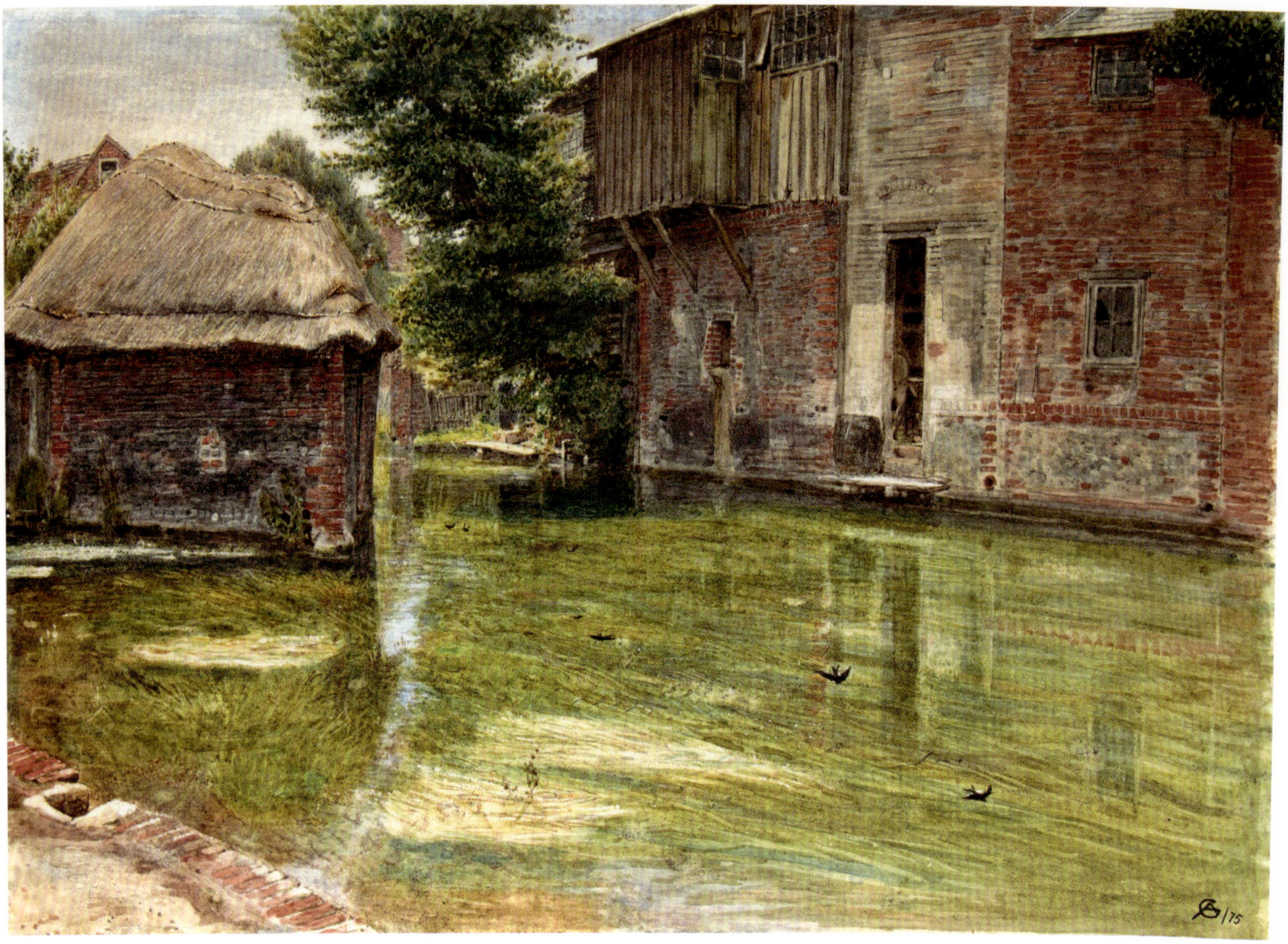

86 Old Mill Near Winchester
Signed with monogram and dated /75
Watercolour and bodycolour
9 x 12 ½ inches
Literature: *Albert Goodwin RWS, 1845-1932*, London: Chris Beetles, 1986, Limited Edition of 1000, Plate 17;
Christopher Newall, *Victorian Watercolours*, Oxford: Phaidon 1987, Plate 34
Exhibited: 'Albert Goodwin RWS 1845-1932. 129 of His Best Works Borrowed From Private Collections', a Museum Tour of the Royal Watercolour Society, Sheffield Mappin Art Gallery, Ruskin Gallery, Stoke on Trent City Museum and Art Gallery, May-October 1986, No 19;
'The Great Age of British Watercolours 1750-1850', Royal Academy, London, January-April 1993, No 157;
'A Watercolourist's Dream. Albert Goodwin (1845-1932) & John Lewis Roget (1828-1908)', The County Gallery, Maidstone, February-March 1999;
'In Search of Sun and Shadow. The Art of Albert Goodwin (1845-1932)', Chris Beetles Gallery, October-November 2019, No 6

Old Mill Near Winchester

Albert Goodwin made a number of visits to the cathedral city of Winchester, from at least as early as 1864, when he was only 19 years old. He seems to have been attracted by both its evocative medieval architecture and its distinctive setting in the valley of the Itchen, a fine example of a chalk stream. Here, in a watercolour of 1875, he focussed on the characteristic breadth, shallowness and crystal clarity of a particular stretch, which powers one of Hampshire's many mills.

Members of the Hampshire Mill Group have made the convincing suggestion that the mill in Goodwin's watercolour is Winchester City Mill as viewed from the north. If it is correct, then the mill itself can only be glimpsed towards the top left of the image, and is mostly obscured by a thatched roof. The thatched roof belonged to a pig sty, which stood on the island that divides the mill race from the main course of the Itchen.

With thanks to the members of the Hampshire Mill Group for their help in the compilation of this note.

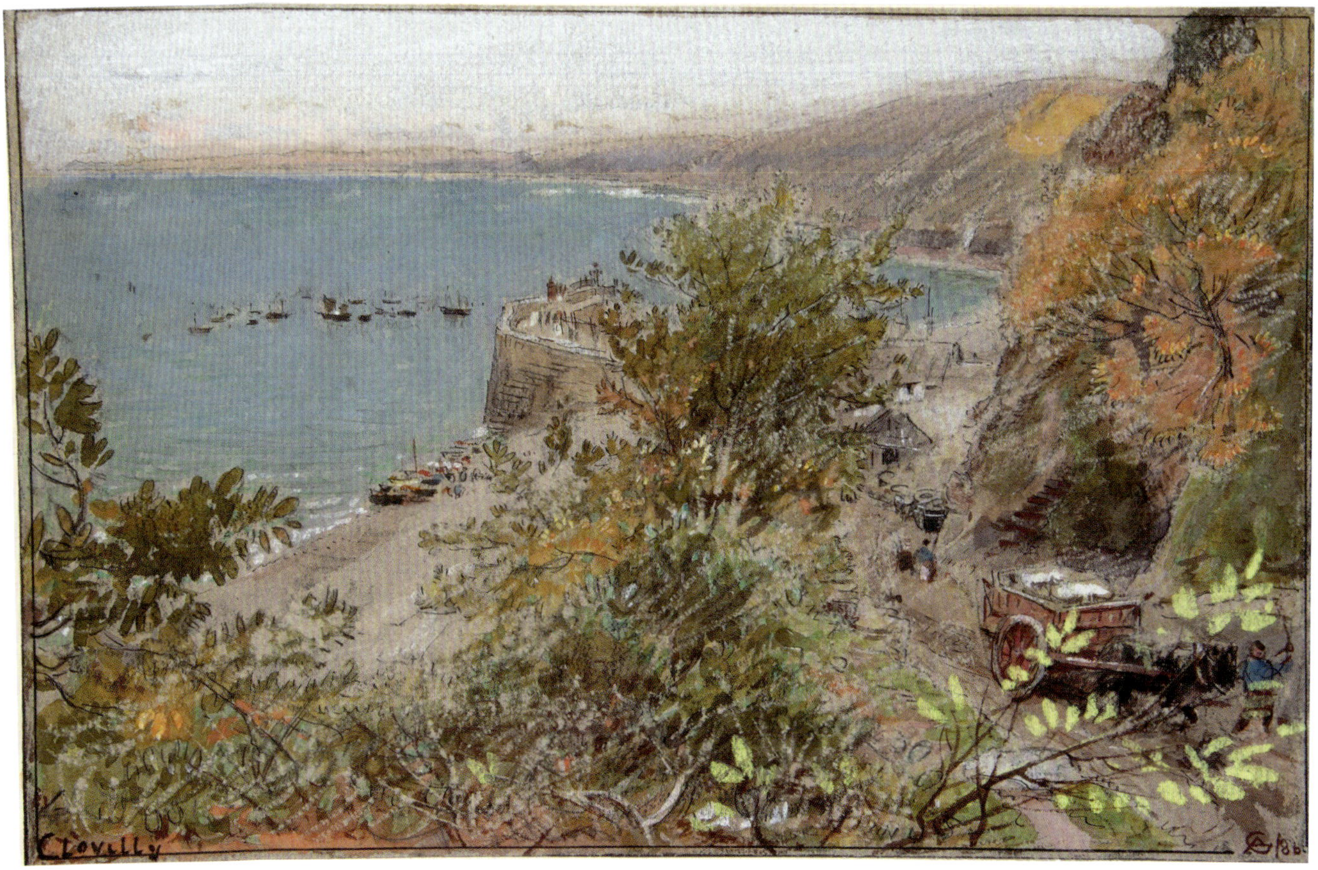

87 Clovelly
Signed with monogram, inscribed with title and dated /86
Watercolour with pen ink, bodycolour and pencil on tinted paper
6 ¼ x 9 inches
Literature: Hammond Smith, 'The Poetical Landscapes of Albert Goodwin RWS (1845-1932)',
Antique Collecting, October 1981, Page 30

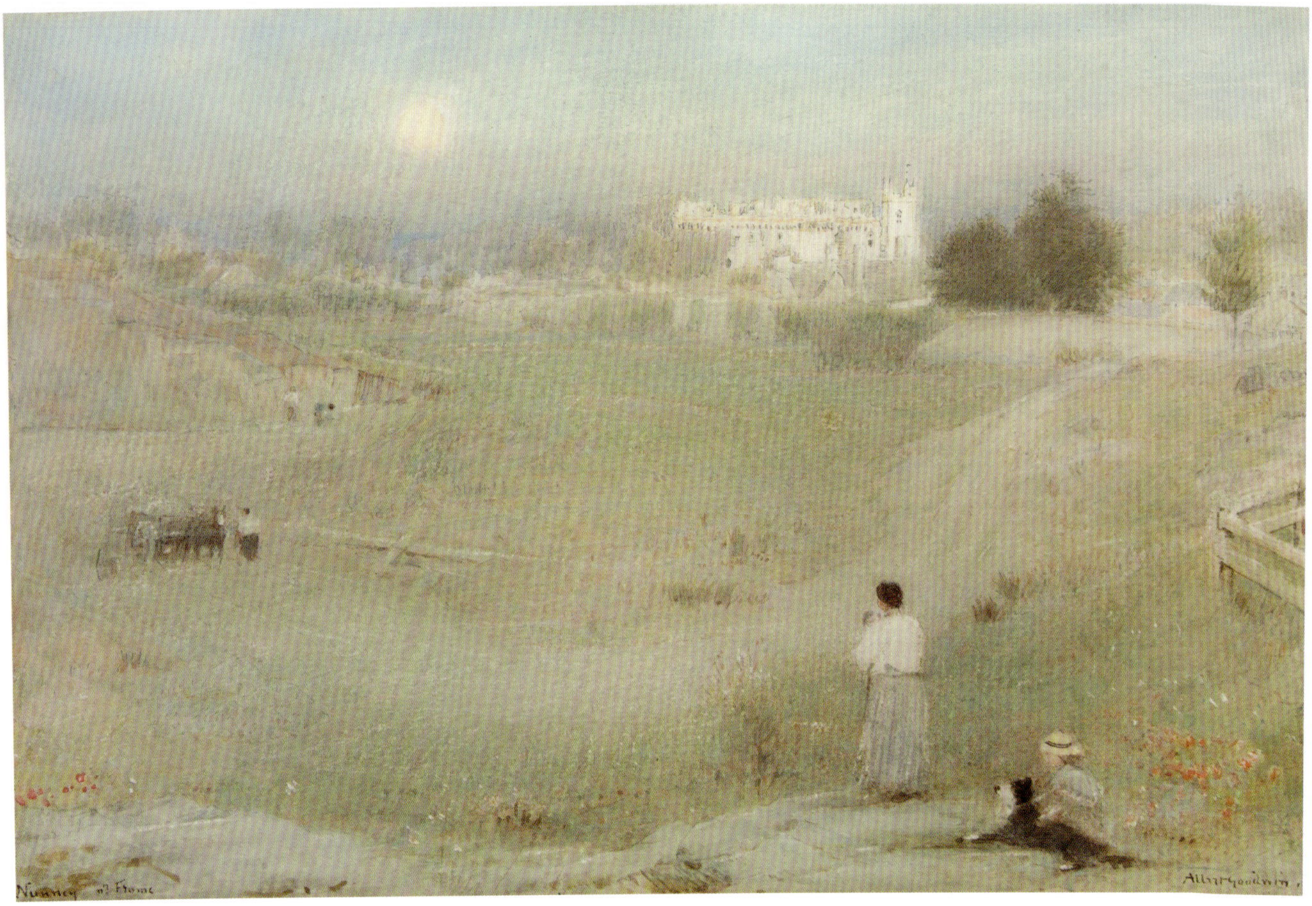

88 **Nunney, near Frome, Somerset**
Signed and inscribed with title
Watercolour with bodycolour and pencil
9 x 14 ¾ inches

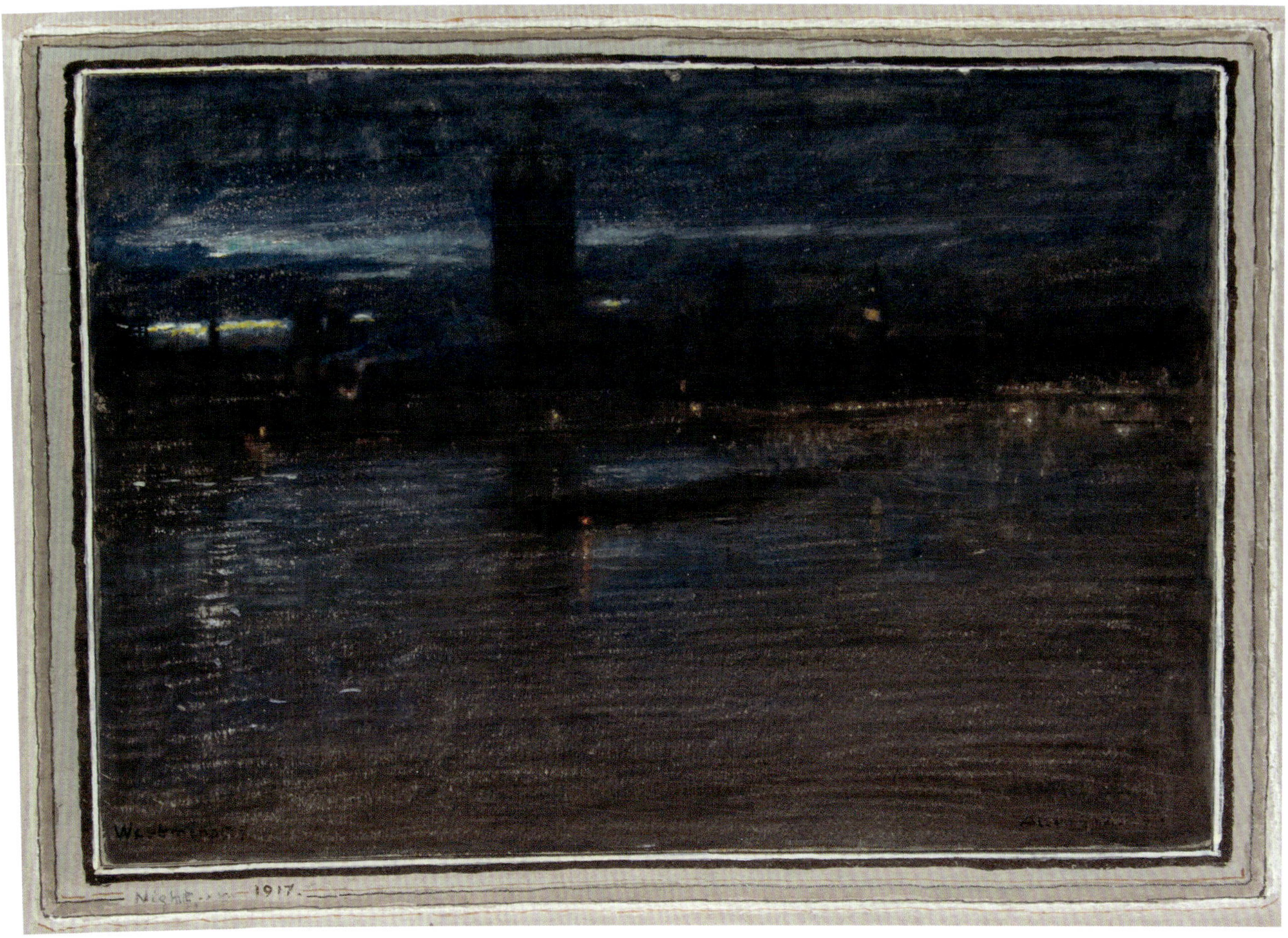

89 **Westminster**
Signed, inscribed with title and dated '17
Inscribed 'Night in 1917' on supporting sheet
Watercolour with bodycolour
10 x 12 ½ inches

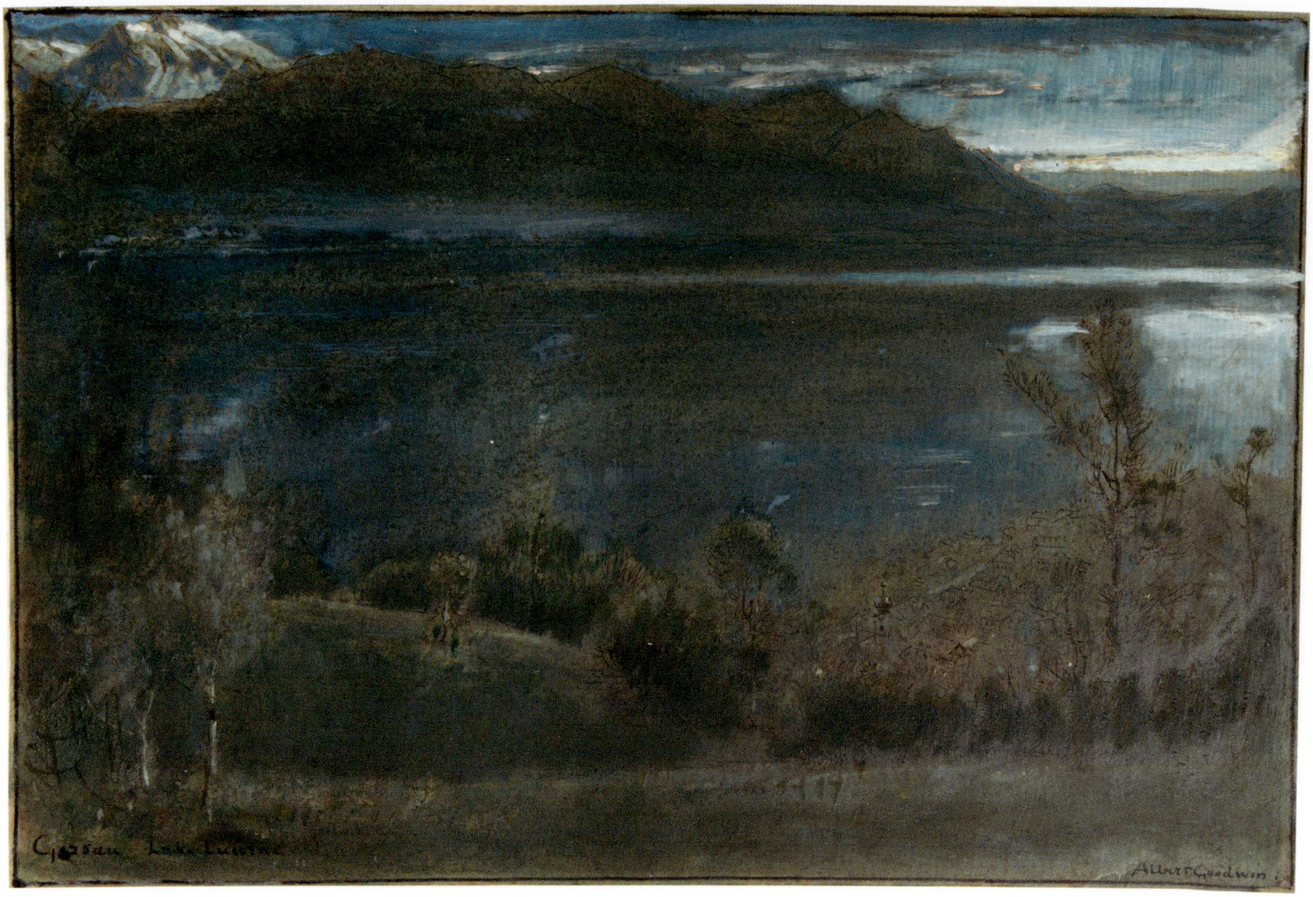

90 Gossau, Lake Lucerne
Signed and inscribed with title
Oil and watercolour with pen ink and bodycolour
on paper on board
10 ½ x 14 ¾ inches

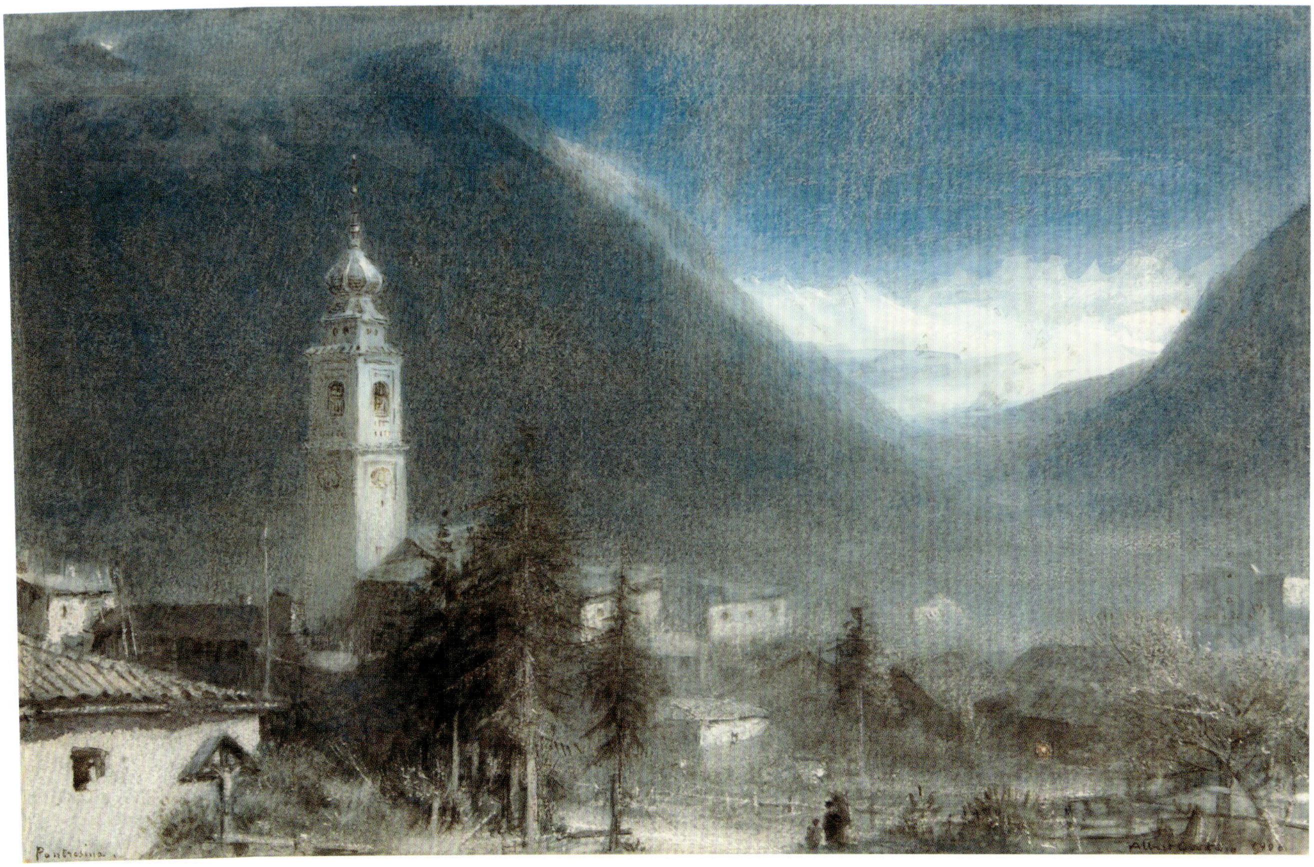

91 Pontresina
Signed, inscribed with title and dated 1906
Signed and inscribed with artist's address on separate wooden panel
Watercolour with pen ink and bodycolour on paper on board
10 x 14 ¾ inches
Probably the work exhibited at the Royal Society of Painters in Water-Colours, Summer 1907, No 121, as 'Pontresina – Summer Moonlight'

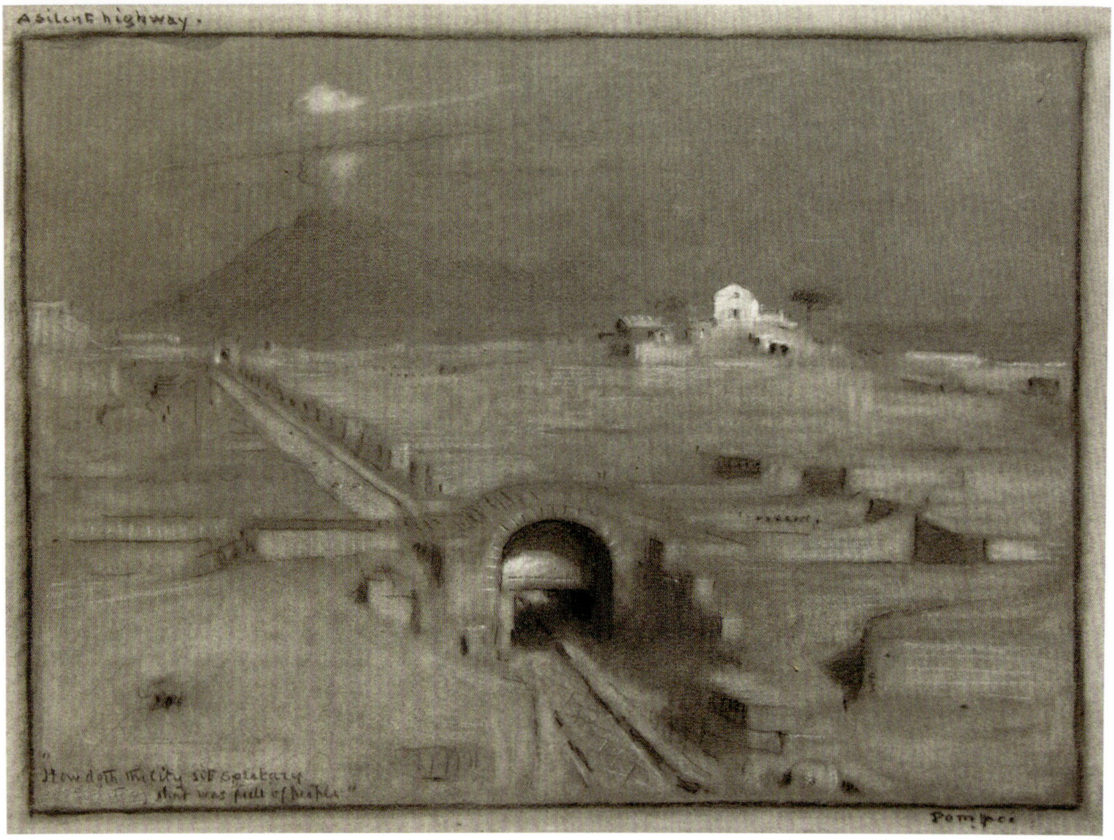

92 A Silent Highway, Pompei
'How doth the city sit solitary that was full of people'
Inscribed with title
Chalk on tinted paper
10 ¼ x 12 ½ inches

This is the preliminary drawing for the 1904 watercolour of the same title, which was exhibited at the Royal Society of Painters in Water-Colours, Summer 1904, No 111, as 'Moonlight Silence, Pompeii'

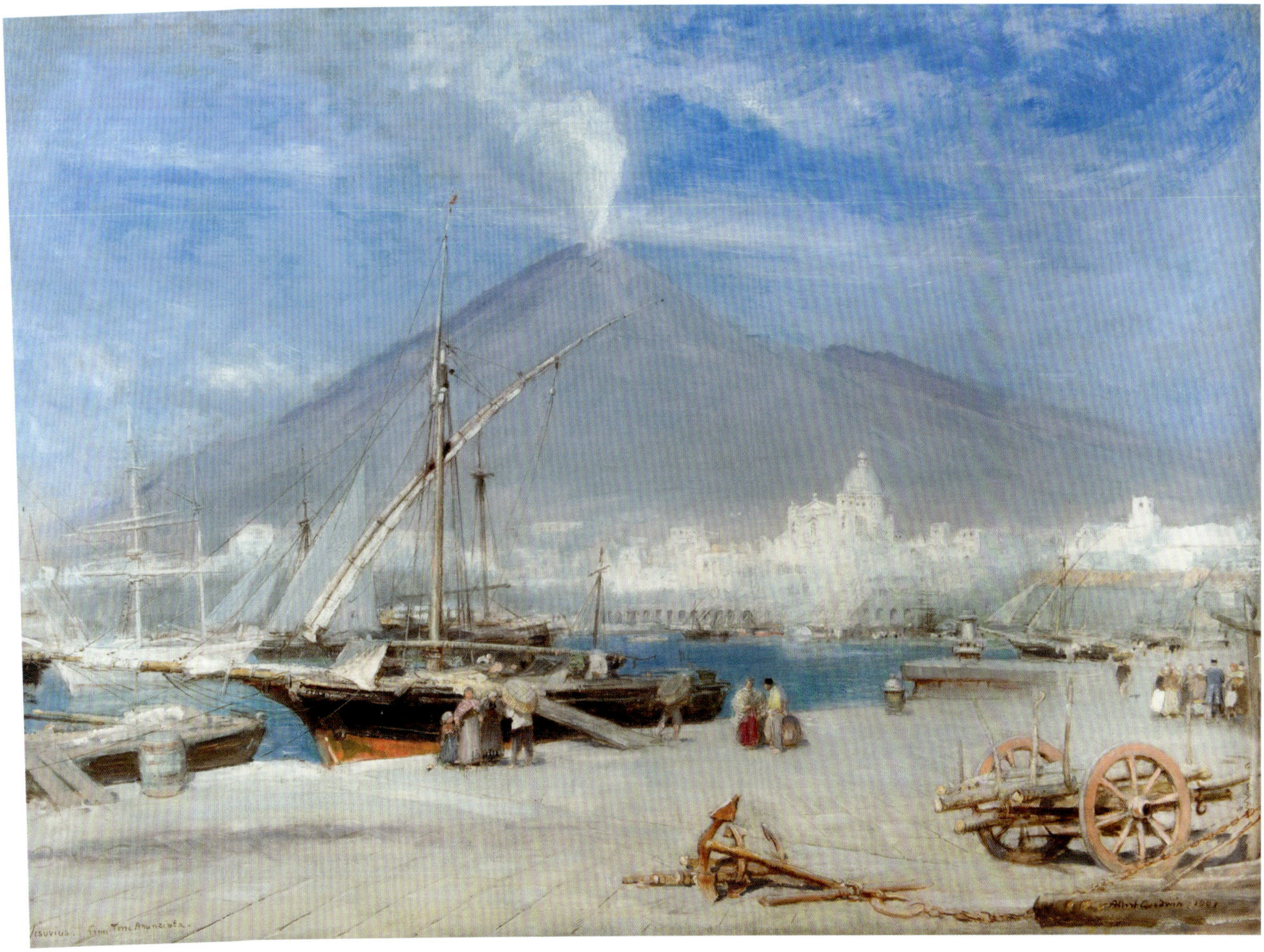

93 Vesuvius from Torre Annunziata
Signed, inscribed with title and dated 1901
Oil on canvas
32 ½ x 44 ½ inches

A watercolour version of this composition was exhibited in 'An Exhibition of Pictures and Watercolours entitled "In Praise of All The Churches" by Albert Goodwin, RWS', Fine Art Society, London, November 1900, No 9, as 'Torre Anunziata, Near Naples'

Vesuvius from Torre Annunziata

From the late eighteenth century, British artists visited Torre Annunziata in order to take in the view of Mount Vesuvius. The town had been built on the remains of Oplontis, one of the settlements destroyed in the eruption of Vesuvius in AD 79. It took its name from a chapel dedicated to the Virgin of the Annunciation, which was founded by Guglielmo di Nocera in 1319. By the time of Albert Goodwin's visit in 1900, it had become an industrial centre specialising in the production of firearms and pasta, especially macaroni, and the processing of other foods. However, he focussed on its picturesque harbour front dominated by the dome of the Chiesa dello Santo Spirito and the looming presence of Vesuvius, and so created something of a symphony in blue, grey and white. He first produced a watercolour of the composition, exhibited at the Fine Art Society in 1900, which provided the basis for the present oil.

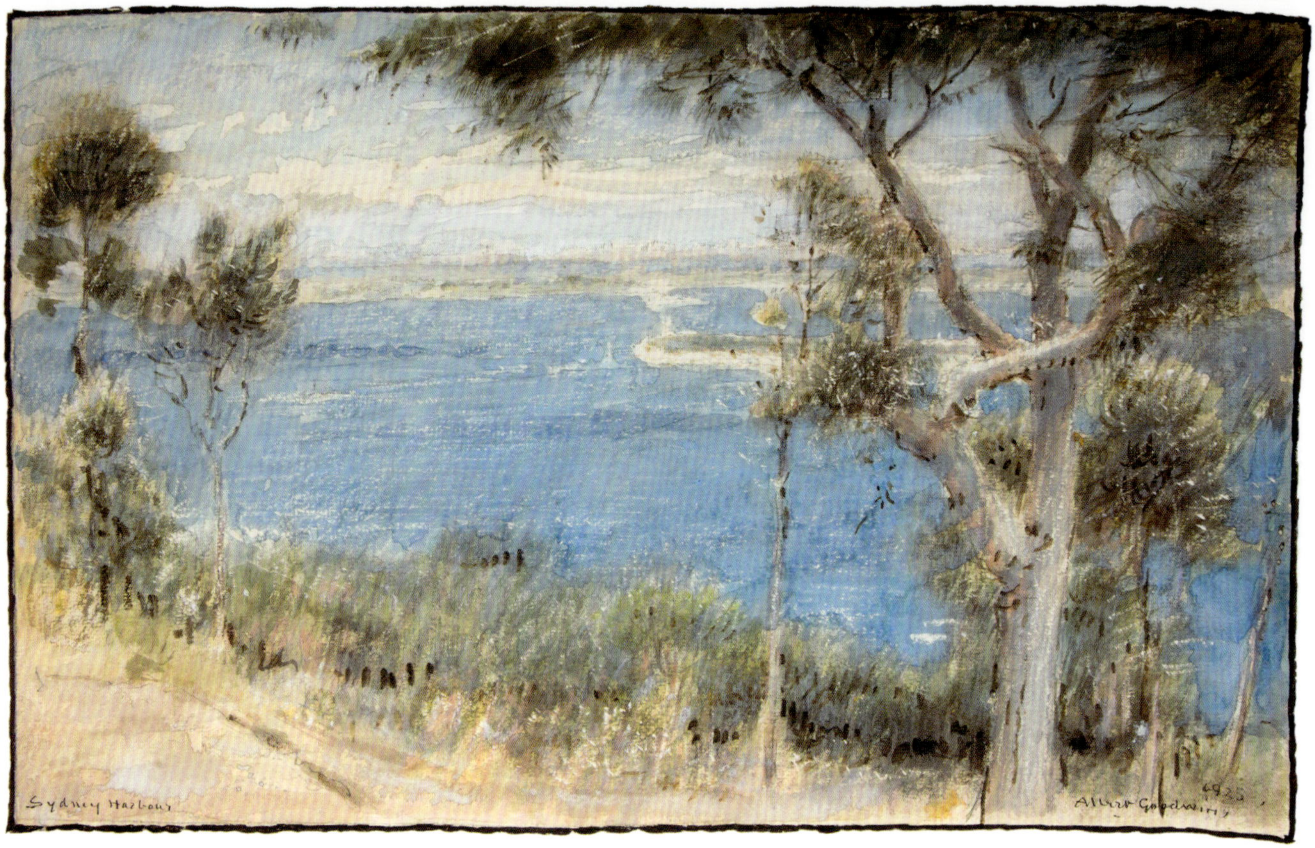

94 Sydney Harbour
Signed, inscribed with title and dated 1925
Watercolour with pencil
10 x 14 ¾ inches

Albert Goodwin's Voyage to Australia in 1916-17

In November 1916, Albert Goodwin sailed – via South Africa and probably Ceylon [95] – to Australia and New Zealand. His son, Arthur Albert Desborough Goodwin, was working as a surveyor in the second of those two countries.

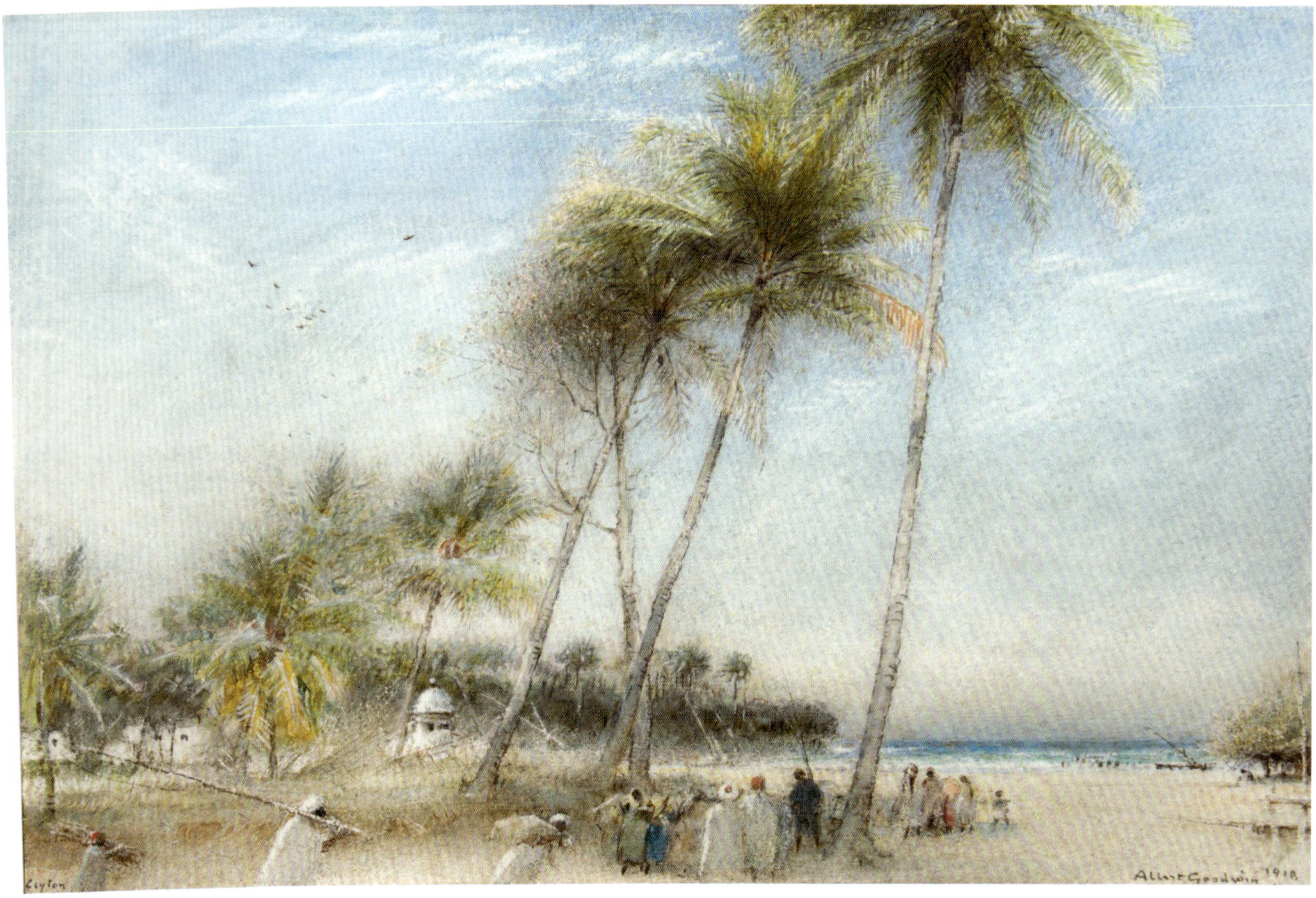

93

95 Ceylon
Signed, inscribed with title and dated 1918
Watercolour
10 x 13 ½ inches

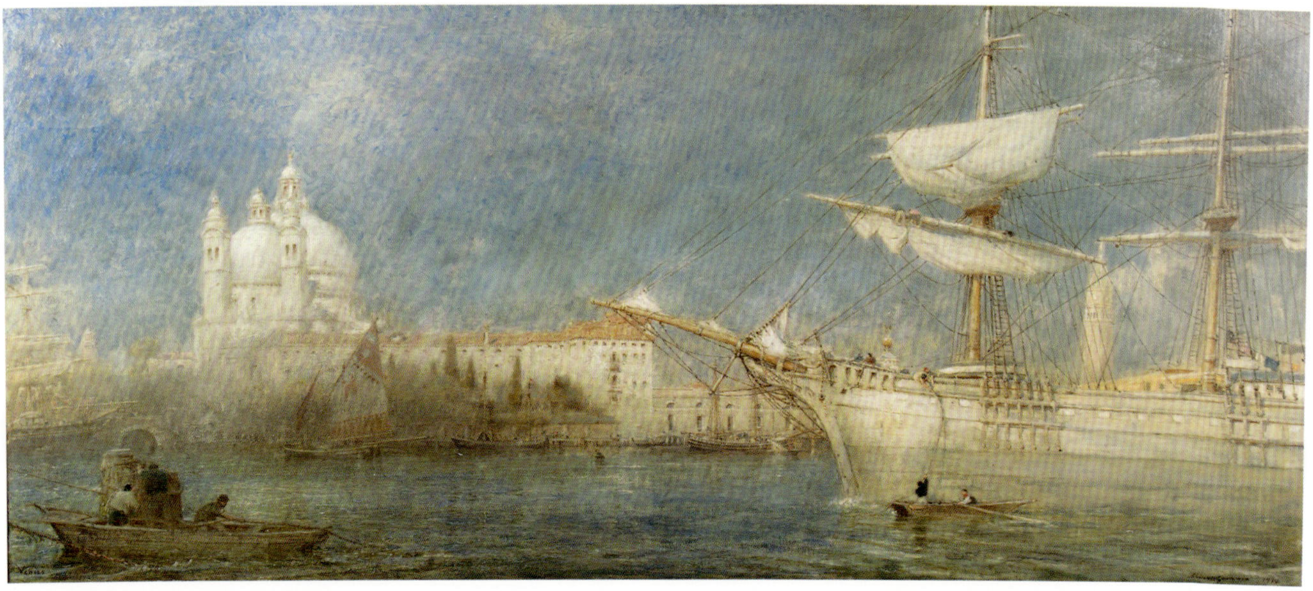

96 The Hardy Norseman at Venice
Signed, inscribed 'Venice' and dated 'Oct 1902' and 1919
Oil on canvas
30 x 60 inches
Exhibited: Royal Academy, Summer Exhibition, 1920, No 600; 'Albert Goodwin, RWS (1845-1932)', Chris Beetles Gallery, May-June 1996, No 165

The Hardy Norseman at Venice
Albert Goodwin's impressive, highly atmospheric panorama of Venice centres on the eastern end of the Canale della Giudecca and takes in the back of Santa Maria della Salute, the Dogana and the Campanile di San Marco, the last through the rigging of the Norseman.

Goodwin probably described this beautiful clipper as 'The Hardy Norseman' because the phrase was in common use among Victorians as descriptive of intrepid explorers, and had been popularised by Robert Lucas de Pearsall (1795-1856) in his English version and harmonisation of a Norwegian national song, 'The Hardy Norseman's House of Yore'. Though many nineteenth-century ships were given the name Norseman, the one depicted is likely to have been the clipper built in 1856 by Robert E Jackson of East Boston, Massachusetts, for the well-known Boston merchants, Cunningham Bros & Co, and was destined for the China trade. However, as it was sold in Siam in 1863, and its subsequent history unknown, its presence in Venice in the early 1890s – when Goodwin painted his watercolour, *The Hardy Norseman* – is conjectural. The watercolour probably provided the basis of the present oil, which was painted between 1902 and 1919, and exhibited at the Royal Academy of Arts in 1920, the last work that the artist showed there.

It is possible that Goodwin was seduced as much by the sight of one of the last large clippers as by the romance of the name Norseman, and considered the ship to be a symbol of a passing age. In that way, it is comparable to J M W Turner's *The Fighting Temeraire, tugged to her last berth to be broken up, 1838* (1839, National Gallery). Strongly influenced by the work of Turner, Goodwin even made his own watercolour copy of *The Fighting Temeraire*.

HERCULES BRABAZON BRABAZON

Hercules Brabazon Brabazon, NEAC PS (1821-1906)

For much of his life, Hercules Brabazon Brabazon pleased himself as a gentleman traveller, producing luminous, loosely-handled watercolours of favourite paintings and places (including India, which he visited in 1870, 1875 and 1876). Admired by John Ruskin as an heir to J M W Turner, he joined the eminent critic on a sketching tour to northern France in 1880. Yet his startling modernity was probably recognised only in the 1890s, by a younger generation of artists, which included John Singer Sargent, Walter Sickert and Philip Wilson Steer. Through their enthusiasm, he was elected a member of the New English Art Club in 1891, and held the first of a series of solo shows at the Goupil Gallery in the following year.

For a biography of Hercules Brabazon Brabazon, please refer to *Chris Beetles Summer Show*, 2016, page 36.

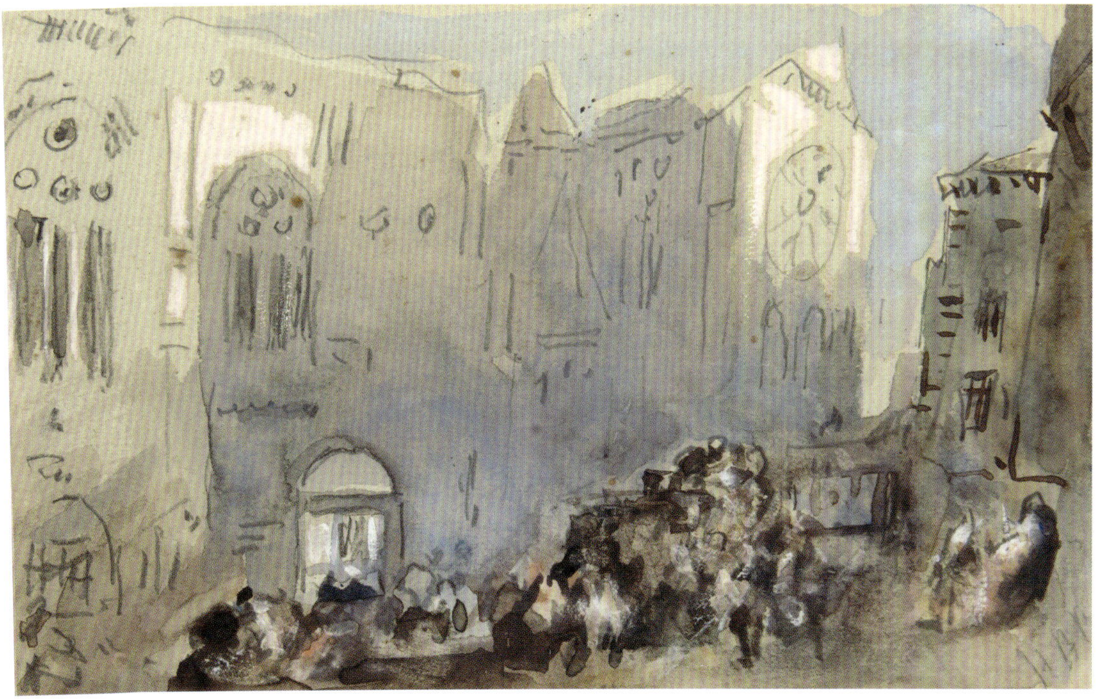

97 **St Julien, Tours**
A Souvenir of J M W Turner
Signed with initials
Watercolour and pencil
4 ½ x 6 ½ inches

Provenance: Sold by Mrs Brabazon Combe, of Oaklands, Sedlescombe, to Martin Hardie in Tunbridge Wells in 1943; Thomas Agnew & Sons
Exhibited: Thomas Agnew & Sons, No 134

St Julien, Tours. A Souvenir of J M W Turner
In 1826, J M W Turner made an extensive tour of north-west France, which culminated in a journey up the River Loire that included a stop at Tours. He found that its mediaeval church of Saint-Julien was being used as a coach house and stable, and had been since the Revolution. Of the drawings that he made of it, one was worked up in watercolour as *St Julian's, Tours*, and engraved by William Radclyffe for the 1833 publication, *Wanderings by the Loire* (the first volume of what became known as 'The Rivers of France'). John Ruskin, the great apologist of Turner, described the engraving as 'especially remarkable for its preservation of deep points of gloom, because the whole picture is of one extended shade (*Modern Painters*, vol I, 1843, part II, section II, chapter III, 'Of Truth of Chiaroscuro'). He owned the original drawing and, in 1861, gave it and others in the series, 'The Rivers of France', to the Ashmolean Museum, Oxford. Hercules Brabazon Brabazon, who was a friend of Ruskin and something of a student of the work of Turner, would have known both the original drawing and the engraving, but the tonal difference between the two suggests that he is more likely to have copied the former than the latter in order to create the present souvenir.

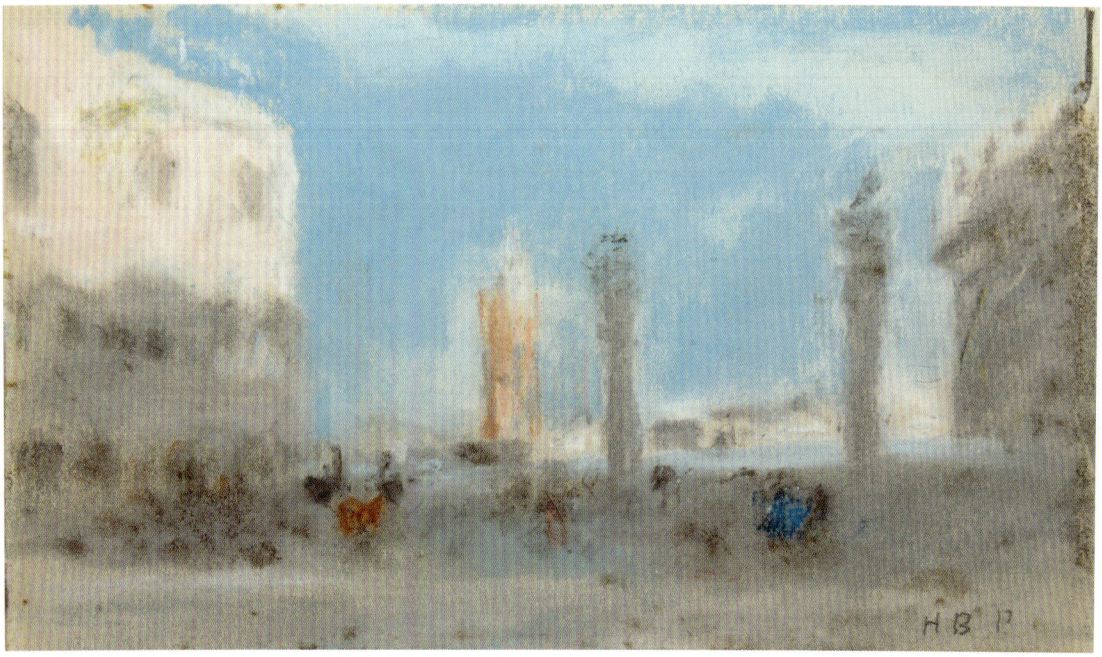

98 Piazzetta San Marco, Venice (above)
Signed with initials
Pastel; 6 x 9 inches
Provenance: Chas A Jackson, Fine Art Dealer, Manchester;
Neville Rawlinson, translator and art collector, Manchester

99 The Lido at Venice (below)
Watercolour and bodycolour with pencil
6 x 9 inches

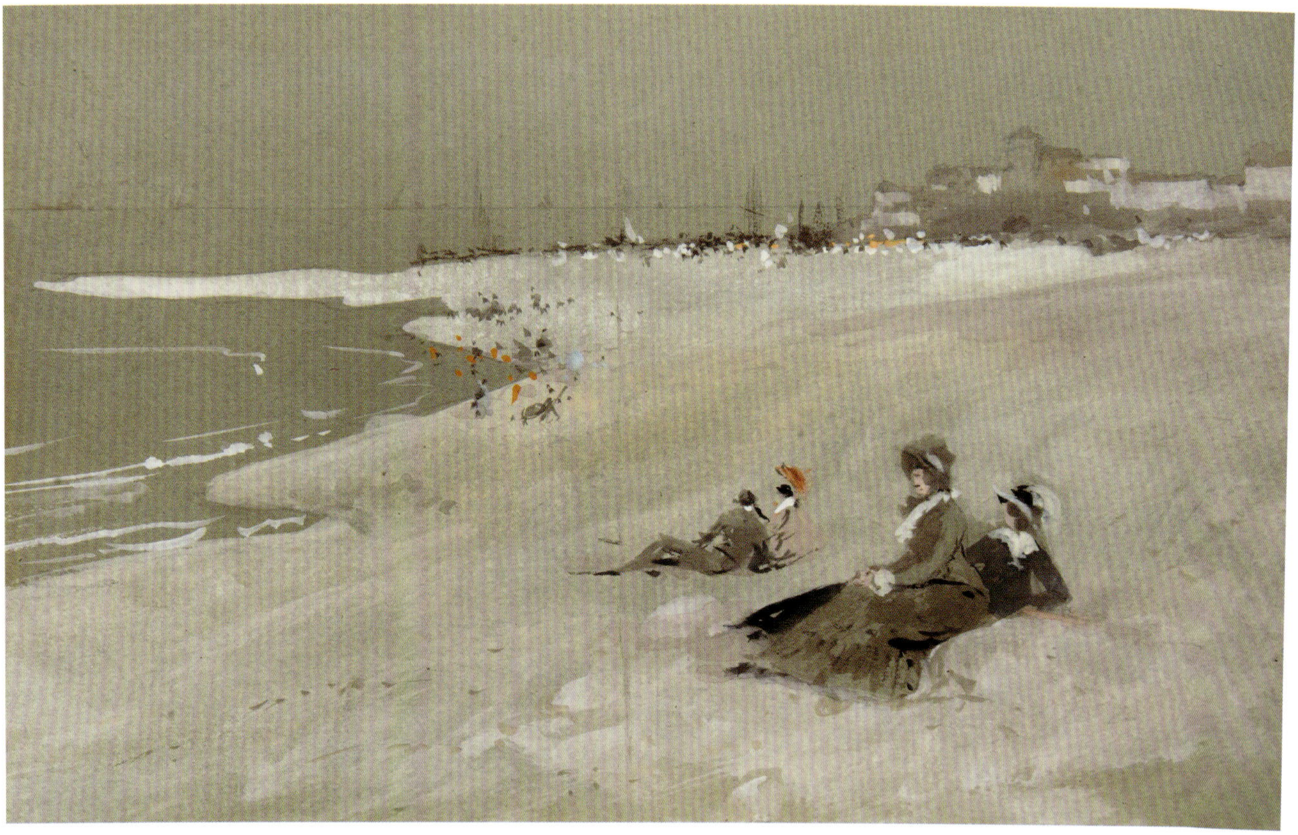

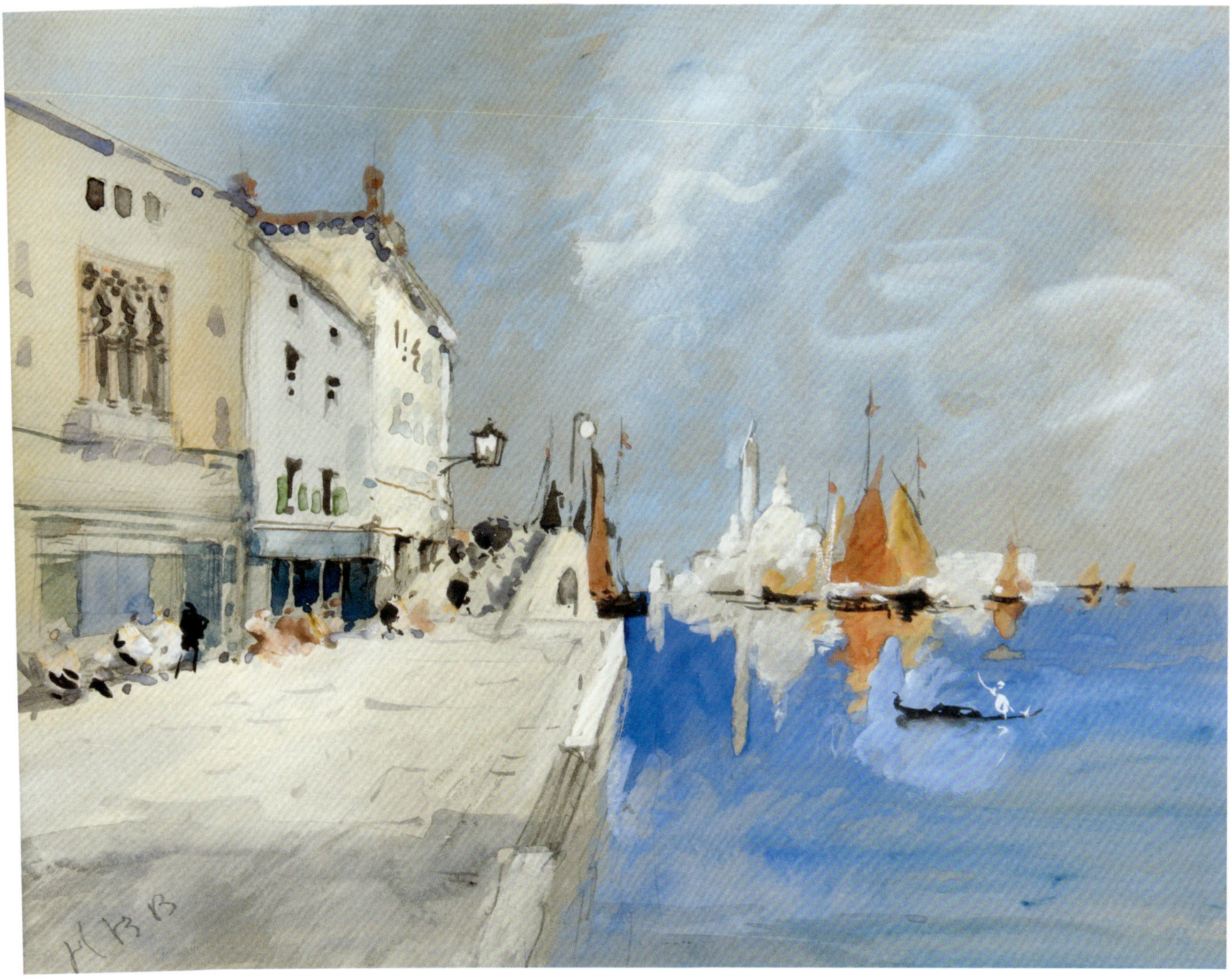

100 Zattere, Venice
Signed with initials
Watercolour with bodycolour
and pencil on tinted paper
9 x 10 ¾ inches

PHILIP WILSON STEER

Philip Wilson Steer, OM NEAC (1860-1942)

Wilson Steer was one of the most interesting and significant British painters working at the turn of the twentieth century. His career subsumed early Impressionist experimentation within a developing traditionalism that emulated Constable and Turner.

For a biography of Philip Wilson Steer, please refer to page 122.

A View at Ludlow

By 1900, Philip Wilson Steer was busy rehearsing the native tradition of landscape painting. Following in the footsteps of J M W Turner, he explored Yorkshire and then the Welsh borders – including the valleys of the Severn, Teme and Wye. Turner's sketchbooks reveal that he had worked in Ludlow, on the Teme, in 1798, and Steer first arrived there exactly a century later.

Yet, despite this homage, many of Steer's paintings of Ludlow reveal the influence of another, Continental and more contemporary, artist. The isolated French Romantic painter, Adolphe Monticelli (1824-1886), was very fashionable in London at the turn of the century, and especially for his unusual technique and chromatic palette, which together had anticipated aspects of Impressionism and other later trends. For instance, D S McColl, the leading critic and champion of Steer, praised Monticelli's 'gem-like' encrustations. When Steer set about producing *A View at Ludlow*, he clearly had Monticelli's technique in mind, as he had three works by the artist in his own collection. While he based the composition on his earlier *Cliffs by the Teme, Ludlow*, he rejected its fluid treatment in favour of a rich impasted handling, and achieved it through a combination of brush, brush handle and palette knife.

According to Bruce Laughton, 'There were basically two different views from the bank of the River Teme that interested Steer, one looking into a left-hand bend and the other into a right-hand bend' (*Philip Wilson Steer 1860-1942*, Oxford: Clarendon Press, 1971, page 94). The recurring motif of a small forked tree suggests to Laughton that Steer concentrated on the right-hand view over a period of two years, 1898-1900. *A View at Ludlow* would seem to one of the later interpretations, in which the tree has been obscured, and the topography generally distilled. Given that the catalogue raisonné by Alfred Yockney (included in McColl's monograph of Steer) dates the painting to 1914, the artist may have worked on it across three decades, returning to the canvas to build up layers in a loving, almost obsessional fashion. If the approach to painting that Ludlow offered Steer seemed at first both retrospective and immediate, it instead became experimental and drenched in memory.

101 A View at Ludlow
Oil on canvas
40 x 50 inches
Provenance: Sale of Steer's Effects, Christie Manson & Woods, 16-17 July 1942, No 124;
Lessore; Lord Molson
Literature: D S MacColl, *Life Work and Setting Of Philip Wilson Steer (with a Full Catalogue of Paintings … by Alfred Yockney)*, London: Faber & Faber, 1945, page 216; Bruce Laughton, *Philip Wilson Steer 1860-1942*, Oxford: Clarendon Press, 1971, Catalogue No 234a and Plate 170, as 'a View at Ludlow, with Three Figures in the Foreground'
Exhibited: 'An Exhibition of Recent and Earlier Works by P Wilson Steer', the Goupil Gallery, March-April, 1924, No 68; and/or 'Modern British Art', the Goupil Gallery, Summer 1924, No 24 as 'the Teme at Ludlow, Sunset' (priced £350)

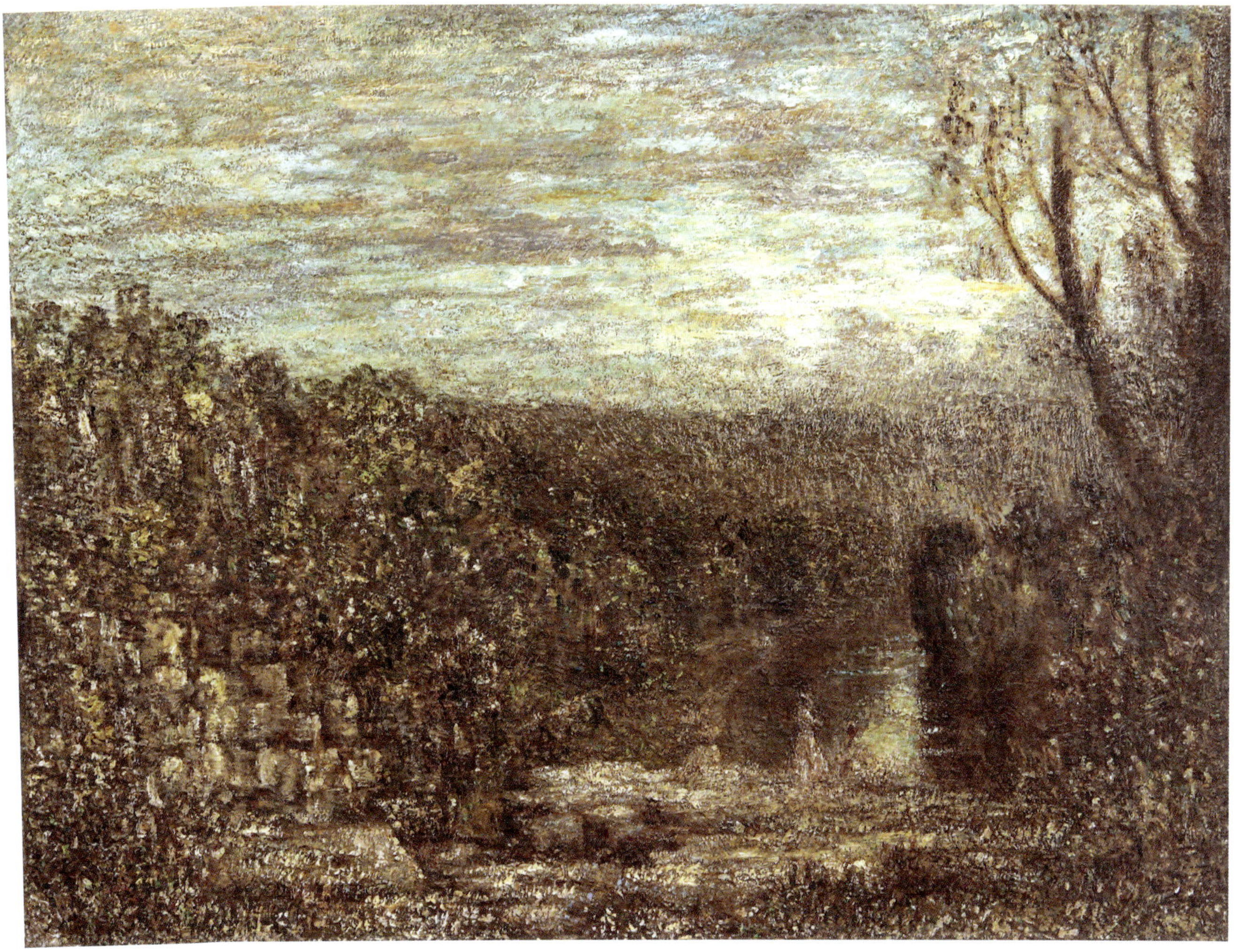

99

HAROLD KNIGHT

Harold Knight, RA ROI RP RWA
PNSA NPS (1874-1961)

Harold Knight was a quiet and gentle man, and his wife, the painter, Laura Knight, feared that she had 'stood in his way', as a result of the strength of her personality and achievement. Nevertheless, he has received acclaim as a painter, both in his lifetime and since, and especially for his sensitive portraits and interior scenes with figures, which emulate those by his favourite artist, Vermeer.

For a biography of Harold Knight, please refer to page 123.

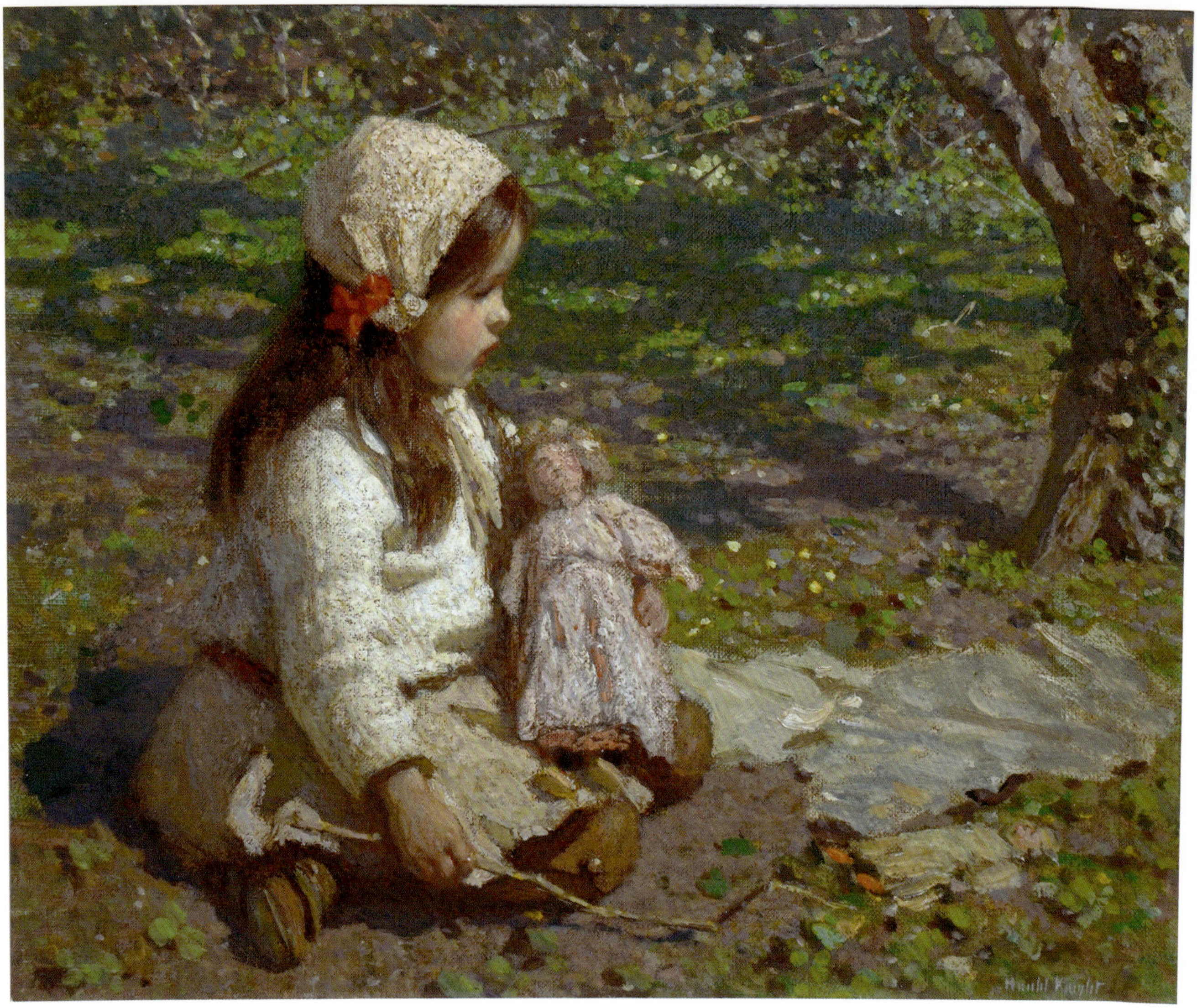

102 **Mornie and Her Doll**
Signed
Oil on canvas
11 ¾ x 13 ¾ inches
Provenance: Samuel John Lamorna Birch, and by descent

MARIA EATON

Maria Eaton (1862-1944)

Maria Eaton was an enterprising painter and printmaker, who initially specialised in sensitive and characterful portrait miniatures. Following her marriage to the architect and artist, Ernest Hampshire, in 1913, she turned increasingly to flower studies, landscapes and townscapes.

For a biography of Maria Eaton, please refer to page 125.

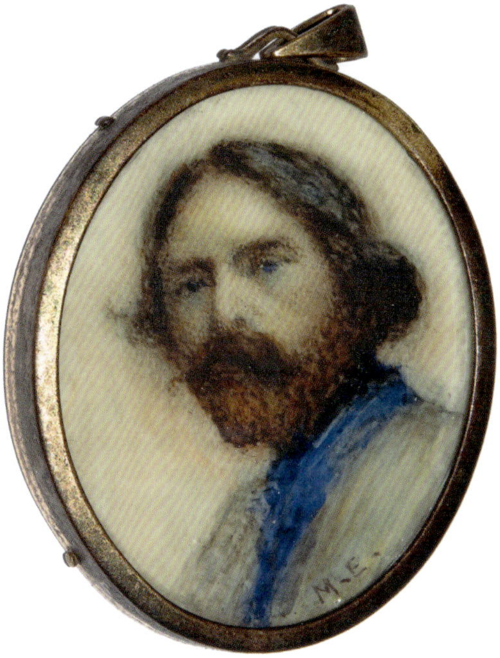

Augustus E John RA

This portrait miniature of the famous, flamboyant Welsh artist, Augustus John OM RA (1878-1961), was probably produced in the years between 1909 and 1913, when John was establishing his name.

103 **Augustus E John, RA**
Signed with initials
Signed, inscribed with title and 'No 2, Royal Academy 1931' on reverse
Watercolour on ivorine
2 x 1 ½ inches

Mornie and Her Doll (opposite)

'Mornie' was the childhood name of Elizabeth Lamorna Birch (1904-1990), the elder daughter of the painter, Samuel John Lamorna Birch, and his wife, Houghton. Birch added 'Lamorna' to his name in 1896, to associate himself with the cove in West Cornwall at which he founded a colony of artists and writers that operated as an outpost of the Newlyn School. Like her younger sister, Joan (1909-1993), Mornie often modelled for painters, including Thomas Cooper Gotch, Harold Harvey, Augustus John and Laura Knight, as well as Harold Knight and her own father. Harold Knight painted the present portrait in the woods at Lamorna, in about 1909, while he and his wife, Laura, were living at Oakhill. Mornie would also became an artist, specialising in flower subjects and landscapes of Lamorna.

WILLIAM WALCOT

William F Walcot, RBA RE (1874-1943)

Working as a painter and printmaker, William Walcot became the most celebrated architectural artist in England during the 1920s and 30s.

For a biography of William Walcot, please refer to *Chris Beetles Summer Show*, 2014, page 42.

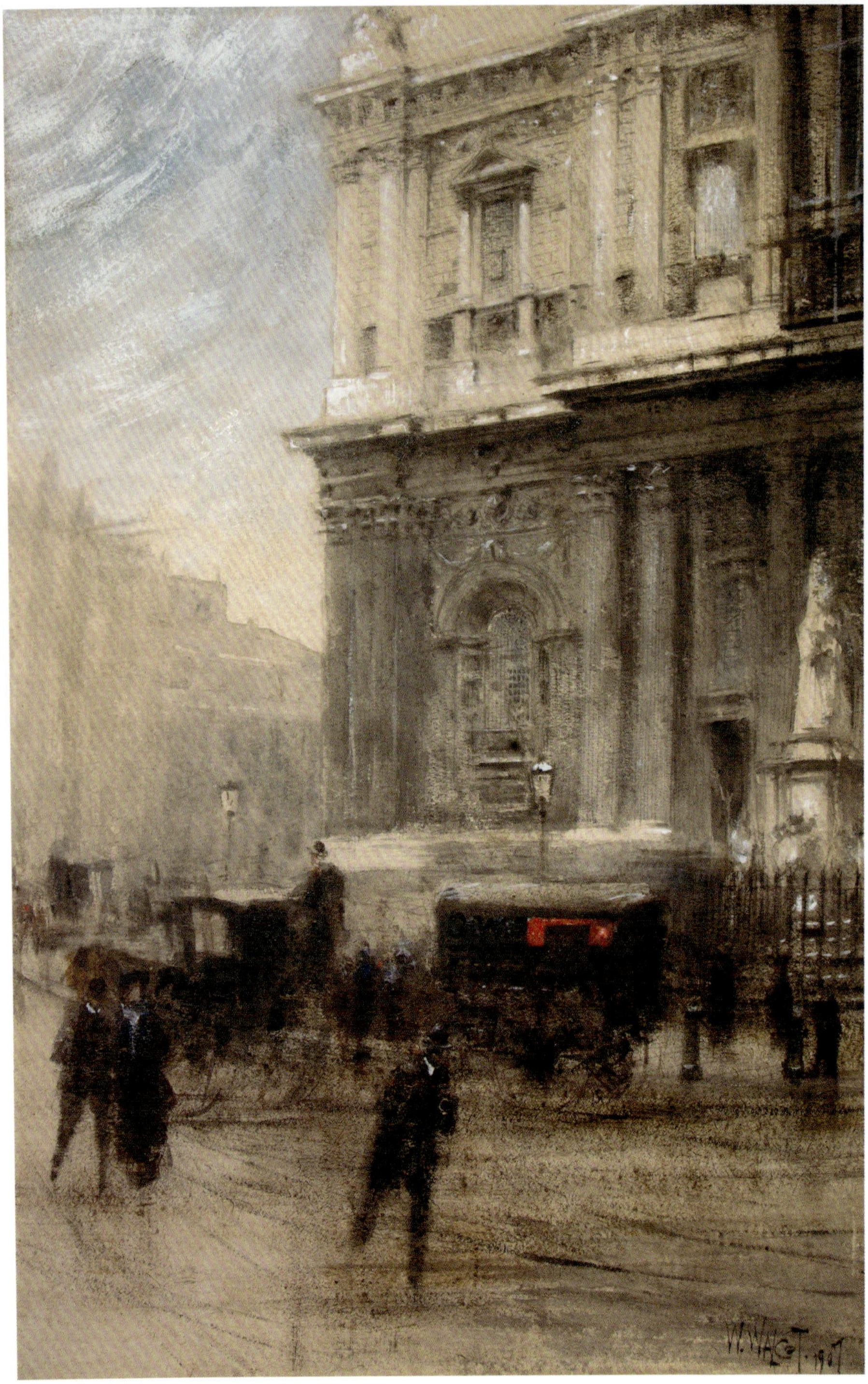

104 **The West Front of St Paul's Cathedral, London**
Signed and dated 1907
Watercolour with bodycolour and gum arabic
29 x 18 ½ inches
Exhibited: 'Exhibition of Paintings and Drawings by Royal Academy Exhibitors', M Newman Ltd London, 10-26 May 1967

ROSE BARTON

Rose Barton, RWS ASWA (1856-1929)

Even her contemporaries appreciated the Anglo-Irish artist, Rose Barton, as the equal of Herbert Menzies Marshall in her work as an urban topographer.

For a biography of Rose Barton, please refer to *Chris Beetles Summer Show*, 2019, Page 69.

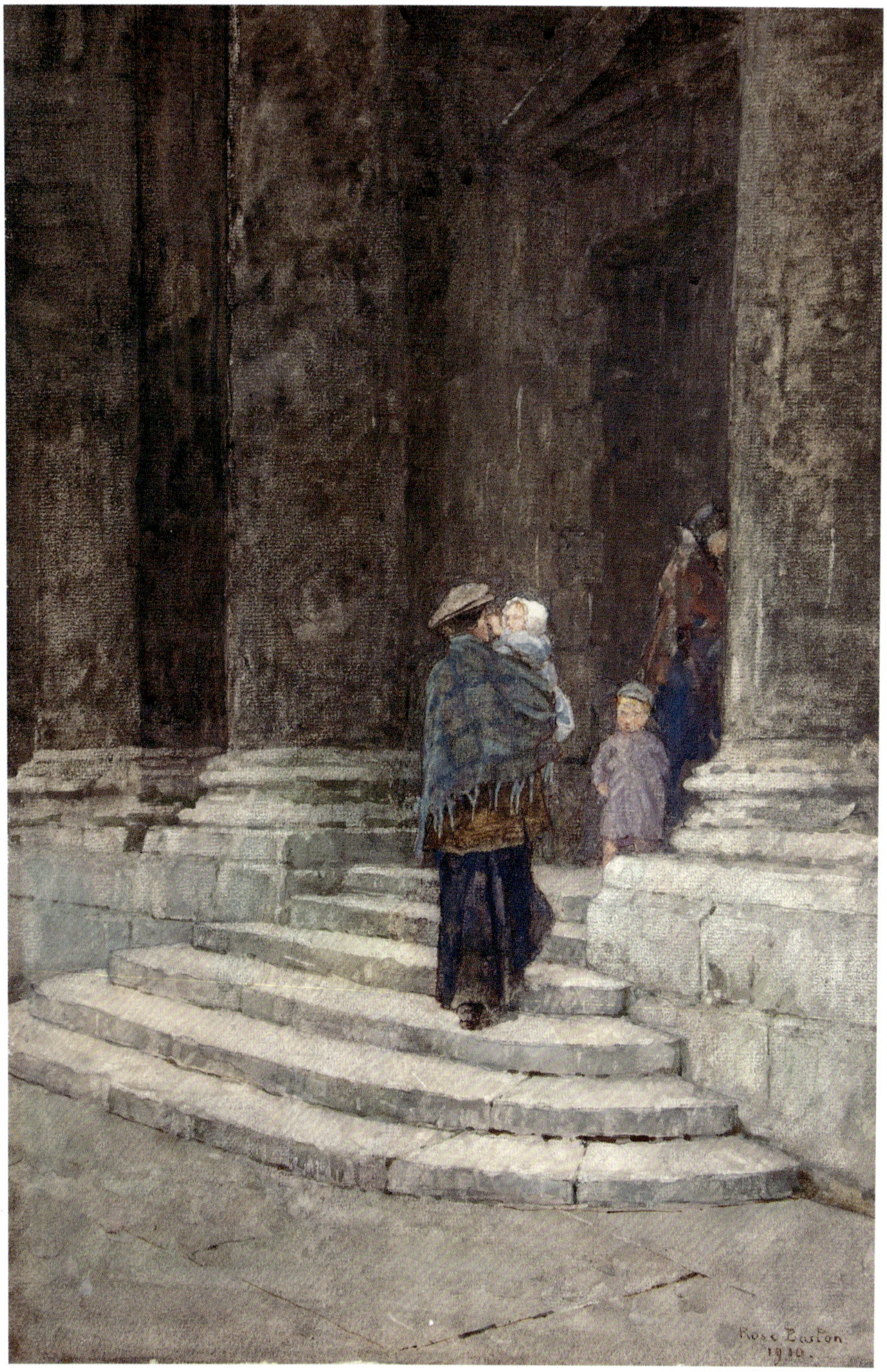

105 **Going to Early Service**
Signed and dated 1900
Watercolour on board
20 x 14 inches

DAVID SHEPHERD

Richard David Shepherd, CBE FRGS FRSA (1931-2017)

David Shepherd was a naturalistic painter in oils of a wide range of subjects, and most notably of African wildlife and steam railways, both of which were dear to his heart. Becoming one of the world's best known and most outspoken environmentalists, he raised millions for conservation through sales of his wildlife paintings. He became so popular with the British public that, during the 1960s, prints of his images of elephants outsold reproductions of works by Canaletto.

For a biography of David Shepherd, please refer to page 126.

Reading Cattle Market

David Shepherd produced this highly atmospheric portrait of the cattle market in Reading, Berkshire, early in his career. It follows in the tradition of works by both William Gunning King (1859-1940) and James Bateman (1893-1959). King's images advertised the animal feed manufacturer, J Bibby, and a poster for the same company can be seen on a wall in Shepherd's painting.

A cattle market has existed on the same site in Reading since 1850, when a public company was established to found such a building as a replacement for the slaughterhouses in the centre of the town. The company chose as its site a meadow south of the railway line and north of Great Knollys Street. To a design by a local architect, John Berry Clacy, the ground was raised above flood level, and the area divided into two parts, for fat and lean stock. The work was completed in eight weeks, and the market opened in the November.

In 1901, the auctioneers, Bailey & Thimbleby, approached the farmer, George Shorland, to run the agricultural side of its business at Reading Cattle Market. By 1903, the firm had become known as Thimbleby & Shorland, and it still operates from the market. The present buildings – including the ring that probably features in Shepherd's painting – were constructed in the late 1930s, by which time Thimbleby & Shorland was bringing loads of Ayrshire cattle from Scotland to the market. However, since the closure of the slaughterhouse in 1996, the focus of sales has been on goods rather than animals, from antiques to contractors' plant.

106 **Reading Cattle Market**
Signed
Oil on canvas
22 x 30 inches

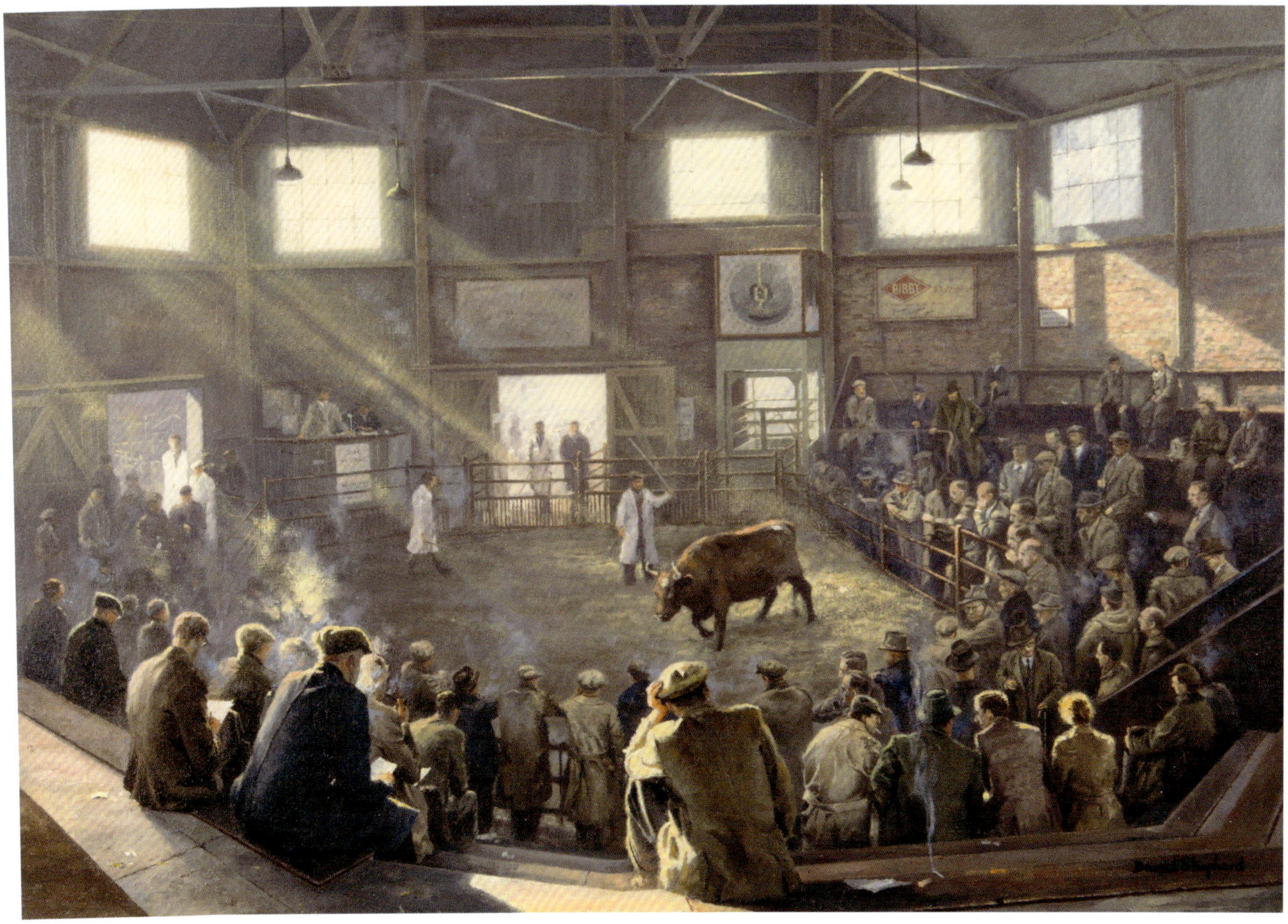
BIBBY

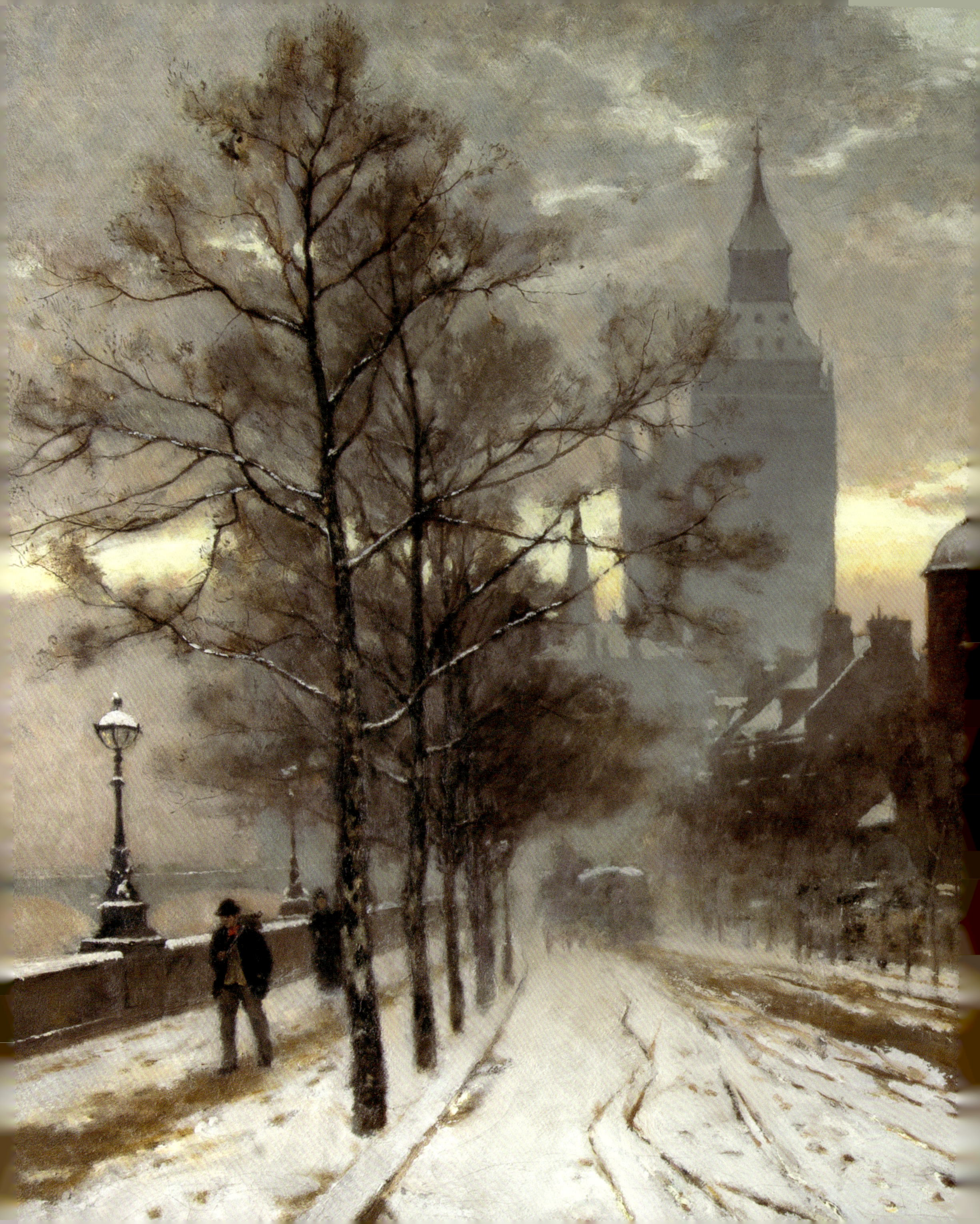

Biographies

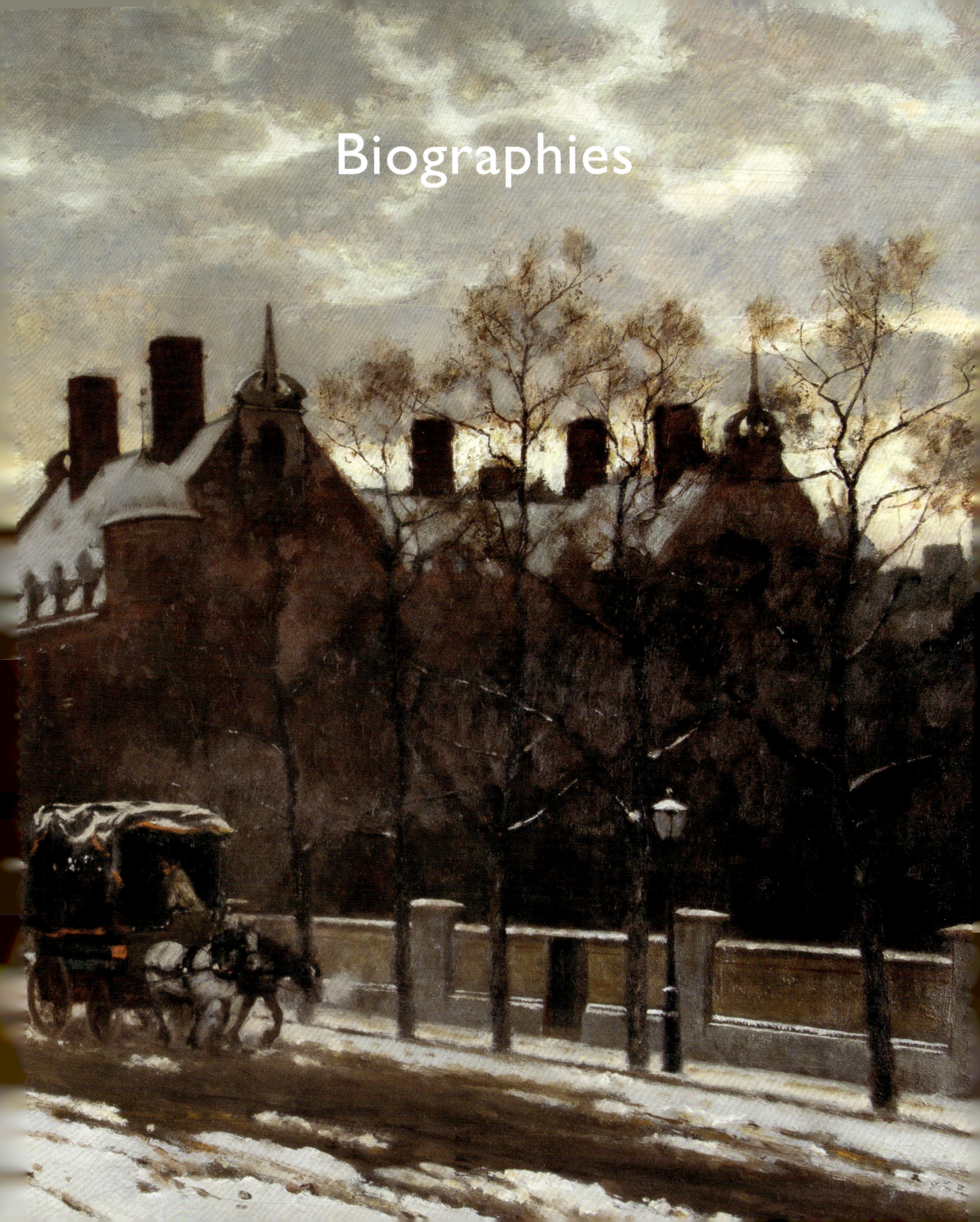

JOHN DOWNMAN

John Downman, ARA (1750-1824)

John Downman was one of the finest and most popular portraitists of the late eighteenth century, who received the patronage of both members of the royal family and icons of fashion. Working mainly in watercolour and pastel, he specialised in small format images that often depicted the half-length of the sitter in profile or semi-profile.

John Downman was born at Ruabon, near Wrexham, in North Wales, the youngest of the five sons of the attorney, Francis Downman, and his wife, Charlotte (née Goodsend), the daughter of the private secretary to George I. During his education at local schools, he began to show an aptitude for art, producing portraits and caricatures of his teachers and fellow pupils. He then probably received early drawing lessons in Chester and Liverpool. In 1767, he moved to London, in order to study under Benjamin West and, in the same year, exhibited for the first time with the Free Society of Artists. In 1769, he entered the recently founded Royal Academy Schools and, in 1770, first showed work at the Royal Academy of Arts, from an address at South Street, Berkeley Square. From the beginning, he specialised in portraiture, in a variety of media, while occasionally producing historical and literary subjects. He also painted a number of fresh and original landscapes between 1773 and 1775, during a period of travel to Italy in the company of Joseph Wright of Derby.

Before 1773, Downman had married his first wife, Elizabeth, and they would have three children: two sons and one daughter, Isabella Chloë, who was baptised at St Anne, Soho, London, on 2 July 1787. Almost nothing is known of this marriage, and Elizabeth seems to have died or disappeared by 1804.

Following his return to England in September 1775, Downman lived initially in Cambridge, where he set up as a portraitist, and received support from the Mortlocks, a local family of bankers (whose portraits he drew in the years 1777-79). Moving to London in 1778, and soon settling at 79 St James's Street, he confirmed his artistic reputation, and developed a characteristic combination of black chalk with additions of red chalk and watercolour that gave vitality to the portrayals of his sitters. He tended to exhibit his small, often oval, portraits in groups of six or nine, and mostly at the Royal Academy. In 1795, he became an associate of the RA, and immediately moved from Leicester Fields, which had been his home for a decade, to Fitzroy Street. Between 1802 and 1804, he lived briefly at a number of addresses in the Piccadilly area, before leaving London to take up residence at Went House, West Malling, Kent, which he had inherited from an uncle.

In 1806, Downman travelled to Devon and, that October, married Mary Jackson, daughter of the composer, William Jackson, in Exeter Cathedral. However, she died in the following year, and he returned to London. In the later phase of his career, he travelled widely in England in order to fulfil portrait commissions, making trips to the Lake District, Northumberland and Yorkshire that may have encouraged a desire to return North. Exhibiting at the Royal Academy for one last time in 1817, he retired first to Chester and finally to Wrexham. In the same year, his one surviving child, Isabella, married a Chester solicitor in Wrexham. He died at home on 24 December 1824.

His work is represented in numerous public collections, including the British Museum, the National Portrait Gallery, Tate, the V&A and The Wallace Collection; the Ashmolean Museum (Oxford), The Fitzwilliam Museum (Cambridge) and Manchester Art Gallery; National Museum Wales (Cardiff); and the Yale Center for British Art (New Haven, CT).

Further reading:

Geoffrey Ashton, 'Downman, John (*b* Ruabon, N Wales, 1750; *d* Wrexham, Dec 24, 1824), Jane Turner (ed), *The Dictionary of Art*, London: Macmillan, 1996, https://doi.org/10.1093/gao/9781884446054.article.T023524;

Jane Munro, 'Downman, John (1750-1824)', H C G Matthew and Brian Harrison (eds), *Oxford Dictionary of National Biography*, Oxford University Press, 2004, https://doi.org/10.1093/ref:odnb/7984;

Jane Munro, *John Downman, 1750-1824: landscape, figure studies and portraits of 'Distinguished persons'*, Cambridge: Fitzwilliam Museum, 1996;

G C Williamson, *John Downman ARA: His Life and Works*, London: Otto, 1907

WILLIAM ALEXANDER

William Alexander (1767-1816)

William Alexander was the only English artist of the late eighteenth century to penetrate the interior of China. As a result, he became well known for his images of the country at a time when Chinoiserie was all the rage. Admired as a technician, he worked as drawing master until 1808, when he accepted a position as one of the first curators at the British Museum.

William Alexander was born in Maidstone, Kent, on 10 April 1767, the son of a coachbuilder. Educated at Maidstone Grammar School, he showed a talent for drawing at an early age. In 1782, he moved to London to study art, and may have taken lessons with Julius Caesar Ibbetson before entering the Royal Academy Schools two years later.

Ibbetson had taken part on the first – abortive – British mission to Beijing. It is therefore likely that he recommended Alexander for the post of junior draughtsman in the embassy of Lord Macartney to China (1792-94), for which the senior draughtsman was the Irish artist, Thomas Hickey. The embassy itself proved a failure, as the Emperor Qianlong was uninterested in trade and communication, but the experience provided an inspiration and springboard for Alexander in his career as a painter and illustrator.

On his return from China, Alexander married on 10 April 1795, but his wife died shortly afterwards, and left no children.

During the ensuing decade, Alexander worked up many of his Chinese sketches into finished watercolours, and exhibited the results at the Royal Academy of Arts. In providing highly skilled representations of unusual subjects, they attracted great interest. In turn, his images were engraved for the official record of the embassy (1797) and other publications, including his own *View of the headlands, islands, etc, taken during a voyage to, and along the eastern coast of China, in the years 1792 & 1793* (1798), and Sir John Barrow's *A Voyage to Cochin China, in the Years 1792, and 1793* (1806).

In the same period, Alexander attended Dr Monro's unofficial 'academy' at his house in Fetcham, Surrey; there he had the opportunity to work alongside such leading contemporaries as Thomas Girtin, in copying exemplars of the art of watercolour collected by Monro and drawing *en plein air* in the surrounding countryside. He was also an active member of Girtin's Sketching Club, 'The Brothers'.

In 1802, Alexander was appointed Professor of Landscape Drawing at the Junior Department of the Royal Military Academy in Great Marlow, Buckinghamshire (the forerunner of Sandhurst). William Delamotte and William Gilpin were the second and third masters.

Six years later, in 1808, Alexander resigned from his professorship in order to become first Keeper of Prints and Drawings, and Assistant Librarian, at the British Museum. In 1810, he began to produce the first inventory of the museum's collection of prints and drawings. The trustees also commissioned him to illustrate items from the Townley collection, in Taylor Combe's *A Description of the Collection of Ancient Terra-cottas in the British Museum* (1810) and a *Description of the Collection of Ancient Marbles in the British Museum* (1812-18). He was a member of the Society of Antiquaries.

Later in life, Alexander produced a number of picturesque landscapes as well as drawings of antiquities.

Alexander died of a brain fever on 23 July 1816 at his uncle's house in Maidstone. He was buried at Boxley, Kent. Some of his collection of contemporary British paintings and drawings was sold at Sotheby's in the following year.

His work is represented in numerous public collections, including the British Library, Tate and the V&A.

Further reading:

Patrick Conner, 'Alexander, William', Jane Turner (ed), *The Dictionary of Art*, London: Macmillan, 1996, vol 1, page 612;
Patrick Conner and Susan Sloman, *William Alexander: An English Artist in Imperial China*, Brighton Museum and Art Gallery, 1981;
Richard Garnett (*rev* Heather M MacLennan), 'Alexander, William (1767-1816)', H C G Matthew and Brian Harrison (eds), *Oxford Dictionary of National Biography*, Oxford University Press, 2004, vol 1, pages 695-696;
Susan Sloman, *Image of China: William Alexander*, London: Jupiter Books, 1980

EDWARD DAYES

Edward Dayes (1763-1804)

Edward Dayes added an often dramatic sense of scale to the elegance and simplicity that he learned from Paul and Thomas Sandby. His topographical mastery became well known through the many engravings that were made from his watercolours.

Edward Dayes was born in Gray's Inn Passage, off Red Lion Square, London, on 6 August 1763, one of the six children of Samuel Dayes, a turner, and his wife, Mary. In about 1771, he moved with his family to the poorer area of Saffron Hill, Clerkenwell, and his father died at Saffron Hill Workhouse in 1774. He studied printmaking under the mezzotinter and miniaturist, William Pether, and, from 1780, at the Royal Academy Schools.

Dayes married Sarah Parker at St Mary's Lambeth on 11 November 1786, and lived first at 75 Long Acre, and later at other addresses in Covent Garden. They had at least one child, George, who was born in 1790, and would become a scene painter.

Dayes exhibited 64 works at the Royal Academy of Arts (from 1786), and others at the Society of Artists (1790-91), in a style developed from that of Paul and Thomas Sandby. In turn, he had a great influence on the younger generation, particularly as a teacher of watercolour. For instance, the young J M W Turner made meticulous copies of his works at Dr Monro's Academy while, from 1789, Thomas Girtin was a direct pupil. Dayes could be a less than generous mentor, being so envious of Girtin's success that it was long believed that he had him imprisoned for unruliness. Nevertheless, he rose to the position of draughtsman to the Duke of York (in about 1791).

In the late 1780s, Dayes recorded the expansion of the capital in four watercolours of new squares, including Hanover Square, which were engraved by Francis Jukes and Robert Pollard. Not only did they pre-empt the similar achievement of Thomas Malton, but also demonstrated Dayes' skill as a draughtsman of figures.

From the early 1790s, Dayes travelled widely in Britain, notably in Northern England and Wales. Responding to the landscape with bold, atmospheric watercolours of picturesque motifs, he also found employment as a topographical illustrator and in working up sketches made by amateurs. One project indicates the way in which he even interpreted terrains that were distant and unknown to him: David Collins' *Account of the Colony in New South Wales* (1798) contains engravings by Dayes after watercolours that Thomas Watling had made in Australia.

In the late 1790s, Dayes changed direction by embarking on a series of large biblical and classical subjects, some in oil, but this venture met with little success, a solo show in 1801 going unnoticed. This failure led him to commit suicide at his home at 5 Francis Street, Bedford Square, London, in late May 1804. His wife had exhibited miniatures at the Royal Academy between 1797 and 1800.

Volumes of his writings were published posthumously in 1805, including the textbook, *Drawing and Colouring Landscape*, and the malicious commentary, *Professional Sketches of Modern Artists*.

His work is represented in numerous public collections, including the British Museum, The Courtauld Gallery, Tate and the V&A; The Fitzwilliam Museum (Cambridge), Leeds Art Gallery and The Whitworth Art Gallery (Manchester); The National Library of Wales (Aberystwyth); and the National Library of Australia (Canberra).

Further reading:

David Blayney Brown, 'Edward Dayes: Historical Draughtsman', *Old Water-Colour Society's Club*, vol 62, 1991, pages 9-21;
Patrick Conner, 'Dayes, Edward (*b* London, 6 Aug 1763; *d* London, May 1804)', Jane Turner (ed), *The Dictionary of Art*, London: Macmillan, 1996, vol 8, page 584;
J Dayes, 'Edward Dayes', *Old Water-Colour Society's Club*, vol 39, 1964, pp 45-55;
Tim Marshall, 'Edward Dayes. His ancestors, family and descendants', *British Art Journal*, Winter 2007/8, pages 31-38;
Greg Smith, 'Dayes, Edward (1763-1704)', H C G Matthew and Brian Harrison (eds), *Oxford Dictionary of National Biography*, Oxford University Press, 2004, vol 15, pages 609-610

COPLEY FIELDING

Anthony Vandyke Copley Fielding, POWS (1787-1855)

Copley Fielding was one of the most technically impressive watercolourists of his day, both popular as an artist and influential as a teacher.

Copley Fielding was born in Sowerby, near Halifax, Yorkshire, on 22 November 1787. He was the third, and best known, of the five artist sons of Nathan Theodore Fielding, a Yorkshire portrait and landscape painter. His full name suggests his father's ambitions for him, as it combines those of Anthony Van Dyck and the history painter, John Singleton Copley RA (though Copley was also a hamlet neighbouring Sowerby).

In 1788, the Fielding family moved to Acton, Middlesex (now in London). Copley attended a local school and, like his brother Frederick, worked as 'an engrossing clerk in the enrolment office of the court of chancery' (Mallalieu, 2004, page 498). After periods in Durham and London, the Fieldings settled in the Lake District in around 1804, first at a cottage in Ambleside and later in Keswick.

Given his first lessons in art by his father, Copley was soon working in a very similar style, though he was sent out each morning to draw from nature. In 1807, he accompanied his father to Liverpool, in order to sell his drawings, and while there began to give drawing lessons. Father and son toured north Wales together in the following year.

In 1809, Copley Fielding settled in London, and lodged at Wells Street, in the artistic quarter north of Oxford Street. He took advice and lessons from John Varley, who may have suggested that he look at the work of Thomas Girtin, which he could have seen at Dr Monro's informal academy. His election as an associate of the Society of Painters in Water Colours in January 1810 indicates the speed of his development.

During the summer, Fielding toured the Borders (visiting his brothers Theodore, in Penrith, and Frederick, in Carlisle), while, in the following year, he revisited Liverpool and north Wales. Further sketching tours in Britain followed through the decade. Though exhibiting eleven oils at the Royal Academy of Arts (1811-42), Fielding strengthened his allegiance to watercolour in becoming a member of the Society of Painters in Water Colours in 1811, its Treasurer in 1813 and its Secretary in 1815. Hugely prolific, he would average over forty exhibits a year there for forty-three years, a total of 1,748 works.

In 1813, Fielding married Susannah Gisborne, the sister of John Varley's wife, and two years later they rented Capo di Monte, a house in Judges Walk, Hampstead (previously occupied by Sarah Siddons, the great tragedienne). In 1817, he also bought a house at 26 Newman Street, north of Oxford Street, 'which was to be the London base of the family business for the next thirty years' (Mallalieu, op cit, page 499) and, particularly, his highly successful practice as a drawing master. His pupils would include William Leighton Leitch, William Andrews Nesfield and John Ruskin, the last a lifelong admirer.

Yet, despite this activity, the ill health of both his wife and elder daughter necessitated a home on the coast, and the family settled at Sandgate, Kent, in 1817. From this time, Fielding not only painted many views of the southern counties, but also many seascapes, especially through the 1820s. At the close of that decade, the family moved to Brighton, living first at 41 Regency Square and, by 1840, at 2 Lansdowne Place. Views of the South Downs then became common to Fielding's repertoire.

Remaining popular and successful throughout his career, Fielding was elected Deputy President of the Society of Painters in Water Colours in 1823, and President in 1831. In 1824, he was awarded a gold medal at the Paris Salon, in the same year as Richard Parkes Bonington and John Constable, although he was the only Fielding brother never to visit France or, indeed travel abroad. His foreign views, such as *Benares*, were developed from the sketches of other artists.

Having made a final move, to 5 Park Crescent, Worthing, in 1847, Copley Fielding died there on 3 March 1855.

His work is represented in numerous public collections, including the British Museum, Tate, the V&A and The Wallace Collection; Brighton & Hove Museums, The Fitzwilliam Museum (Cambridge), Manchester Art Gallery, Southampton Art Gallery and Tyne & Wear Museums; and the Art Gallery of New South Wales (Sydney).

Further reading:

Solomon Charles Kaines-Smith, 'Anthony Vandyke Copley Fielding', *Old Water-Colour Society's Club*, vol 3, 1925, pages 8-30;
Huon Mallalieu, 'Fielding (Anthony Vandyke) Copley (1787-1855)', H C G Matthew and Brian Harrison (eds), *Oxford Dictionary of National Biography*, Oxford University Press, 2004, vol 19, pages 498-499;
Terence Mullaly, 'Copley Fielding, *The Sussex County Magazine*, vol 26, 1952, pages 574-578;
Marcia Pointon, 'Fielding (3) (Anthony Van Dyck) Copley Fielding (*b* Sowerby Bridge, W Yorks, 1787; *d* Worthing, W Sussex, March 2, 1855)', Jane Turner (ed), *The Dictionary of Art*, London: Macmillan, 1996, vol 11, page 60

ALFRED JOSEPH WOOLMER

Alfred Joseph Woolmer, RBA (1805-1892)

The painter and sculptor, Alfred Joseph Woolmer, was best known for his distinctive genre subjects, and especially 'elegant courtship scenes in light dappled gardens and shady bowers' and 'sensuous, mildly erotic images of ladies at their *toilette*' (Asleson, 2018). While he sometimes illustrated specific episodes from literature, he focussed more often on the evocation of a poetic atmosphere through the fluid handling of a rich palette. Initially emulating 'the romantic historical costume pieces' (Asleson, op cit) that were popular in the 1820s and 30s, he gradually developed a personal approach through the assimilation of an eclectic range of influences that most notably included Watteau.

Alfred Joseph Woolmer was born in Chelsea, London, on 20 December 1805, the fifth of six children of the picture dealer, William Ferrers Woolmer, of Hamilton Street, Piccadilly, and his wife, Jane (née Stringer).

Tradition has recorded that Woolmer studied art in Italy, and, though it is uncertain how formal a training this was, it is known that he undertook a number of sketching tours on the Continent during his career. While living at 50 Earl Street, Paddington, in 1827, he began to show work in London, contributing to the exhibitions of the Royal Academy of Arts, the British Institution and especially the Society of British Artists. He was elected to the membership of the latter in 1841, and for the following decade would contribute between 10 and 16 paintings a year to its annual exhibitions.

Having lived at several different addresses early in his career, Woolmer settled at Fortis Green, in Finchley, in 1849. Four years later, he married Mary Anne Tuffield, daughter of Edward Tuffield, a painter and glazier. From that time, he halved the number of his submissions to the Society of British Artists. He and his wife would have at least three sons and a daughter called Marion, who also became an artist. The family lived at two different addresses in Upper Holloway during the mid 1860s, before moving to 9 Chester Road, New Highgate, in 1868.

From 1875, Woolmer lived at The Limes, 34 Dartmouth Park Avenue, Kentish Town. While further reducing his output from that date, he continued to exhibit regularly at the Society of British Artists until 1887 (the year in which the society received its royal charter). During a career of six decades, he exhibited over 350 works.

Alfred Joseph Woolmer died in London on 19 April 1892.

His work is represented in numerous public collections, including the Russell-Cotes Art Gallery & Museum (Bournemouth).

Further reading:

Robyn Asleson, 'Woolmer, Alfred Joseph (1805–1892)', H C G Matthew and Brian Harrison (eds), *Oxford Dictionary of National Biography*, Oxford University Press, 2018, https://doi.org /10.1093/ref:odnb/64286

GEORGE FREDERIC WATTS

George Frederic Watts, OM RA (1817-1904)

By the end his long career, George Frederic Watts had become the most revered figure in British art, and was one of first to hold the Order of Merit, when it was instituted in 1902. Inspired by the example of the Renaissance masters, he attempted to revive the tradition of history painting by producing ambitious allegories that promoted a moral message, stating that 'I paint ideas, not things'. The allusive, often expressive results reveal an association with the Continental Symbolist movement. In addition, he was a distinctive and penetrating portraitist, and an occasional, but invariably impressive sculptor.

The final home, studio and gallery of George Frederic Watts and his second wife, Mary Seton Watts, in the Surrey village of Compton, are open to the public as the Watts Gallery – Artists' Village, and hold the largest collection of his work.

His work is also represented in numerous public collections, including the National Portrait Gallery, Tate and the V&A; the Ashmolean Museum (Oxford), Birmingham Museums Trust, Manchester Art Gallery, the Walker Art Gallery (Liverpool) and York Art Gallery; and The Art Institute of Chicago (IL).

Further reading:

Emilie Isabel Barrington, *G F Watts: Reminiscences*, London: George Allen, 1905;
Mark Bills and Barbara Bryant, *G F Watts: Victorian Visionary*, New Haven/London: Yale University Press/Watts Gallery Compton, 2008;
Barbara Bryant, 'Watts, G(eorge) F(rederic) (*b* London, Feb 23, 1817; *d* London, July 1, 1904)', Jane Turner (ed), *The Dictionary of Art*, London: Macmillan, 2003, https://doi.org/10.1093/gao/9781884446054.article.T090866;
Barbara Bryant, 'Watts, George Frederic (1817-1904)', H C G Matthew and Brian Harrison (eds), *Oxford Dictionary of National Biography*, Oxford University Press, 2007, https://doi.org/10.1093/ref:odnb/36781;
Wilfrid Blunt, *'England's Michelangelo': A Biography of George Frederic Watts, OM, RA*, London: Hamish Hamilton, 1975;
John Gage and Chris Mullen, *G F Watts, 1817–1904: A Nineteenth Century Phenomenon*, London: Whitechapel Art Gallery, 1974;
Mary Seton Watts, *George Frederic Watts: The Annals of an Artist's Life*, London: Macmillan & Co, 3 vols, 1912

JOSEPH NOEL PATON

Sir Joseph Noel Paton, RSA (1821-1901)

Joseph Noel Paton was the leading Scottish artist of the Victorian period to specialise in imaginative figure subjects, and notably fairies. In producing such masterpieces as *The Quarrel of Oberon and Titania*, he capitalised on his mimetic skills in order to represent the supernatural with great conviction.

Joseph Noel Paton was born in Dunfermline, Fife, on 13 December 1821, the second of three children of a damask designer and manufacturer. His father's interests as an antiquarian and collector provided early inspiration. (The collection, inherited by Paton, is now in the National Museum of Scotland, Edinburgh.) From his earliest years, his reading fired his imagination, and he made drawings based on tales of Celtic romance and legend, in addition to episodes from the Bible and ancient history. He developed talents for both literature and art, and would become a poet and critic as well as a painter and sculptor.

On completing his education at Dunfermline School and Dunfermline Art Academy, Paton spent three years in his father's profession, becoming director of design at Brown, Sharp & Co's sewn-muslin factory at Paisley, Strathclyde. Then, in 1842, he left Scotland for London where, in the following year, he entered the Royal Academy Schools. Though he did not take up a studentship, his time at the Schools proved important to his artistic development, for he met and befriended a younger, precocious student, John Everett Millais.

Paton's aptitude for literary subjects enabled him to work as both illustrator and painter. He contributed to Samuel Carter Hall's *The Book of British Ballads* (1842 & 1844) and Mrs Anna Maria Hall's *Midsummer Eve: A Fairy Tale of Love* (1847), two landmarks in the construction of the Victorian imagination. He also entered the competitions for the decoration of the rebuilt Houses of Parliament, a project on which the health of British history painting seemed so strongly to depend. He established his reputation in England with his two prizewinning entries, *The Spirit of Religion* (1845) and especially *The Reconciliation of Oberon and Titania* (1847). He had already exhibited his first, small version of its pendant, *The Quarrel of Oberon and Titania*, in Edinburgh in 1846, as his diploma work on becoming an associate of the Royal Scottish Academy.

Paton was invited by Millais to join the newly founded Pre-Raphaelite Brotherhood. Though sympathetic to its ideals, he declined, for he disliked London and preferred to return to Scotland. As a result, he practised and promoted its principles in the Scottish capital, recording the natural world in almost uncanny detail, and capitalising on his mimetic skills in order to convincingly represent the supernatural.

This he demonstrated triumphantly with the large version of *The Quarrel of Oberon and Titania*, judged to be *the* painting of the exhibition when shown, in 1850, at the Royal Scottish Academy. He was elected a full academician in the same year.

Paton's approach to landscape painting was influenced not only by the example of the Pre-Raphaelites but by the writings of their champion, John Ruskin. Paton met Ruskin through Millais and, in 1853, attended the lectures that he gave in Edinburgh on Architecture and Painting. Soon after, he went on painting trips with his brother, the artist Waller Hugh Paton, to the Isle of Arran (1854, 1855), possibly to Loch Lomond (1858), and later to the Continent (1861, 1868).

By the late 1850s, Paton was as well known and admired in England as in Scotland, through his exhibits at the Royal Academy of Arts (1856-83) and his illustrations to Charles Kingsley's *The Water Babies* (1863). He was appointed Queen's Limner for Scotland in 1866, and knighted a year later.

His work as an original imaginative painter culminated in 1867, with the completion of *The Fairy Raid* and its exhibition at the Royal Academy. Five years later, he declined the invitation of Lewis Carroll to illustrate *Through the Looking-Glass and What Alice Found There*, the author's second great work of fantasy, stating that John Tenniel remained the ideal artist for the job. Instead, he devoted his remaining time to painting religious subjects in an academic manner comparable to that of his compatriot, William Dyce. He died at his home in Edinburgh on 26 December 1901. Of the eleven children from his marriage to Margaret Gourlay Ferrier (died 1900), his sons Frederick Noel Paton and Ronald Noel Paton also became artists.

His work is represented in the collections of the British Museum; and the Art Gallery and Museum, Kelvingrove (Glasgow) and the National Gallery of Scotland (Edinburgh).

Further reading:

Alasdair A Auld, *Fact and Fancy: Drawings and Paintings by Joseph Noel Paton, 1821-1901*, Scottish Arts Council, 1967;
Alasdair A Auld, 'Paton, Sir (Joseph) Noel [Noël] (*b* Dunfermline, Fife, 1821; *d* Edinburgh, 25 Dec 1901)', Jane Turner (ed), *The Dictionary of Art*, London: Macmillan, 1996, vol 24, page 266;
Nicola Bown, 'Paton, Sir Joseph Noël (1821-1901)', H C G Matthew and Brian Harrison (eds), *Oxford Dictionary of National Biography*, Oxford University Press, 2004, vol 43, pages 62-63;
Francina Irwin (ed), M H Noel-Paton and J P Campbell, *Noel Paton, 1821-1901*, Edinburgh: The Ramsay Head Press, 1990

CHARLES GREEN

Charles Green, RI (1840-1898)

Charles Green was a painter and illustrator of genre and historical subjects. He is now best remembered for images illustrating, or inspired by, the work of Charles Dickens.

Charles Green was born in Well Walk, Hampstead, on 17 August 1840, and baptised twice: at St John's, Hampstead, on 4 September 1840 (possibly because he was sickly), and again at St Mary's, Islington, on 8 April 1842. He was the youngest of five children of Henry Gilson Green, then a gentleman of independent means, and his wife, Mary Anne or Marianne (née Reynolds). Mary Anne had a number of interesting literary connections. Her mother was related to the Hamilton family, which included William Beckford; her elder brother was John Hamilton Reynolds, poet, critic, journalist, playwright, satirist, and, like Mary Anne, a friend of the poet, John Keats; their sister, Jane, was married to Thomas Hood.

Charles Green spent his early years at the house in Well Walk. However, by 1851, the family had moved to 22 Richmond Road (now Richmond Avenue), Islington, to live with his mother's father, George Reynolds, and her sister, Charlotte. His father was working as an attorney solicitor's general clerk, and he took up a position in the same office. He made drawings in his spare time, including some in classes at James Mathews Leigh's School of Fine Art, at 79 Newman Street, north of Oxford Street. In 1857, his father wrote to the leading wood engraver and illustrator, John Gilbert, enclosing some of Charles's drawings and asking his advice. Gilbert was sufficiently encouraging that, two years later, in May 1859, Charles began an apprenticeship with the wood engraver, Josiah Whymper, at 20 Canterbury Place (now 45 Lambeth Road), Lambeth, and lived next door to the studio. He worked alongside, and befriended, James Mahoney, J W North, G J Pinwell and Frederick Walker. They were paid ten shillings for three days' work each week, and encouraged to work in 'the Gilbert style'.

By the time that the census was taken in 1861, Charles Green had returned to live with his family, which had moved across Islington to 15 College Terrace (now College Cross). His elder brother, Henry Towneley Green, who would also become a watercolour artist, was then working as an insurance clerk. Charles quickly established himself as an illustrator, and made the most of opportunities afforded by the growth in the number of illustrated books and magazines.

Among books, Charles Green contributed to *Cassell's Illustrated Family Bible* (1859-63), *English Sacred Poetry of the Olden Times* (1864), *The Life and Lessons of Our Lord* (1864), the Choice Series of selections from the poets (1864) and Isaac Watts' *Divine and Moral Songs* (1865). Among magazines, he contributed to *Once a Week* (from 1860), *The Cornhill Magazine* (including 1862), *The Churchman's Family Magazine* (1863-64), *London Society* (1863, 1867), *The Illustrated London News* (1866), *Cassell's Family Magazine* (1867), *The Sunday at Home* (1867, 1869), *The Leisure Hour* (1869), and *Good Words for the Young* (1870). His contribution of contemporary subjects to the early numbers of *The Graphic* (from 1869) were admired by Van Gogh.

As a watercolourist, Charles Green specialised in literary and other genre scenes, often with period settings. He transformed some of his delicate pen and ink illustrations by adding watercolour, and often used a stippled technique influenced by William Henry Hunt. He joined the Langham Sketching Club (by 1864) and Savage Club, and was elected to the Royal Institute of Painters in Water Colours (ARI 1864; RI 1867), of which his brother, Towneley, was also a member. Also painting in oils, he exhibited at the Royal Academy until 1883. In 1878, he was elected an honorary member of the Imperial Royal Academy of Vienna.

Charles Green was probably best known for his illustrations to works by Charles Dickens, and for watercolours inspired by them. Notable among these were *The Old Curiosity Shop* for Chapman and Hall's 'Household Edition' in 1871, *A Christmas Carol* for *Pears Christmas Annual* in 1892, and, his last work, *Great Expectations* for Chapman and Hall's 'Gadshill Edition' in 1898. He also became known for theatrical subjects, including scenes from plays, glimpses backstage and views of auditoria.

By 1881, Charles Green was living with his siblings, Marianne and Towneley, and their aunt, Charlotte Reynolds, at 78 Park Road, Haverstock Hill. On visits to the house, such friends as the actor, Frank Archer, would enjoy listening to Charlotte reminisce about Keats, Charles Lamb, Leigh Hunt and Dickens. Charles also had a studio at Charlecote, 3 Hampstead Hill Gardens, which was designed especially for him by the architects, Batterbury and Huxley, in 1878. He and Towneley hosted 'smoking parties' there, and it eventually became their home. He died there 15 years later, early in May 1898 (and possibly the first of the month), and was buried in Hampstead Cemetery. In October 1899, the Fine Art Society held a memorial exhibition. Towneley died in December 1899, and a large sale of the works of the two brothers was held at Christie Manson & Woods, London, in 1900.

His work is represented in numerous public collections, including the V&A; and the Mercer Art Gallery (Harrogate).

Further reading:

John Fulleylove, 'Personal recollections of two Hampstead artists: Charles and Towneley Green', *The Hampstead Annual*, 1900, pages 94-105

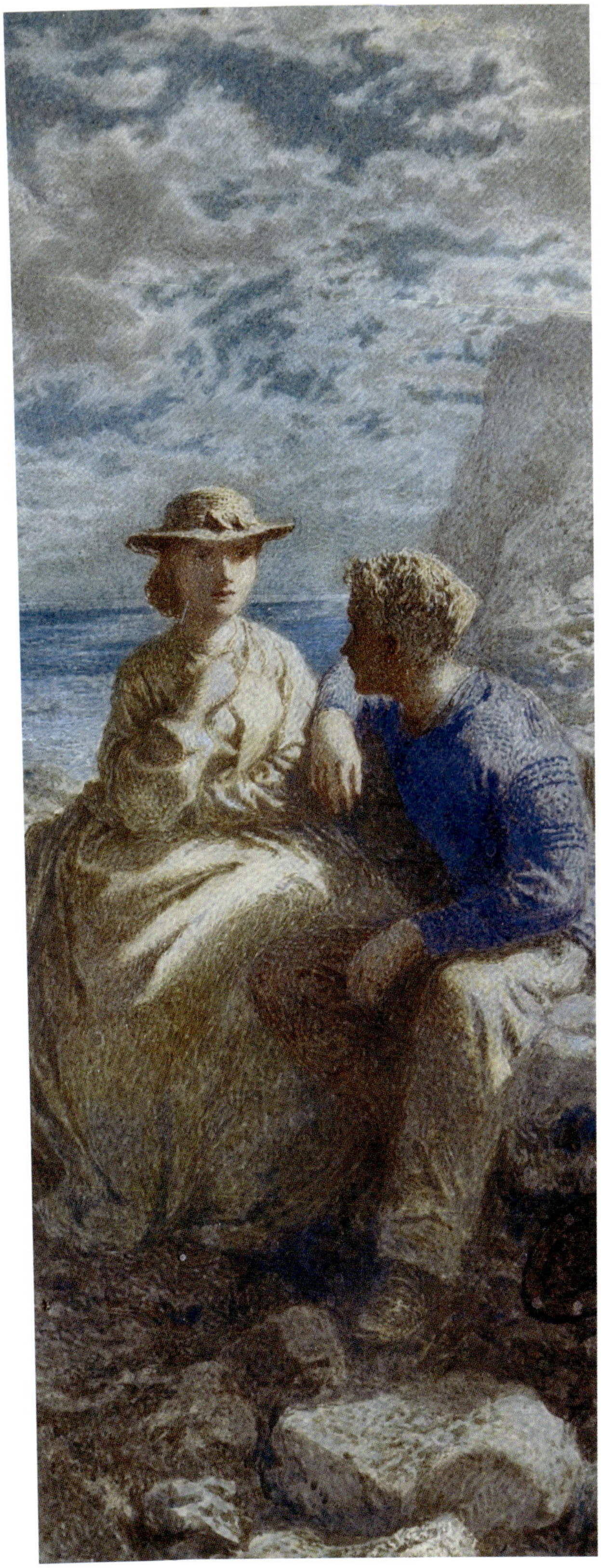

Detail of Charles Green, *By the Sea* [52]

FRANK WILLIAM WARWICK TOPHAM

Francis William Warwick Topham, RI ROI (1838-1924)

Frank William Warwick Topham was best known as a painter of charming genre scenes in oil and watercolour, especially those with Italian settings. In addition, he produced a number of portraits.

Frank William Warwick Topham was born at 32 Fortress Terrace, Kentish Town, the second of ten children of the genre painter, Francis William Topham, and his wife, Mary Anne (née Beckwith). He studied art under his father from an early age, before entering the Royal Academy Schools. Later, he went to Paris, to work in the atelier of the academic painter, Charles Gleyre.

From 1860, Topham exhibited widely at London and provincial venues that included the Royal Academy of Arts, the British Institution, the Royal Society of British Artists, the Institute of Painters in Water Colours, the Grosvenor Gallery and the New Gallery.

Topham enjoyed the company of his father, and undertook sketching tours with him to Ireland in 1860, and to Rome and Capri in 1863. Developing a particular love of Italy, he returned to the country on several occasions, and made its people the chief subject of his paintings. One documented trip was that of 1865, when he went to Ravenna with fellow painters, E S Lundgren and Frank Dillon.

In 1870, Topham married Helen Lemon, in Horsham, Sussex. She was the daughter of his father's friend, Mark Lemon, the first editor of *Punch*. They settled together at 58 Queen's Road, St John's Wood, but, in 1877, moved to Ifield, Prince Arthur Road, Hampstead. They had five daughters and three sons.

In 1879, Topham was elected a member of the Institute of Painters in Water Colours. (Six years later, the institute would receive its royal charter.) Then, in 1883, he was elected to the membership of the Institute of Painters in Oil Colours, only two years after its foundation. (In turn, it would receive its royal charter, becoming the Royal Institute of Oil Painters in 1909.)

Around 1890, Topham and his family moved to Coneyhurst, a Tudor manor house in the village of Ewhurst, in Surrey, which he had modernised and extended. However, he retained a studio in London at Garden Chambers, 32 Great Ormond Street, and continued to paint and exhibit into the early years of the twentieth century. He died at home on 25 May 1924, at the age 86.

Further reading:

Tom Pocock, *Topham and Son. A Family of Artists*, London: Burgh House Museum, 1985

BEATRICE HEWITT

Beatrice Marion Hewitt (1859-1908)

Beatrice Hewitt is best known as a painter of sensitive miniature portraits. However, her early watercolours of flowers and the present impressive figure study in oil demonstrate that she was an artist of range as well as skill.

Beatrice Hewitt was born in Hanwell, Middlesex, and baptised on 18 September 1859 as the fifth of seven children of the medical doctor, Joseph Hewitt, and his wife, Charlotte (née Waterhouse). When Joseph Hewitt died six years later, in Eton, his addresses were given as 7 Southwick Place, Hyde Park Square, London, and Heath Lodge, Iver, Buckinghamshire.

Almost nothing is known of the childhood of Beatrice Hewitt; however, by the time of the taking of the 1871 census, she and her six siblings were living with their widowed mother and a maternal aunt, Eliza Waterhouse, 'on interest of money &c' at Chestham (now Chestham Park), a large Regency house to the north of Henfield, Sussex, which they possibly rented.

By 1878, Beatrice Hewitt and her family had returned to London, and were living at 18 Delamere Crescent (now part of the Warwick Estate), in Paddington, which her mother kept as a boarding house. On the census taken at Delamere Crescent three years later, in 1881, Beatrice and an elder sister, Florence, are each identified as being 'artist pr [painter]'. While nothing is known of the artistic training of either woman before this date, Florence is singled out for praise two years later; an article in the *Bazaar Exchange and Mart* for 7 December 1883 states that 'The work of Miss Florence Hewitt as a flower painter has already been for several years before the public, and her designs upon calendars, letter wallets and Christmas cards, are universally admired'.

It seems that Beatrice Hewitt also first came to public notice as a flower painter, two studies of roses being exhibited at the Royal Institute of Painters in Water Colours in 1884. Her address at the time was 'St Aubyns, Kew Gardens', which proved to be 'a superior educational home' of which she was Principal, and possibly founder, 'where a limited number of pupils are received, and for whom a thorough and finished education is provided'. She was assisted in this by both her mother and 'resident Foreign Governesses and visiting Professors' (F S D de Carteret Bisson, *Our Schools and Colleges*, London: Simpkin, Marshall, 1884, page 554). However, there is no evidence that this finishing school flourished for more than a year and, by the end of the 1880s, Beatrice Hewitt was focussing on her artistic career.

Between 1888 and 1895, Beatrice Hewitt is known to have lived in the Balham area of South London, and initially at 70 Cheriton Square, 'Upper Tooting'. While there, she exhibited at the Royal Academy of Arts for the first time, showing *An Academy Model* (which might be the present work) in 1888. The title, 'An Academy Model', suggests that she was undergoing a course of study at this point, but there is no evidence for this.

By 1890, Beatrice Hewitt had moved, with her mother, to 7 Ryde Vale Road, which was closer to Tooting Common. In that year, she exhibited at the Royal Academy for a second time with two portrait miniatures, and these established her artistic identity. Similar works were shown each year at the RA until 1893, and then again in the years 1895, 1901 and 1902. Most of her sitters came from the upper middle classes, though, by the turn of the century, she was also being patronised by members of the aristocracy, namely the Duchess of Newcastle (1901) and Mary, Countess of Mar and Kellie (1902).

In 1893, Beatrice Hewitt moved a few streets away to Linkfield House, 30 Fontenoy Road, which was the home of the architect, Edwin J Munt and his family. In 1895, her exhibits at the RA were singled out in the magazine, *The Athenaeum*, as demonstrating the beauty of the contemporary miniature. Apart from her work as miniaturist, she contributed 'A Study in Colour', for use as a frontispiece, to *The Pall Mall Magazine*, in 1894.

By 1898, Beatrice Hewitt had begun a new phase of her life when she moved north of the River Thames to live at one of the three artists' studios at 12a Edith Terrace, Chelsea. She then studied at the Slade School of Art, and at the end of her first year of was awarded a prize of £3 for Fine Art Anatomy, a course that was taught by Professor G D Thane.

By 1901, Beatrice Hewitt had moved to 4 Addison Studios, Blythe Road, West Kensington, with her younger sister, Constance. She remained there until at least 1904, the year in which Constance died, in Hailsham, Sussex, at the age of 39. It is likely that, on becoming ill, Constance had joined her mother, aunt and sisters, Margaret and Florence, who together had taken Oldbury Farm, Hooe, which is five miles east of Hailsham, and which Margaret ran as a dairy farm.

In turn, Beatrice Hewitt also became ill, and her burgeoning artistic career was cut short. She joined her family at Oldbury Farm, dying there on 30 August 1908, aged 49.

ALICE MARY CHAMBERS

Alice Mary Chambers (1854/55-1920)

Alice Mary Chambers was a significant figure in British artistic circles of the late nineteenth century, and was in particular a valued friend of the infamous artists' agent, Charles Augustus Howell. Her beautiful drawings and watercolours reveal a debt to both Pre-Raphaelitism and Aestheticism, and especially to the work of Dante Gabriel Rossetti.

Alice Mary Chambers was born in Harlow, Essex, in either 1854 or 1855, the daughter of the Rev John Charles Chambers, a controversial figure in the Anglican Church, and his wife, Mary (née Upton). Their two older children had both died in infancy in 1852. At the time of her birth, Alice's father was vicar of St Mary Magdalene in Harlow, but, in 1856, he became perpetual curate of St Mary's, Crown Street, and warden of the House of Charity, both in Soho, London, positions that he retained until his death. He has been described as turning 'St Mary's into a model for managing a parish along ritualist [or Anglo-Catholic] lines' (Morris, 2004). By consent, he and his wife separated 'each to live crypto-monastic lives of celibacy and charity' (Mumm, 2001, page 3).

The census for 1861 records that Alice and her mother were living at Fernley Bank, West Hill (now Westwood Hill), Sydenham, a school for young ladies run by her mother's sisters, Sarah, Martha and Anna, and at which her mother also taught.

A decade later, the census for 1871 records that Alice and her mother were again living with her father – at 16 Upper Woburn Place, Bloomsbury. However, within the next three years, both her mother and father had died (in 1873 and 1874). In his will, J C Chambers made his brother, the Rev Oswald Littleton Chambers (Vicar of Hook, Yorkshire), guardian of his daughter, and left the income from a substantial sum – between two and three thousand pounds – for his daughter's 'maintenance and education'. In 1877, J C Chambers became posthumously controversial, when his two-volume publication, *The Priest in Absolution* (1866 & 1870), was condemned in the House of Lords by the Earl of Redesdale for its promotion of auricular confession.

Nothing is known of the artistic education of Alice Mary Chambers, but she had certainly emerged as a painter by 1875, when she produced her earliest dated work, a watercolour of a young woman entitled *Contemplation*. However, it is only from the 1880s that her career can be charted in any detail.

Before 1881, Chambers had begun to establish a close relationship with the artists' agent, Charles Augustus Howell, who may be considered one of the most colourful characters of the Victorian age. The friend and agent of Dante Gabriel Rossetti, it was Howell who, in 1869, persuaded the Pre-Raphaelite artist and writer to dig up the poems that he had buried with his wife, Elizabeth Siddal. Through Rossetti, he met John Ruskin and, during the late 1860s, acted as his secretary, specifically managing his discreet charitable donations. He had a mixed reputation in his lifetime, being regarded as both a 'gifted raconteur' and a 'prodigious liar' and worse (Merrill, 2011).

Chambers became a member of a close circle around Howell that also included his wife, Kitty, and his mistresses, the artist, Rosa Corder, and Clara Vaughan. Together they were described by James McNeill Whistler as 'the Cock and his Hens'. It has been suggested that Chambers was the third of these mistresses, though somehow she managed to stay loyal to Howell and retain something of her respectability. In 1885, both she and Corder even provided promissory notes in order to help Howell, when the art collector, Samuel Wreford Paddon, took legal action against him for fraud.

Chambers was at her most artistically productive during the years of her friendship with Howell and his circle, as if she needed the support of a likeminded community. By 1881, she was living at 17 Red Lion Square – an address with significant Pre-Raphaelite associations – and describing herself as 'an artist in drawing and painting'. From that year until 1893, she exhibited nine works at the Royal Academy of Arts, most of which were either portraits or images of women from literature and myth. In the same period, she also provided the frontispiece illustration for Mary Hullah's *The Lion Battalion* (1885), a collection of stories for children.

When Howell died in 1890, he and Chambers were living at the same address in Southampton Row, and possibly in a ménage with Rosa Corder. Chambers was named as one of the two executors and trustees of his will, along with the auctioneer, Frederick John Bonham, and as one of the two guardians of Rosalind, his daughter by Kitty, along with Corder. (In 1883, Corder had given birth to his other daughter, who was christened Beatrice Ellen Howell.)

Through the 1890s, Chambers lived a peripatetic life, spending a lot of time in France and Spain. In 1892, she angered Corder by taking Rosalind on a trip to Normandy, and a lawsuit followed. The result was that the girl 'was made a Ward in Chancery and was sent to Harrow to be educated and reared by a clergyman's widow' (Cline, 1978, page 28). Following the death of Corder in 1893, Rosalind was placed with the widow and daughters of a West Indian judge. Despite these distractions, Chambers continued to produce work and exhibit it at the New Gallery and the Royal Institute of Painters in Water Colours, and also in the provinces.

In 1901, when she was living at 15 Ann's Villas, West London, Chambers described herself in the census as 'living on own means' rather than as 'artist'. From that time, she retained an address in London – including one at Brook Green in 1906, and one at Vincent Square in 1912 – but spent most of her time either at Rose Cottage, Church Norton, Selsey, in Sussex, or abroad in Italy or Spain. Selsey must have been of particular significance, as Howell had also had a house there. When Elizabeth Pennell visited her to talk about her memories of Whistler, she found 'a woman of about fifty, stout, pleasantly ugly, with no endeavour to dress so as to improve matters' (*The Whistler Journal*, Philadelphia: J B Lippincott, 1921, page 69). In doing homage to the artists that she had known, she also donated a plaster death mask of Rossetti to the National Portrait Gallery.

Alice Mary Chambers died at Pomona House, 111 New Kings Road, Fulham, on 5 May 1920.

Further reading:

Clarence Lee Cline, *The Owl and the Rossettis: Letters of Charles A Howell and Dante Gabriel, Christina and William Michael Rossetti*, Pennsylvania State University Press, 1978;

Thomas McLean, 'Family Portraits: The Life and Art of Alice Mary Chambers', *Victorians: A Journal of Culture and Literature*, The Ohio State University Press, Number 133, Summer 2018, pages 69-81;

Linda Merrill, 'Howell, Charles Augustus (1840?–1890)', H C G Matthew and Brian Harrison (eds), *Oxford Dictionary of National Biography*, Oxford University Press, 2011, https://doi.org/10.1093/ref:odnb/39340;

Jeremy Morris, 'Chambers, John Charles (1817-1874)', H C G Matthew and Brian Harrison (eds), *Oxford Dictionary of National Biography*, Oxford University Press, 2004, https://doi.org/10.1093/ref:odnb/5074;

Susan Mumm (ed), *All Saints Sisters of the Poor: An Anglican Sisterhood in the Nineteenth Century*, Woodbridge: The Boydell Press/Church of England Record Society, 2001

ALBERT CHEVALLIER TAYLER

Albert Chevallier Tayler, RBA RBC ROI NEAC (1862-1925)

Albert Chevallier Tayler painted a variety of figure subjects, both contemporary and historical. He became best known for his interior scenes, including dinner parties and domestic celebrations, and was admired for the high finish of his canvases. Absorbing Continental influences through study in Paris, he established himself as a member of the Newlyn School by producing social realist scenes *en plein air*. Then, following his conversion to Catholicism in 1887, and his move to London in 1895, he focussed increasingly on religious imagery, middle class settings and portraiture.

Albert Chevallier Tayler was born in Leytonstone, Essex, on 5 April 1862, the seventh of eight children of the solicitor, William Moseley Tayler, and his wife, Elizabeth Sarah (née Warren). He was educated at All Saints' Grammar School, Bloxham, Oxfordshire, and began to study art in London at Heatherley's School of Art. In 1879, he won a three-year scholarship to the Slade School of Art, where he was taught by Alphonse Legros. Moving to Paris, he studied for a year in the atelier of the history painter, Jean-Paul Laurens, alongside other former students of the Slade, including Thomas Cooper Gotch, George Percy Jacomb-Hood and Henry Scott Tuke. He then studied for a further year in the atelier of the celebrated portrait painter, Carolus-Duran, alongside Norman Garstin.

In September 1884, Tayler joined the colony of artists based in the Cornish fishing village of Newlyn, and lived there intermittently for over a decade. He settled at Belle Vue House (now called Boase Castle House), where he shared lodgings with Stanhope Forbes and William Blandford Fletcher. Other Newlyn friends included Garstin, Tuke and Gotch. (He would live with Gotch at The Malt House before moving to Parc Terrace). An avid cricketer, who began painting cricketing subjects in 1886, he played in the annual Newlyn vs St Ives artists' cricket match, and would later become a member of the Artists' Cricket Club.

In 1884, Tayler began to exhibit at the Royal Academy of Arts, the most established exhibiting society of the day (and would continue to do so until his death). However, in 1885, he became a founder member of the New English Art Club, as a progressive alternative to the academy, which could promote the interests of the Newlyn painters, among others. Exhibiting widely, he also became a member of the Royal Institute of Painters in Oils (1890), the Art Workers' Guild (1905-7), the Royal Society of British Artists (1908) and the Royal British Colonial Society of Artists (of which he became the Honorary Secretary). He showed frequently at major Parisian exhibitions, including the Salon, which awarded him a 2nd class medal in 1891.

Possibly prompted by the conversion of his youngest sibling, Mary, Tayler became a Roman Catholic in 1887, and began to concentrate on religious imagery. Then from 1895, when he moved to London and settled at 23 Orsett Terrace, Bayswater, he relaxed into a more genteel, urban lifestyle, and produced a greater number of scenes of middle class life. However, in that year, he served on the provisional committee of artists during the opening of the Newlyn Art Gallery (and, from 1904, he would use it as a venue for the sale of his work). In 1896, he married Mrs Elizabeth Christiana Cotes, the widowed daughter of William Allingham, surgeon to the household of the Prince of Wales. Having had one daughter by her first husband, Charles Edward Henry Cotes MB, she would have two sons with Tayler.

By the turn of the century, Tayler had gained a significant reputation for his history paintings, among other subjects. These included the ambitious *'Honi soit qui mal y pense': the Origin of the Order of the Garter, 1349*, which was shown at the Royal Academy in 1901, and the large panel entitled *The Vintners Company Entertaining the Five Kings*, which was commissioned for the Royal Exchange, London, in 1903. At around the same time, he began to paint an increasing number of portraits, including one in 1906 of E W Hornung, author of the E J Raffles stories.

With a studio at 61 Carlton Hill, St John's Wood – close to Lord's cricket ground – Tayler was well placed to paint cricketing subjects. In 1905, he produced a set of 12 watercolours of famous, mostly aristocratic cricket players, and these were turned into lithographs by Lever Brothers for a campaign to advertise its soap products (as was an earlier painting, *The Dress Rehearsal* of 1888). In 1906, he painted the impressive *Kent vs Lancashire at Canterbury*, which was commissioned by Kent County Cricket Club in order to celebrate the club becoming county champions for the first time in that year. This has been described as the only painting 'of a real cricket match in progress in which all the players on the fielding side are portrayed and are clearly recognisable' (Jonathan Rice, *Stories of Cricket's Finest Painting: Kent v Lancashire 1906*, Durrington: Pitch Publishing, 2019).

Tayler's two sons were killed on active service in the First World War, the younger in the RAF in August 1918, and the older, an army officer, in the Dvina relief force in north Russia in 1919. Tayler received the commission for the Dvina relief force memorial painting, a triptych that portrays a memorial service. Unveiled at the Crystal Palace in 1921, it is now in the collections of the Imperial War Museums. His later portraits, include those of Admiral Earl Beatty and Field-Marshal Earl Haig.

Tayler died at home on 20 December 1925, and was buried at St Mary's Roman Catholic cemetery, Kensal Green.

His work is represented in numerous public collections, including the Imperial War Museums; and the Alfred East Art Gallery (Kettering) and the Penlee House Gallery & Museum (Penzance).

Further reading:

Anne Anderson, 'Tayler, Albert Chevallier (1862-1925)', H C G Matthew and Brian Harrison (eds), *Oxford Dictionary of National Biography*, Oxford University Press, 2011, https://doi.org/10.1093/ref:odnb/101045

HUBERT VON HERKOMER

Sir Hubert von Herkomer, CVO RA VPRWS RE RI (1849-1914)

Bavarian-born Hubert von Herkomer was a leading and sometimes controversial figure in the cultural life of Victorian Britain. He first made his name as a Social Realist, with wood-engraved illustrations for *The Graphic* and paintings exhibited at the Royal Academy of Arts. Broadening both his methods and his subject matter, he became particularly well known as a portraitist. He set up his own School of Art in Bushey, in 1883 and, two years later, was appointed Slade Professor Fine Art at Oxford University. Ever energetic and forward thinking, he produced 'pictorial-music-plays' in his own theatre and, at the end of his life, became a pioneering film-maker.

His work is represented in numerous public collections, including Guildhall Art Gallery, the National Portrait Gallery and Tate; the Ashmolean Museum (Oxford), Bushey Museum and Art Gallery, Chesterfield Museum & Art Gallery, Leeds Art Gallery, Russell-Cotes Art Gallery & Museum (Bournemouth), Southampton City Art Gallery, Touchstones Rochdale; and Yale Center for British Art (New Haven, CT); and also Christ Church College (Oxford), the Examinations School (Oxford), Trinity College (Cambridge) and the University of Manchester.

Further reading:

Lee M Edwards, *Herkomer: A Victorian Artist*, Aldershot: Ashgate, 1999;
Lee M Edwards, 'Herkomer, Sir Hubert von (1849-1914)', H C G Matthew and Brian Harrison (eds), *Oxford Dictionary of National Biography*, Oxford University Press, 2011, https://doi.org/10.1093/ref:odnb/33836;
Lee M Edwards, 'Herkomer, Sir Hubert von (*b* Waal, Bavaria, May 26, 1849; *d* Budleigh Salterton, Devon, March 31, 1914)', Jane Turner (ed), *The Dictionary of Art*, London: Macmillan, 2004, https://doi.org/10.1093/gao/9781884446054.article.T037756;
Grant Longman: *The Beginning of the Herkomer Art School*, Bushey: E G Longman, 1983;
J Saxon Mills, *The Life and Letters of Sir Hubert Herkomer, CVO RA: A Study in Struggle and Success*, London: Hutchinson, 1923

CARLTON ALFRED SMITH

Carlton Alfred Smith, RBA RI ROI (1853-1946)

Carlton Alfred Smith was a painter, mainly in watercolour, of gentle rural genre scenes, including many of mothers and daughters.

Carlton Alfred Smith was born in Camden Town, London, on 27 August 1853, the son of a steel engraver. He was educated in France, and then studied at the Slade School of Fine Art, winning gold and silver medals. Initially, he worked as a lithographer before turning to painting. He exhibited mainly at the Royal Society of British Artists (being elected a member in 1879), the Royal Institute of Painters in Water Colours (RI 1889) and the Royal Institute of Oil Painters (ROI 1890), and also at the Royal Academy of Arts.

By 1891, Smith was married to the coastal painter, Martha (née King), and they were living at 72 Park Road, Hampstead, with their two young daughters. A decade later, in 1901, they had moved to Surrey, and were living at Vine Cottage, Witley Crossways, Witley. Then, by 1911, they had moved again, and were living at 31 Fairfax Road, Chiswick, their daughters having grown up and left home.

Smith spent the years between 1916 and 1923 in India, during which time he produced both portraits and fascinating scenes of street life.

Carlton Alfred Smith died in London on 3 December 1946.

ROBERT THORNE WAITE

Robert Thorne Waite, RWS RBC ROI (1843-1935)

Robert Thorne Waite was a painter, mostly in watercolour, of bright and airy landscapes and pastoral scenes. He was particularly fond of the corn and hay fields of the South Downs.

Robert Thorne Waite was born in Cheltenham, Gloucestershire on 18 April 1842, the seventh of eight children of the watchmaker, Thomas Waite, and his wife, Elizabeth (née Amphlett). He was educated at Cheltenham Grammar School, and then, from 1860, he studied art at the National Art Training School, South Kensington, London. During the mid 1860s, he worked at Bettws-y-Coed, North Wales, alongside his close contemporary, Thomas Collier, developing a style that emulated the work of David Cox and Copley Fielding.

Thorne Waite exhibited mainly at the Royal Society of Painters in Water-Colours, being elected an associate in 1876 and a full member in 1884. He showed at a range of venues, including the Royal Academy of Arts and a number of dealers, and was also elected to the Royal British Colonial Society of Artists and the Royal Institute of Oil Painters, the latter in 1883. In that year, he was living with his wife, Marian (née Parkman), and two daughters at 35 Dartmouth Park Road, Kentish Town. About a decade later, in 1891, they moved a couple of miles west to Maitland Park Villas, Maitland Park Road. By that date, they also had a son. (However, one of the daughters may have died in infancy, as Waite later records, in his entry in *Who's Who*, that he had one son and one daughter.)

By the outbreak of the First World War, Thorne Waite had moved to Bournemouth and was living at Greta, 12 Queen's Park, West Drive. He died in Bournemouth on 28 February 1935.

GEORGE MARKS

George Marks (1857-1938)

Working in oil and watercolour, George Marks produced landscapes that imbued many of the secluded places of Southern England with a quiet poetry, be they gorse bushes on the downs or primrose patches in the dells.

George Marks was born in Bristol, the eldest of three sons of the artist, George Marks. By 1869, he and his family had moved to Kentish Town, London, and in 1879 they were living at Rose Villa, Maple Road, Penge. He exhibited at the principal London galleries from 1876 – including the Royal Academy of Arts (1878-1904), the Royal Society of British Artists and the Royal Institute of Painters in Water Colours – with a number of London dealers and in the provinces. His later addresses included Flackwell Heath, near High Wycombe, Buckinghamshire (1883), Greenwich (1885), Shere, near Guildford, Surrey (1887-93) and Ross-on-Wye, Herefordshire (1927). He died in Kidderminster, Worcestershire.

Detail of George Marks, *The Edge of a Sussex Common* [73]

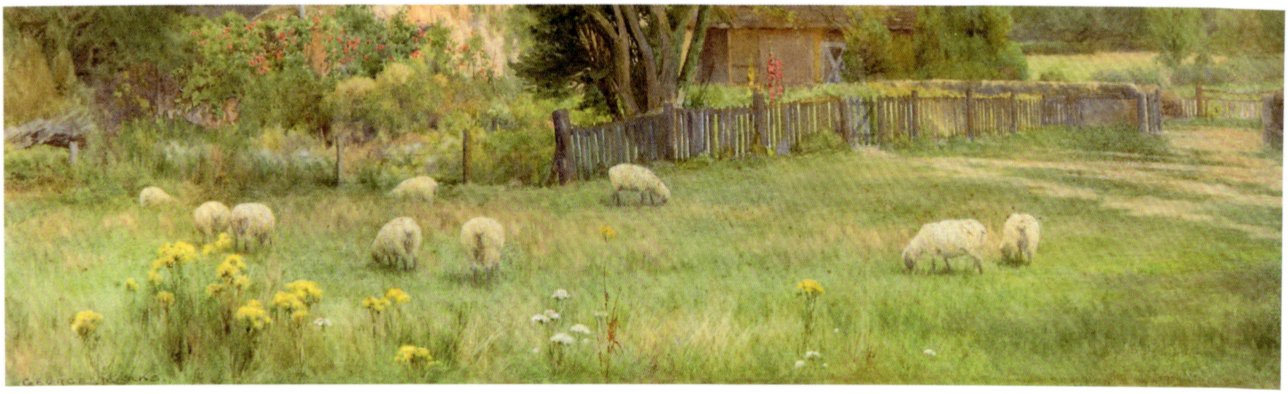

SAMUEL READ

Samuel Read, RWS (1815-1883)

Samuel Read was a painter and illustrator, specialising in architectural subjects and, to a lesser extent, coastal views. He was particularly fond of producing images of the interiors and exteriors of cathedrals, many of which were reproduced in *The Illustrated London News*, for which he worked as its first Special Artist (a visual journalist sent to record major news stories for illustrated publications).

Samuel Read was born in Needham Market, Suffolk, the eldest of ten children of the bootmaker, Thomas Read, and his wife, Mary. He was baptised at the local Congregational church on 20 December 1815. Educated at Theobald's Grammar School, in Needham Market, he was articled as a clerk in 1830 to John Eddowes Sparrowe, attorney of Ancient House, Ipswich, and town clerk. During his time with Sparrowe, he produced both political caricatures and pencil portraits of the leading men of Ipswich. In 1839, he moved to the office of William Mason, the borough surveyor, possibly with the intention of becoming an architect.

In 1841, Read moved to London to learn wood-engraving from Josiah Whymper, and also studied painting with the watercolourist, W Collingwood Smith. In 1843 – and annually between 1846 and 1857 – he began to send architectural drawings to the Royal Academy of Arts, mainly of the interiors of English and Belgian churches. In the following year, while living in Greenwich, he began to illustrate books, the first being *Zoological Studies*, and also contributed to *The Illustrated London News*. He became the first Special Artist for that magazine, and in that capacity was sent to Constantinople in 1853, just before the outbreak of the Crimean War.

In 1857, Read was elected as an associate of the Society of Painters in Water Colours, and from then on contributed to every one of its exhibitions. Three years later, he married Isabella Carruthers, the daughter of the proprietor of the Inverness Courier, and they would have one son and one daughter.

Read made a number of British and Continental sketching tours, and during the 1870s produced coastal scenes and other landscapes, though they proved less successful than his architectural subjects. In June 1865, while returning from a sketching trip abroad, he was – like fellow passenger, Charles Dickens – involved in the Staplehurst railway disaster, and narrowly escaped death.

In 1880, Read became a full member of the Society of Painters in Water Colours (the year before the society received its Royal Charter). He also retained an unofficial position as art editor of *The Illustrated London News*. In his later years he lived at Parkside in Bromley, though he died at Fort Cottage, Sidmouth, Devon, on 6 May 1883, following a stroke. His studio sale was held at Christie's on 29 February 1884.

His work is represented in the collections of the V&A.

Further reading:

Anne Pimlott Baker, 'Read, Samuel (1815-1883)', H C G Matthew and Brian Harrison (eds), *Oxford Dictionary of National Biography*, Oxford University Press, 2010, https://doi.org/10.1093/ref:odnb/23220

BAIRD FRASER

Gilbert Baird Fraser (1866-1947)

The watercolours of Baird Fraser tend to be both looser and warmer than those of his brothers.

Baird Fraser was born in Bedford on 23 July 1865. Between 1876 and 1881, he attended the local grammar school and, while there, studied art under Bradford Rudge. Describing himself as a landscape artist from the time he left school, he probably exhibited watercolours at the Bedford Rooms between 1883 and 1886. In 1887, he moved with his parents to Hemingford Grey, Huntingdonshire. Three years later, he helped his brother, Anderson, found the White Cockade Club at nearby Holywell. Following his marriage in 1897, he settled in Holywell. During the First World War, he worked at Fowells Engineering and Munitions Factory, St Ives. He died at his home in Holywell on 6 February 1947.

Further reading:

Charles Lane, *The Fraser Family*, London: Chris Beetles Ltd, 2010

PHILIP WILSON STEER

Philip Wilson Steer, OM NEAC (1860-1942)

Wilson Steer was one of the most interesting and significant British painters working at the turn of the twentieth century. His career subsumed early Impressionist experimentation within a developing traditionalism that emulated Constable and Turner.

Philip Wilson Steer was born in Birkenhead, Cheshire, on 28 December 1860, the youngest of three children of the painter, Philip Steer, and his wife, Emma (née Harrison). In 1864, he moved with his family to Apsley House, Whitchurch, Herefordshire, and was initially educated at home by a governess. In 1871, the year that his father died, he began to attend a local preparatory school, and, in 1875, advanced to Hereford Cathedral School, remaining there for two years. While there, he obtained a nomination to join the Department of Coins and Medals at the British Museum, as he had an interest in coins. In order to gain that position, he spent some months in Whitchurch with Dr Purcell, a private tutor from whom he learned more than from any other teacher. Then, from January 1878, he undertook an intensive course in London in order to prepare for the rigorous Civil Service examination. Not naturally academic, this proved to be too much for him, so he gave up the idea and turned instead to painting.

Having started to draw and paint at about the age of 16, Steer went to Gloucester School of Art two years later, in 1878, and there studied under John Kemp. Once his mother had sold their house in Whitchurch, and moved her household to 23 Brunswick Road, Gloucester, he became a full-time student. In April 1881, he gained a second class certificate in perspective from the National Art Training School, South Kensington, and this led him to attempt to enter the Royal Academy Schools, but without success. As a result, he decided to go to Paris, a city he had first visited in 1876, on the return journey from a holiday in Germany.

So, in the autumn of 1882, Steer settled at the Hôtel du Beau-séjour, in the boulevard Poissonnière, soon moving to the even more central Britannique, in the avenue Victoria. Enrolling at the Académie Julian, he studied ostensibly under William-Adolphe Bouguereau, though really worked harder on his own. Among his fellow students, he developed close friendships with James Christie and T B Kennington, and would remain within a circle of English and American artists. In January 1883, he transferred to the Ecole des Beaux-Arts, where he 'received a more strict and effective training' (*The Studio,* 1930, page 254) under Alexandre Cabanel, and alongside students that included the outstanding Edward Stott. That spring, he returned briefly to London, where he may have seen the exhibition of Impressionism at the Dowdeswell Galleries, and certainly exhibited for the first time at the Royal Academy of Arts. (He showed again at the RA in 1884 and 1885, but, on being skied and rejected in successive years, he chose not to submit to its exhibition again until 1940.) Visiting the posthumous exhibition of Manet's work at the Ecole des Beaux-Arts in January 1884, he remained in the French capital until the summer, and exhibited at the Paris Salon. He left after he failed an examination in the French language which had been newly introduced at the Ecole.

On his return to England in 1884, Steer made the first of many painting expeditions to Walberswick, on the Suffolk coast, making many studies from nature, and so instigating a series of seaside subjects. In the following year – when he acquired a London studio at 6 Trafalgar Studios, Manresa Road, Chelsea – he made the first of several visits to towns on or close to the north French coast, including Etaples, Dannes, Boulogne and Montreuil-sur-Mer. Initially, the paintings that he produced, such as *At the Well, Walberswick,* reflected the influence of the rural naturalism of Jules Bastien-Lepage. However, by the end of the 1880s and into the next decade, they revealed an interest in various styles of Impressionism, including those of James McNeill Whistler, Claude Monet and the Divisionists.

In 1886, Steer helped to found the New English Art Club with artists of a similarly innovative character, including his friend, Walter Sickert, and also sold work through dealers. Exhibitions of his seaside subjects at such venues as the Goupil Gallery (notably 'London Impressionists' in 1889 and a solo show in 1894) were particularly helpful in developing his reputation as both the leading follower of French Impressionism in England and a figure of great originality. In turn, from 1893, he conveyed his approach to art to the younger generation through his teaching at the Slade School as an assistant to Professor Fred Brown. If his early work was continually attacked by conservative critics, he gradually gained support from such enlightened individuals as his friends, D S MacColl and George Moore, who were then writing in *The Spectator* and *The Saturday Review*, among other journals.

Following the death of his mother in 1898, Steer moved to 109 Cheyne Walk, Chelsea, and would remain there, as a bachelor, for the rest of his life. By this time, he had begun to react to his growing success by looking to the more established native tradition of landscape painting, as represented by Thomas Gainsborough, John Constable and J M W Turner. He rehearsed the eighteenth-century picturesque tour by working in Yorkshire, North Wales and the West Country, and favouring river and coastal scenes. He exhibited the large, impressive canvases that resulted mainly at the New English Art Club. In 1906, he was elected an honorary member of the Liverpool Academy of Arts.

From the turn of the century, Steer also produced independent watercolours, having previously used the medium only for preliminary studies. In 1918, as an Official War Artist, he produced masterly watercolours of the manoeuvres of the British fleet. Owing to his failing eyesight, he worked increasingly in this medium and, in the process, emulated Turner's late, near abstract achievements.

In 1929, Steer was given a major retrospective exhibition at the Tate Gallery, becoming the first artist in his lifetime to receive this honour. The exhibition included a portrait of Margaret Raynes (Tate, 1922), who had been his childhood nurse and had remained his housekeeper until her death at the age of 91 in 1929.

Steer retired from the Slade in 1930, after teaching there for nearly 40 years, and in 1931 reluctantly accepted the Order of Merit. For a few years, he continued to produce refined watercolours during excursions to Kent and Essex, and exhibited them in a series of solo shows at Barbizon House and other venues. However, he was forced to give up painting in 1938, as the result of near blindness. A number of memorial shows followed his death at home in London on 21 March 1942.

His work is represented in numerous public collections, including the British Museum, Tate and the V&A; the Ashmolean Museum (Oxford), Birmingham Museums, Christchurch Mansion (Ipswich), The Fitzwilliam Museum (Cambridge), Leeds Art Gallery, Lotherton Hall (Leeds), Manchester Art Gallery, Museum of Gloucester, Norwich Castle Museum & Art Gallery, Southampton City Art Gallery, Williamson Art Gallery & Museum (Birkenhead) and York Art Gallery; National Museum Wales (Cardiff); Dublin City Gallery The Hugh Lane; and Yale Center for British Art (New Haven, CT).

Further reading:

Ysanne Holt, *Philip Wilson Steer*, Bridgend: Seren, 1992;
Ysanne Holt, 'Steer, Philip Wilson (1860-1942)', H C G Matthew and Brian Harrison (eds), *Oxford Dictionary of National Biography*, Oxford University Press, 2004, https://doi.org/10.1093/ref:odnb/36264;
Robin Ironside, *Philip Wilson Steer*, Oxford: Phaidon, 1943;
Bruce Laughton, *Philip Wilson Steer 1860-1942*, Oxford: Clarendon Press, 1971;
D S MacColl, *The Life and Work and Setting of Philip Wilson Steer (with a Full Catalogue of Paintings … by Alfred Yockney)*, London: Faber and Faber, 1945;
Jane Munro, 'Steer, Philip Wilson (*b* Birkenhead, Dec 28, 1860; *d* London, March 18, 1942)', Jane Turner (ed), *The Dictionary of Art*, London: Macmillan, 2003, https://doi.org/10.1093/gao/9781884446054.article.T081168

HAROLD KNIGHT

Harold Knight, RA ROI RP RWA PNSA NPS (1874-1961)

Harold Knight was a quiet and gentle man, and his wife, the painter, Laura Knight, feared that she had 'stood in his way', as a result of the strength of her personality and achievement. Nevertheless, he has received acclaim as a painter, both in his lifetime and since, and especially for his sensitive portraits and interior scenes with figures, which emulate those by his favourite artist, Vermeer.

Harold Knight was born in Nottingham on 27 January 1874, the second of five children of the architect and amateur painter, William Knight, and his wife, Elizabeth (née Symington). His mother has been described as having a 'rigid puritan temperament', which 'did not make for a happy home life for the family' and 'sternly repressed' Harold's 'natural instincts' (Janet Dunbar, 2004).

Between 1881 and 1888, Knight attended Nottingham High School. Then, at the age of only 14, he began to train at Nottingham Municipal School of Art and Design, one of the oldest and best of the provincial art schools. While there, he met his future wife, Laura Johnson, and they both studied under Herbert Wilson Foster. Knight was considered the best student at the school, and won a number of prizes, including a Prince of Wales Silver Medal in 1894, and gold, silver and bronze medals at the annual National Competitions held by the Science and Art Department, South Kensington. He exhibited at the Royal Academy of Arts for the first time in 1896.

As the result of receiving a British Institute Scholarship in 1895, Knight went to Paris in 1896, and studied at the Académie Julian under Benjamin Constant and Jean-Paul Laurens. However, he left after nine months, either, or perhaps both, because he 'did not find the French ateliers congenial' (Janet Dunbar, 2004) or had 'run out of funds' (Kenneth McConkey, *Impressionism in Britain*, Yale University Press/Barbican Art Gallery, 1995, Page 143).

In 1897, Knight joined Laura Johnson, her elder sister, Eva (known as 'Sis'), and their great aunt West, on a holiday to Staithes, a fishing village on the Yorkshire coast. Deciding to remain there to paint, he became a member of a burgeoning artistic colony, which included Arthur Friedenson and Fred Mayor, with whom he shared lodgings at the Porritts' cottage in Gun Gutter. He produced paintings of the daily lives of local fisher folk, which he sold to dealers in Nottingham.

From 1899, Laura also began to live in Staithes on a more permanent basis, settling into Ebor Cottage with her elder sisters, Nellie and Sis. Harold and Laura then both established a routine, and worked extremely hard. Two years later, in ☞

☞ 1901, they broke away from the Yorkshire Union of Artists, based in nearby Whitby, and founded the Staithes Art Club, which held exhibitions in the Fisherman's Institute.

In 1903, Harold Knight married Laura Johnson at St Helena's Church, West Leake, Nottinghamshire. Initially, they remained in Staithes, but achieved additional stimulation by taking trips to the Netherlands. They made their first, six-week visit, in June 1904, with Henry Silkstone Hopwood, a fellow member of the Staithes Group. They stayed in Amsterdam – where Harold studied the work of Vermeer, the artist that he most admired – and then moved on to the artists' colony of Laren in North Holland. In the following year, the Knights returned to Laren for a period of six months and, as before, lodged at the English-speaking pension run by Vrow Kam. As a result of these visits, Harold's paintings increasingly revealed the influence of members of the Hague School, including Josef Israels.

Knight had his first success in 1905, when *A Cup of Tea*, showing a poor family grouped around a table, was bought from the Royal Academy by Queensland Art Gallery, Brisbane, Australia. His ability was recognised in the following year when he was elected to the membership of the Institute of Oil Painters, and further marked by his first London exhibition, entitled 'Dutch Life and Landscape', which was held jointly with Laura at the Leicester Galleries. Sales from that enabled them to make their third and longest trip to the Netherlands. When they returned in January 1907, they brought with them 'a large number of canvases, some of which they sold', and others which they 'burnt or painted over' (Janet Dunbar, 2004).

In November 1907, the Knights left Staithes and moved to Newlyn, in Cornwall. In 1908, they settled into permanent lodgings with Mrs Beer at Penzer House, and remained with her for a year. Harold continued to produce the genre scenes with which he had established his name, but responded to the Cornish light by brightening his palette, and became integrated into the local artistic community, being elected a member of the Newlyn Society of Artists.

In 1909, the Knights became tenants at Trewarveneth Farm, and Harold began a series of paintings of women in interiors that were inspired by the example of Vermeer and would help define his oeuvre. In 1912, both Harold and Laura became seriously ill, and had to refrain from painting for a period of six months. Nevertheless, they were championed by Norman Garstin, a fellow member of the Newlyn Society of Artists, who later the same year published an appreciation of their 'unconscious collaboration' in the magazine, *The Studio*. In 1913, they made something of a fresh start, when they moved to Oakhill, Lamorna Gate, St Buryan, and Harold began to gain commissions for portraits and exhibit more widely, including at the Paris Salon in 1914, and at the short-lived National Portrait Society, of which he was a member. By the outbreak of the First World War, they had become key members of the Lamorna Group, comprising the second wave of Newlyn artists headed by Samuel John 'Lamorna' Birch, who took his epithet from the cove just south of Newlyn.

During the war, Knight took a pacifist stance as a conscientious objector and, as a result, was shunned by colleagues and former friends, a situation that put a strain on his health. In 1916, he was called to report for service and, after several meetings to review his case, was forced to work on farms in North Cornwall. However, by 1917, his health had so deteriorated that he was excused further labour.

In 1919, the Knights moved to London, and soon settled at 1 & 2 Queen's Road (now Queen's Grove), St Johns Wood (while returning to Cornwall in the summer months throughout the 1920s). In 1922, they moved a short distance to 9 Langford Place (later changed to No 16), which became their permanent home, and where each had a studio. They would purchase it in 1937.

Harold consolidated his reputation as a portrait painter and, in 1925, was both elected to the Royal Society of Portrait Painters and received a silver medal from the Paris Salon for his painting of the pianist, Ethel Bartlett. Then, in September 1926, he received an invitation to go to Baltimore to paint Dr John Finney of the Johns Hopkins Memorial Hospital. Laura joined him at the end of the year, and they stayed in the United States until April 1927. In 1928, Harold was elected an associate of the Royal Academy, and almost a decade later, in 1937 would become a full academician (on each occasion a year after his wife). Between 1936 and 1945, he was also President of Nottingham Society of Artists.

From 1929, the Knights had regularly attended the annual Malvern Festival, which was founded by their friend, Sir Barry Jackson, primarily as a showcase for the work of George Bernard Shaw. Following the outbreak of the Second World War, they returned to the Worcestershire-Herefordshire borders, staying initially at the British Camp Hotel, Colwall, and then moving to the nearby Park Hotel. In the post-war period, they would spend most of their summers at this hotel, and in their final years together spend almost all their time there. Harold died at the hotel on 3 October 1961.

His work is represented in numerous public collections, including the National Portrait Gallery; Laing Art Gallery (Newcastle upon Tyne) and Nottingham Castle Museum & Art Gallery; and the City Hall (Cardiff) and National Museum Wales (Cardiff).

Further reading:

Janet Dunbar (rev), 'Knight [née Johnson], Dame Laura (1877–1970)', H C G Matthew and Brian Harrison (eds), *Oxford Dictionary of National Biography*, Oxford University Press, 2009, https://doi.org/10.1093/ref:odnb/34349

MARIA EATON

Maria Eaton (1862-1944)

Maria Eaton was an enterprising painter and printmaker, who initially specialised in sensitive and characterful portrait miniatures. Following her marriage to the architect and artist, Ernest Hampshire, in 1913, she turned increasingly to flower studies, landscapes and townscapes.

Maria Eaton was born in Macclesfield, Cheshire, the youngest of six children of the drysalter, Edward Eaton, and his wife, Ellen (née McDonnell). Baptised on 4 June 1862, she grew up at Upton Cottage, Upton, near Macclesfield. By 1881, the family was living at Lower Beech House, Tytherington. Though little is known of her education, Eaton was awarded a medal by the South Kensington Schools.

It seems that Maria Eaton visited Canada during the 1880s, and in 1889 exhibited a work at the Art Association of Montreal. However, by early in 1891, she had returned to England and had set herself up at Mr Head's bookshop in the High Street, Congleton, Cheshire, first holding an exhibition and then giving classes in painting and drawing. A decade later, she was based at Burlington House, 238 Oxford Street, Manchester (now Oxford Road), and describing herself, in the Census of 1901, as an 'artist photographer [on her] own acc[ount]', though nothing is known of her photography. She painted miniatures of Sir Alfred Hopkinson (Vice-Chancellor of the Victoria University of Manchester between 1901 and 1913) and Edwin Waugh (a Lancashire poet), showing the latter in 1904, as her first exhibit at the Royal Academy. In 1905, she held a solo show of miniatures at Burlington House.

By 1906, Maria Eaton had moved to London, and settled at the Studio, 49 College Road, Haverstock Hill. However, in 1907, she was living at 5 Adelaide Road, South Hampstead, and in 1908 at 240 High Holborn. This period of her career culminated in 1912 with a solo show of watercolours of Badminton House and its surroundings at Frost & Reed, 8 Clare Street, Bristol.

In 1913, Maria Eaton married the architect and artist, Ernest Llewellyn Hampshire, who was 20 years her junior, at Holy Trinity Church, Vauxhall Bridge Road, close to her home at 11 Ponsonby Terrace. Hampshire was living with his parents at 20 Thrale Road, Streatham, and the bridal couple may have begun their married life at this address, as it is inscribed on the reverse of her depiction of Augustus John, which may have been one of her last portrait miniatures [103]. However, within a year, they moved into 193c Alexandra Road, St John's Wood. For the first years of their marriage, at least until 1922, they stayed each summer, at the Studio, Baldrine, Lonan, on the Isle of Man, in order to paint.

In 1914, they held a joint exhibition of landscapes of the Isle of Man with Yeend King at their London studio.

Working increasingly as a painter of landscapes and flowers, Maria exhibited at the Society of Women Artists (from 1919), the Salon des Artistes Françaises, Paris (from 1928) and especially the Royal Institute of Painters in Water Colours (from which Queen Mary bought *Spring Flowers* in 1922).

In 1931, the Hampshires moved into the former home of Ernest's parents at 20 Thrale Road, Streatham. Continuing to exhibit until 1937, Maria probably died in 1944.

DAVID SHEPHERD

Richard David Shepherd, CBE FRGS FRSA (1931-2017)

David Shepherd was a naturalistic painter in oils of a wide range of subjects, and most notably of African wildlife and steam railways, both of which were dear to his heart. Becoming one of the world's best known and most outspoken environmentalists, he raised millions for conservation through sales of his wildlife paintings. He became so popular with the public that, during the 1960s, prints of his images of elephants outsold reproductions of works by Canaletto.

David Shepherd was born in Hendon, North London, on 25 April 1931, the second of three children of Raymond Shepherd, who worked in advertising, and his wife, Margaret (née Williamson). At the age of eight, while growing up with his family in Totteridge, he showed a glimpse of his later artistic success by winning a children's painting competition in the magazine, *Nursery World*. Later, he attended Stowe School, in Buckinghamshire, but failed to shine academically. Throughout his childhood, his only ambition had been to become a game warden; so, on leaving school, in 1949, his father paid for him to travel to Kenya to follow his dream. However, when he arrived at Nairobi National Park, he was politely told by the warden that he was unqualified. After a brief period in which he worked as a hotel receptionist on the Kenyan coast, he returned home.

Shepherd turned almost desperately to art, and applied for a place at the Slade School of Art, only to be told that he had no talent. However, he met Robin Goodwin, a painter of portraits and marine subjects, at a party, and was taken on as his assistant at his Chelsea studio. He stayed with him for three years, from 1950 to 1953, and, painting every day from dawn to dusk, learned much from him. He soon developed a speciality in aeronautical subjects, becoming a founder member of the Society of Aviation Artists in 1953, and winning commissions from airline companies that enabled him to travel the world. The results were showcased at his first solo exhibition, held at the Parsons Gallery, in London, in 1955.

During this time, Shepherd met Avril Gaywood, a secretary for Capital Airlines, and his parents encouraged them to get engaged by giving him a Victorian cottage, with more than an acre of land, next to their own house in Frensham, Surrey. He and Avril married in 1957, and would have four daughters, including Mandy, who would also become a wildlife and military artist.

In 1960, the Royal Air Force invited Shepherd to paint for the services in Aden, and then to depict life in Kenya. This proved to be a turning point in his career, as he produced his first wildlife painting, a rhinoceros chasing a Twin Pioneer down a runway. Soon after, he became a conservationist, after finding a herd of dead zebra at a Tanzanian waterhole, which had been poisoned by poachers.

Though Shepherd exhibited only once at the Royal Academy, in 1956, his second solo show – held at the Tryon Gallery, London, in 1962 – proved a great success. At the same time, his work gained in popularity through its reproduction as prints, an early example being *Wise Old Elephant*, which was published by Boots the Chemist in 1962, and sold a quarter of a million copies. Further solo shows – in London (1965 and subsequently), Johannesburg (1966 and 1969) and New York (1967) – confirmed his international reputation. Soon Shepherd was producing the portraits of statesmen and stateswomen, notably Kenneth Kaunda, President of Zambia (1967), Queen Elizabeth, the Queen Mother (1969) and Sheikh Zayed of Abu Dhabi (1970). As a result of his success, he was able to buy an Elizabethan farmhouse set in 16 acres at Hascombe, in Surrey.

Shepherd was interested in conserving trains as well as wildlife. In 1967, he bought two mainline steam locomotives – The Green Knight and Black Prince – from British Railways, and sold the former to North Yorkshire Moors Railway to finance the restoration of the latter, which was eventually sold to North Norfolk Railway in 2015. In the early 1970s, he received two further locomotives from President Kaunda in gratitude for his raising the funds, through the auction of five wildlife paintings, to purchase a Bell Jet Ranger helicopter that would be used to combat game poaching in Zambia. The return of one of these locomotives to Britain was the subject of the 1974 BBC documentary, *Last Train to Mulobezi*, one of several television programmes made about the artist. During the same period, he helped found the preserved steam railway, East Somerset Railway.

Shepherd had a major fund-raising success in 1973, when his painting, *Tiger Fire*, raised £127,000 for Indira Gandhi's Operation Tiger. His exceptional talent for raising awareness through his art was recognised in the same year, when Prince Bernhard of the Netherlands conferred on him the Most Excellent Order of the Golden Ark for services to nature conservation. At the end of the decade, in 1980, he was awarded an OBE. In 1984, he founded the David Shepherd Conservation Foundation (now known as the David Shepherd Wildlife Foundation) both to channel his own conservation efforts and to fund vital enforcement and community projects. His achievements were further acknowledged during the late 1980s and 90s: he was made a Fellow of both the Royal Society of Arts (1986) and the Royal Geographical Society (1989), and an Officer of the Order of St John (1996), and received the Order of Distinguished Service from President Kaunda (1988).

In 2000, David and Avril Shepherd moved to Hammerwood, in West Sussex, and settled into another Elizabethan farmhouse. As he entered his seventies, David continued to work as hard as ever in the fields of art and animal conservation, and his achievements were acknowledged by his being made a Freeman of the City of London (2004) and awarded a CBE (2008).

In 2011, during the year of his eightieth birthday, Shepherd launched a new campaign to save the tiger in the wild. A year later, he was awarded both the Conservation Award in the Wetnose Animal Aid Awards and the True Englishman Award at the St George's Day Club annual gathering. He also took up an invitation to open Zambia's first elephant orphanage nursery at a ceremony officiated by Dr Guy Scott, Vice-President of Zambia. In 2014, he held his last solo show, at the Rountree Tryon Galleries, In 2016, he was awarded the Lifetime Achievement Award, as one of the Mirror's Animal Hero Awards.

Shepherd produced a number of books that promoted interest in both his art and its subjects, beginning with *An Artist in Africa* (1969). Those that followed included his autobiography, *The Man Who Loves Giants* (1975), *Paintings of Africa and India* (1978), *A Brush with Steam: David Shepherd's Railway Story* (1983), *David Shepherd: The Man and his Paintings* (1985), *An Artist in Conservation* (1992), *David Shepherd: My Painting Life* (1995), the autobiography, *Only One World* (1995), and *Painting with David Shepherd* (with Brenda Howley, 2004)

David Shepherd died on 19 September 2017.

Further reading:
Theo Cowdell, 'Shepherd, (Richard) David (*b* London, April 25, 1931)', Jane Turner (ed), *The Dictionary of Art*, London: Macmillan, 2003, https://doi.org/10.1093/gao/9781884446054.article.T078184;
Olivier Holmey, 'David Shepherd: Artist and conservationist sneered at by critics but whose work sold in droves' [Obituary], *Independent*, 25 September 2017;
Michael McNay, 'David Shepherd' [Obituary], *Guardian*, 21 September 2017

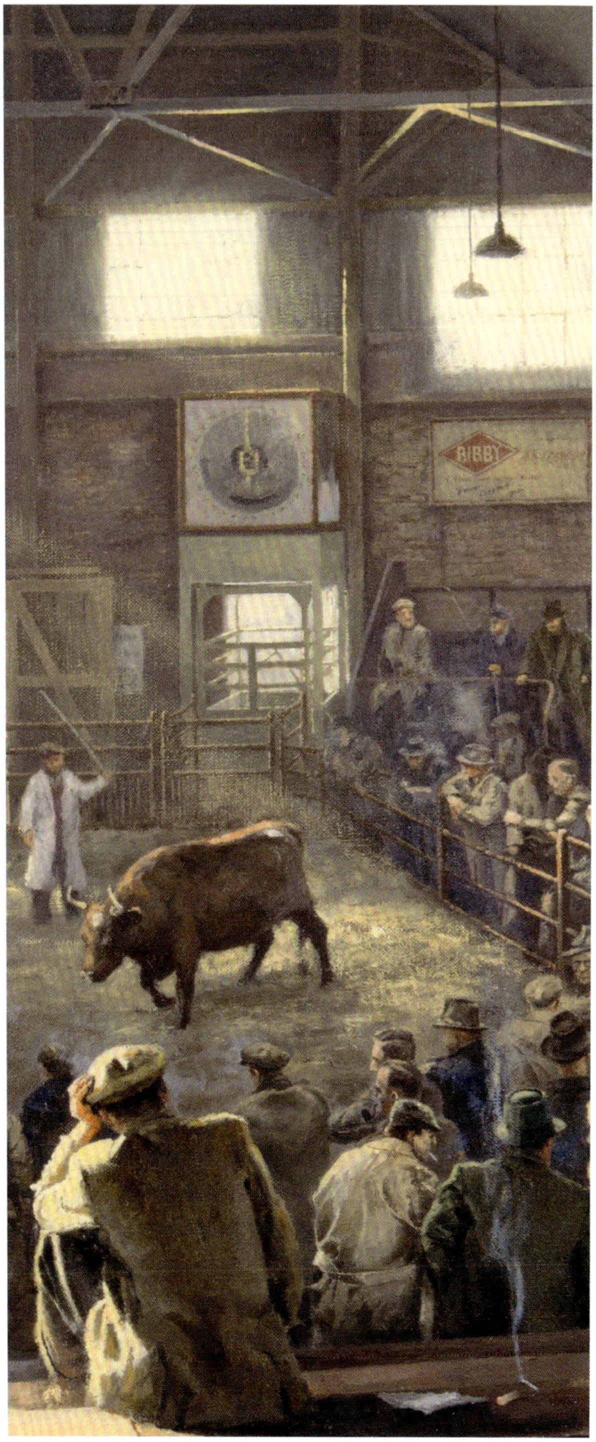

Detail of David Shepherd, *Reading Cattle Market* [106]

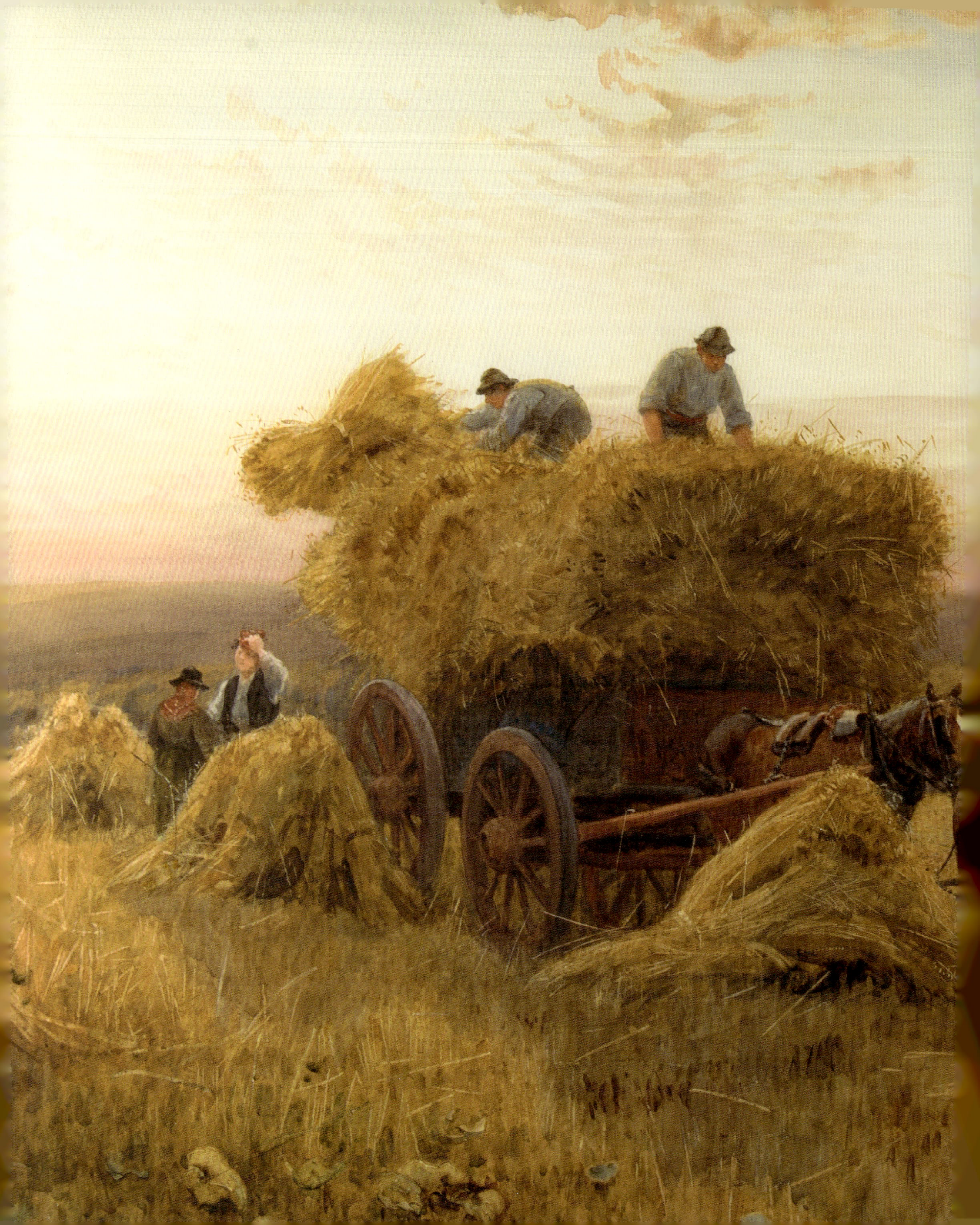